The

FLIP

The FLIP

Turn Your World Around!

JARED ROSEN
DAVID RIPPE

HAMPTON ROADS
PUBLISHING COMPANY, INC.
for the evolving human spirit

Front cover art and design by Anne Dunn Louque
Back cover design by Jane Hagaman

Hampton Roads Publishing Company, Inc.
1125 Stoney Ridge Road
Charlottesville, VA 22902

434-296-2772
fax: 434-296-5096
e-mail: hrpc@hrpub.com
www.hrpub.com

If you are unable to order this book from your local
bookseller, you may order directly from the publisher.
Call 1-800-766-8009, toll-free.

Library of Congress Cataloging-in-Publication Data

Rosen, Jared, 1955-
  The flip : turn your world around / Jared Rosen and David H. Rippe.
      p. cm.
  Summary: "Rosen and Rippe use wit and insight to highlight the transformation from
an upside-down to a right-side up world. The Flip offers interviews and wisdom from
leading thinkers and visionaries, including Oscar Arias, Paul Ray, John Gray, Ed Begley
Jr., and Dr. Christiane Northrup, who illuminate the influential shifts in our corporations,
media, politics, food, medicine, and beliefs"--Provided by publisher.
  Includes index.
  ISBN 1-57174-474-6 (6 x 9 tcwflp : alk. paper)
  1. Social ethics. 2. Social values. 3. Human ecology. 4. Holism. 5.
Conduct of life. I. Rippe, David H., 1958- II. Title.
  HM665.R67 2006
  303.3'72--dc22
                              2006006988

ISBN 1-57174-474-6
10 9 8 7 6 5 4 3 2 1
Printed on acid-free paper in the United States

I dedicate this book to my daughter, Kylea, who holds the vision of *The Flip* for the coming generation.

—Jared

This book is dedicated to Patti, always my light; and to my children, the future of the Right-Side Up world.

—David

CONTENTS

Acknowledgments xiii

Introduction. The Bridge xv
    The Other Side of the Bridge
    The Choice

***One.* Flipping Your Life—From Flipped Out to Flipped In** 1
    A Millennium of Contradiction
    Making the Flip
    Operating under the Influence
    Equal Opportunity Flipsters
    Meet the Flipsters—Conversations on the Bridge
    A Conversation on the Bridge with Dr. Paul Ray
    A Conversation on the Bridge with Byron Katie
    A Conversation on the Bridge with Yolanda King
    A Conversation on the Bridge with Dr. Barbara De Angelis
    Life, Love, Laughter
    Flip Tips

***Two.* Flipping the Mind—From Fragmented
      Thought to Whole Thinking** 19
    A Brain Teaser
    Welcome to the Great Divide
    Striking the Balance
    Somehow We Know
    Making the Flip
    Conversations on the Bridge
    A Conversation on the Bridge with Dianne Collins
    A Conversation on the Bridge with Dr. John Selby
    A Conversation on the Bridge with Dr. Peter Russell
    A Conversation on the Bridge with Gary Zukav
    It's Time to Change Your Mind
    Flip Tips

***Three.* Flipping the Emotions—From Emotional Resistance
      to Emotional Flow** 37
    Who's in Charge Here?
    The Big Secret

Welcome to the Club
What's Mary Up To?
Go with the Flow
Imagine Your Life
What's Your Pleasure?
Conversations on the Bridge
A Conversation on the Bridge with Dr. Carista Luminare-Rosen
A Conversation on the Bridge with Dr. Faye Mandell
A Conversation on the Bridge with Daphne Rose Kingma
A Conversation on the Bridge with Dr. John Gray
A Conversation on the Bridge with Dr. Candace Pert
A Conversation on the Bridge with Ayman Sawaf
The Journey of a Thousand Miles . . .
Flip Tips

**Four. Flipping the Channels—From Mindless
    Programming to Mindful Media** 59
Cocktail Anyone?
The Dark Ages
What's Wrong with This Picture?
Our Constant Companion
Lights! Camera! Action!
Hungry for Substance
Nowhere to Go but Up
Conversations on the Bridge
A Conversation on the Bridge with Barnet Bain
A Conversation on the Bridge with Debbie Levin
A Conversation on the Bridge with Sheldon Drobny
A Conversation on the Bridge with John Raatz
Is This Thing On?
Flip Tips

**Five. Flipping Burgers—From Processed Foods
    to Natural Wholesomeness** 79
The Diet and the Damage Done
Thanks for the Memories
Table for Two, Dinner for Four
Fast-Food Junkies Unite!
But Weight! There's More!
From Bad to Worse
The Most Natural Thing in the World
A World of Choices
Conversations on the Bridge
A Conversation on the Bridge with John Robbins
A Conversation on the Bridge with Nell Newman
A Conversation on the Bridge with Udo Erasmus

A Conversation on the Bridge with Dr. Vandana Shiva
Check Please!
Flip Tips

Six. Flipping Pills—From Treating Symptoms
to Maintaining Health 101
Two Camps along the Same River
An Ugly Bit of Business
The Three Horsemen of the Apothecary
Better Living through Chemistry
Pop Quiz
Paying the Tab
Putting the Person Back into Personal Health Care
The Times They Are a Changin'
Conversations on the Bridge
A Conversation on the Bridge with Dr. Christiane Northrup
A Conversation on the Bridge with Dr. Kenneth R. Pelletier
A Conversation on the Bridge with Dr. O. Carl Simonton
A Conversation on the Bridge with Dr. Dolores Krieger
Natural, Logical, Powerful
Flip Tips

Seven. Flipping the Switch—From Nonrenewable
to Sustainable Energy 123
Is It Hot in Here?
Energize Me
No Rest for the Wicked
More Answers Than Questions
Winds of Change
The Most Abundant Element
Three . . . Two . . . One . . . Blast Off
Conversations on the Bridge
A Conversation on the Bridge with Daryl Hannah
A Conversation on the Bridge with L. Hunter Lovins
A Conversation on the Bridge with Philippe Cousteau
A Conversation on the Bridge with Ed Begley, Jr.
We Have the Power!
Flip Tips

Eight. Flipping the Coin—From Scarcity to Abundance 145
Do You Come Here Often?
The Finer Things in Life
Dad, Can I Borrow a Trillion Bucks?
What Are They Up To?
Put It on My Tab
All That Glitters Is Not Gold

A Fortuitous Flip of Fortune
Conversations on the Bridge
A Conversation on the Bridge with Stu Zimmerman
A Conversation on the Bridge with Dr. Hazel Henderson
A Conversation on the Bridge with Dr. Danah Zohar
A Conversation on the Bridge with Lynne Twist
Try This at Home
Flip Tips

Nine. **Flipping the Corporation—From Pirates to Stewards** **169**
You Are Not Alone
Corporations Are People, Too
A Delicate Balance
Legalized Gambling
Making the Flip
Not a Single, Not a Double, but a Triple Bottom Line
Conversations on the Bridge
A Conversation on the Bridge with Patricia Aburdene
A Conversation on the Bridge with Ray Anderson
A Conversation on the Bridge with Marilyn Tam
A Conversation on the Bridge with Dr. Peter Senge
A Conversation on the Bridge with Terry Mollner
Take This Job and Love It
Flip Tips

Ten. **Flipping the Trigger—From Tribal Warfare to Global Tribe** **190**
Fooled Again
Irrational Defense
The Undisputed Heavyweight Champion of the World
All Is Not Lost
Deep Roots
Don't Know Much about History
Conversations on the Bridge
A Conversation on the Bridge with Dr. Oscar Arias
A Conversation on the Bridge with Dr. Marshall Rosenberg
A Conversation on the Bridge with Barbara Marx Hubbard
It's a Matter of Culture
Flip Tips

Eleven. **Flipping the Light—From God-Fearing**
          Believers to Spiritual Human Beings **211**
More Than 6.5 Billion Served
Members Only, Others Need Not Apply
24/7 Armageddon
A Single Faith and a World of Possibilities
Conversations on the Bridge

A Conversation on the Bridge with Rabbi Zalman Schachter-
   Shalomi
A Conversation on the Bridge with Venerable Dhyani Ywahoo
A Conversation on the Bridge with Dr. Elisabet Sahtouris
A Conversation on the Bridge with Bishop Alden Hathaway
A Conversation on the Bridge with Her Holiness Sai Maa Lakshmi
   Devi
Metaphors Be with You
Flip Tips

Index 233

ACKNOWLEDGMENTS

The authors gratefully acknowledge the contributions of many. We thank all of the contributors to *The Flip* for their dedication to creating a more compassionate, healthy, and enlightened world. Special thanks to our agent, Bill Gladstone, for his vision and enthusiasm—you're a great friend, Bill. Thank you to Ming Russell for her insights and suggestions. We are grateful to the Hampton Roads Publishing team for their dedication and hard work in giving this book life. Thank you to our editor Patrick Miller for his expert wordsmithing. We extend warm thanks and appreciation to Cat Pancero for listening to and transcribing hours of interviews.

My deepest heartfelt gratitude to my wife, Carista, for her pure love and ceaseless support. To Audrey Philpot for being the master networker that she is. To Jullian Jannus for her gentle guidance and holding the vision for *The Flip* movie. To Mary Cosgrove for her friendship and inspiration for the first draft of the book. To Gary Tomchuk, Peter Matthies, and Stu Zimmerman for being true brothers dedicated to building the Right-Side Up world. To Lorrie Kazan and Judith Avalon for their loving support. To Sai Maa for her blessing of light and love.

—Jared

I want to acknowledge my wonderful family for allowing the space for this book to create itself. Thank you to all who have believed in me through the years. Thanks to Herb and Susan for being there when it mattered. I want to acknowledge all searchers and seekers wherever you are on your path— never give up the quest. And lastly, I want to thank the Universe for its bounty and its blessing. Namasté.

—David

THE BRIDGE

Imagine yourself standing on a bridge between two worlds. On one side of the bridge is an upside-down world. Why is it upside-down? It is upside-down because people have lost their intimate connection to the whole and feel isolated and separate from society. Even their thoughts are fragmented. That world is upside-down because fear has trumped love as the dominant emotion—even though love is what we all seek. It has been turned topsy-turvy because sources of news and entertainment paint dark pictures of violence and murder instead of celebrating the best that people can bring to life.

In the upside-down world, more money is spent on war than on all social-service programs—for children, the elderly, education, the homeless, the hungry, the disabled—combined. The good people of the upside-down world willingly consume toxins through their water, air, and food supply and wonder why they feel tired and ill most of the time.

In the upside-down world, people say they value children, yet parking-lot attendants make more money than child-care workers and sports figures make more in one season than educators do over an entire career. It is an upside-down world because children are taught computer literacy but not emotional literacy. Faced with an inability to cope in a contradictory world, kids act out their unresolved emotions. The upside-down answer is to give them drugs rather than honestly dealing with their issues. Having taught our youth to self-medicate through pharmaceuticals, we later jail them after they have taken illicit drugs to numb the feelings they never learned to express.

The world is upside-down because people kill each other to control limited underground resources—oil, ore, minerals, water, and precious metals—while they ignore unlimited resources such as the sun and wind that can be harnessed for an endless supply of energy.

Trust is a rare commodity in the upside-down world, and intentional deception is commonplace. Our institutions—government, religion, media, education—claim to provide comfort and aid to society while in fact serving their own interests.

In this crazy world, despair turns to desperation. We feel more alone, more isolated, and ever more over our heads—upside-down. The world feels like it is spinning out of control, into chaos, and collapse.

THE OTHER SIDE OF THE BRIDGE

On the other side of the bridge, there is a world that is Right-Side Up. People walk in balance with the Earth and honor all living beings. People know that everything and everyone are interconnected. They realize that love is to be treasured and shared as the highest form of acceptance.

The people in the Right-Side Up world teach their children that emotions are to be expressed, not repressed. They learn that it is safe to speak their truth, and trust is a natural outcome of their relationships.

In the Right-Side Up world, food is more wholesome and nutritious because the seeds are not altered and the food is not processed with a range of untested chemicals whose names are unpronounceable and interactions unknown. People grow their own flavorful food, rich in nutrients, in their own backyard or community garden. Rain is not heavy with pollution because people in the Right-Side Up world do not rely on burning oil and gas for energy. Instead, they count on the power of the sun, wind, and tides as well as other clean, renewable energy sources for their energy needs.

The Right-Side Up world values diversity and self-expression. Communities celebrate the human spirit through their art forms, which have become a way of life, blended harmoniously with spirituality. Humankind rejoices in the spirit within everyone and everything—and they have evolved beyond their fascination with darkness and evil.

The Right-Side Uppers adhere to a Second Bill of Rights that gives all people:

- The right to a useful job that pays a living wage for adequate food, clothing, and recreation
- The right for every businessperson, large and small, to trade in an atmosphere of freedom from unfair competition
- The right to a decent home
- The right to medical care and the ability to achieve good health
- The right to a good education
- The right to adequate protection from the economic fears of old age, sickness, accident, and unemployment

Does this sound like the impossibly idealistic ravings of a left-leaning lunatic? Think again. The Second Bill of Rights was proposed by Franklin Delano Roosevelt in his State of the Union speech on January 11, 1944. How far we have regressed in sixty-odd years!

Yes, the Right-Side Up world encourages acceptance, tolerance, and freedom to live the way one wants as long as it harms no other. Conflict is met with compassion, and human unity is the guiding principle for society.

THE CHOICE

You are standing on this bridge between two worlds—one is upside-down, the other is Right-Side Up. The bridge is about to collapse. You must make a choice to go in one or the other direction. Which side would you go to?

Most people would choose the Right-Side Up world. It is the obvious choice for a better place to live in. Yet many people view the Right-Side Up world as idealistic and unattainable and thus accept living in the upside-down world. Is it the gravity of fear that holds them in this destructive state? Is it lack of faith? Or have the forces of the upside-down world so skewed our perceptions that we do not believe a Right-Side Up world is possible?

We live in an amazing age. It is a point in the evolution of humankind when a massive shift in consciousness, which we call "the flip," is taking place. The flip is happening in nearly every facet of our global society. This book offers the insights and views of the leading thinkers of our time giving their impressions on what the coming flip means and how it will impact not only our immediate time, but the lives of future generations.

The flip is occurring whether we embrace it or not, whether we believe it or not. The question is whether you will be a willing participant and active proponent of the flip, or if will you struggle to hang onto an outmoded, broken world that serves the darker parts of our being. By choosing to believe in the possibilities of the human spirit, by embracing the flip, you can become free to express yourself and work for a balanced world and a wholehearted life.

The choice is yours.

ONE

FLIPPING YOUR LIFE

From Flipped Out to Flipped In

Barry U., a troubled resident of the upside-down world, groans and hits the snooze button, hoping for ten more minutes of peace before beginning another dreaded day. After a quick shower while CNN blurts news of the latest bombings, celebrity scandals, government cuts, and corporate malfeasance, Barry slams back a cup of coffee. He prays the caffeine will kick in and change his mood. As he navigates rush-hour traffic, Barry's pulse quickens. He frets over his mounting debts—first and second mortgages, three credit cards near their limit, car payments, and a plethora of other "necessary" expenses. He turns on the radio to calm his anxiety, only to find his mobile inner sanctum invaded by news, sports, weather, stocks, and shock-jocks.

At work, sixty-three emails and seventeen voice mails await. He desperately wants to escape to the Caribbean, if just for a long weekend. Barry deserves a vacation but is so afraid of being downsized or outsourced—despite being "Employee of the Year" last year—that he doesn't dare take a much-needed respite. He'll soldier on, valiantly trying to make sense of his chaotic circumstances.

Sound familiar? Perhaps you know someone like that. We do—lots of them. People in our day and age are flipped out! Flipped out about job security, social security, and homeland security. They watch the news about flipped-out people doing flipped-out things sponsored by companies selling products and pills to calm and protect them from further flipping out. It's a crowded place, this upside-down world.

A MILLENNIUM OF CONTRADICTION

Life at the dawn of the new millennium is filled with contradictions and distractions. Our lives are measured by possessions and productivity, by quantity rather than quality. We tell ourselves we have to work harder, faster, longer. We are tethered to our jobs, willfully enslaved by technology—cell phones, pagers, PDAs, email, the Internet, text messaging—so that even when we are out of the office, we never escape the pressure of business. Our predicament is like the popular parable of the circus elephant. At a young, age the elephant's leg is tied to a stake, forcing it walk round in a circle, entraining it. As a large, formidable adult it could easily pull the stake and run free, but it does not, having been programmed to walk in a circle. And so it is for people and their belief that they cannot be far from the responsibilities of their job. For many, work defines our identity and sets us on a dangerous path of frenetic pace, exaggerated self-importance, and perpetual crisis invention.

> **Every morning I wake up torn between a desire to save the world and an inclination to savor it. This makes it hard to plan the day.**
> —E. B. White

Have we fallen victim to the insatiable call of consumerism, which brings on debt, which brings on the need to earn more money, which forces us into servitude in jobs that greedily demand more and more of our time? Are we caught in a vicious cycle of our making?

It's a competitive world, to be sure. But does it have to be?

Try this. Close your eyes and ask yourself what the three most important things are in your life. Just three. C'mon, close your eyes. Don't think about it too long; just quickly name three things. Now look at the list and place a checkmark by the items you named.

❏ Money	❏ Family
❏ Car	❏ Friends
❏ Job	❏ Love
❏ Status	❏ Home
❏ Fashion	❏ Nature
❏ Fame	❏ Music
❏ Clothes	❏ God/Higher Power
❏ Food	❏ Health
❏ Sex	❏ Intimacy

On which side do your checkmarks predominate? If the three things you named are not on the example above, on which side of the grid do you honestly feel they belong? The left side represents material or ego-related needs, the right side a set of ideas and experiences related to spirituality. You can probably guess which one is upside-down and which is Right-Side Up. How did you do?

Now ask yourself how balanced your lifestyle is, especially in relation to the things you say are the most important to you. A simple calculation of where you spend your free time will tell you where your life is compared to where you want it to be—in which world are you standing. Here goes:

24 hours in a day
- 9 hours working, including the optional luxury of a one-hour lunch
- 1 hour of drive time to and from work
- <u>8</u> hours sleeping
= 6 hours remaining in your waking hours

How do you spend those precious six hours? In front of the TV? Drinking in a bar? Shopping? Catching up on paperwork from the office? Having a nutritious, pleasant dinner with loved ones? Taking a walk? Reading a book? Volunteering for a worthwhile social cause? The answers are important because they represent the decisions you've made that have led to your happiness or hollowness.

Make no mistake, these are your choices—no one else's.

Another way to determine on which side you're living is to consider the things that preoccupy your mind. Are you thinking about the mortgage? Are you fretting over the bills? Worried about whether your boss will approve of your work on the project of the moment? Or are you thinking about bringing flowers to your partner? Perhaps calling a friend to express how much he or she means to you? Planning to join a yoga class with your mother?

The level of general agitation or stress you feel is an excellent compass for what direction your life is heading, or in which world you currently reside. Is it Right-Side Up or upside-down?

MAKING THE FLIP

Mary R. is a contented citizen of the Right-Side Up world. She awakens invigorated and opens her window for a deep breath of fresh air. She admires the flowers in her garden as she listens to the birds chirp in nearby maples. She puts on a kettle for a relaxing cup of organic green tea and reads a passage from a favorite book. After a leisurely shower she meditates for half an hour. Dressing for work, Mary looks forward to meeting new people and discovering unexpected opportunities. She knows there will be problems to challenge her, but she also knows that whatever situation arises she will ably deal with it. She is confident, happy, and fulfilled.

Sound far-fetched?

Hardly. Mary is one of millions of actual people who have made the flip to the Right-Side Up world. They have come to terms with the daily requirements of living in these times and have developed individual methods of nurturing themselves. They have mastered being mindful in a hustle-bustle age. Mary and other Flipsters have each created a personalized plan that enables them to feel whole in the fragmented upside-down world. To the millions who have already flipped, that other polarized, divided world is simply a crazy memory of an antiquated age.

Flipsters have recognized their responsibility for happiness. The TVs and radios have been turned off. The consumption of mindless mass media has been reduced or eliminated. They read books. They take walks. They are open to yoga, pottery, meditation, energy healing or a dozen other interests. They are active in that which serves their well-being and that of society. They contribute to good causes. They pitch in when needed. They practice the faith of their preference, or none at all. The Flipsters are the embodiment of mastering duality in recognition of our Oneness.

Does this mean Flipsters don't have problems? Of course not. Hello . . . we are living on planet Earth after all. No one is immune to life's dramas. But those who have made the flip are ready for what life deals them. They know that the duality of existence will present continual challenges and opportunities.

OPERATING UNDER THE INFLUENCE

Since this chapter is about flipping your life, we need to delve deeper into the influences—both conscious and subconscious—that affect us. It is important to recognize that we don't all respond exactly the same to similar stimuli. One may love vanilla ice cream while another may have an allergic reaction to it. Each of us has individual needs, wants, and desires. But there are overarching societal forces that exert powerful influences over most of us, many causing serious detriment to ourselves and the planet. These influences affect the way we think and the way we feel—both topics we will address in chapters 2 and 3, respectively.

What we take into our mind and body virtually controls all aspects of our lives and our happiness. We ingest massive doses of negative daily news and watch show upon show (the average American watches eight hours of TV per day) of "programming" that promotes the darker sides of our nature.

We further corrupt our lifestyles with processed foods full of chemical preservatives and additives meant to ensure a longer shelf life, but definitely not a longer human life. Then, feeling bad, we trudge to the doctor for this pill or that injection, not to cure, but to mask the symptoms we are feeling. You can see where this is going, can't you?

The homes, cars, places of work, and industries of America selfishly consume 40 percent of the world's energy, using sources that pollute our air, land, and water—further adversely affecting our health. To secure our energy needs we wage war. Most wars are fought for economic reasons, and the dominant driver of contemporary economies is energy in the form of oil.

Yes, we need a strong defense to protect us from hostile countries, but we have recently crossed the Rubicon and begun launching preemptive wars on the flimsiest of excuses. Lest you think we are unpatriotic, we are not. We love our country. But we also love the Earth and care about all its people. And there is strong evidence dating back at least a hundred years to support the notion that our leaders take us into war for profit and power. This information will be discussed in chapter 10, "Flipping the Trigger: From Tribal Warfare to Global Tribe."

> **Only a life lived for others is worth living.**
> —Author Unknown

To change the unfortunate "profit over people" priority, corporations must be accountable and responsible for their impact not only economically, but socially and environmentally as well. The movement is already substantially underway in many business sectors, with only a handful of industries dominated by the world's largest corporations resisting the flip.

Sadly, in our upside-down world, children can name more corporate logos than indigenous trees. Thirty years ago this was not the case. But there is hope. And progress. And momentum. Even as the Earth heats up and the threat of human extinction hangs over us like the sword of Damocles, there is another kind of global warming—that of the human heart. We are living at a time in history when the evolutionary shift is rapidly taking all of us from the materialistic, mechanistic age to one of mindful awareness and enlightenment.

To hasten this we must change our relationship with money. Not that money in and of itself is bad, but it should not and cannot be the primary motivator of our decisions. Chapters 8 and 9 discuss how we can flip our approach to both money and business—in a positive, healthy manner.

And finally, in chapter 11 we return full circle to the inner beliefs we hold in the form of religion and spirituality—to the core essence of our faith and how a true understanding of the realities and illusions of belief can lead us to contentment and fulfillment.

Sounds like a lot to cover, doesn't it? Well, we're up for it. We've been preparing for this our entire lives—as have you. Plus, we have millions of Flipsters already living in the Right-Side Up world, leading the way by example.

EQUAL OPPORTUNITY FLIPSTERS

Becoming a Flipster, participating in one of the greatest shifts in consciousness in humankind, does not require credentials. No shoes, no shirt—no problem. It doesn't matter whether you are a suburban housewife in Denver, a bachelor in New York City, an heiress in Beverly Hills, or a father of five in Topeka—the flip is waiting for you to embrace it.

Political affiliations are meaningless. Christians, Buddhists, Hindus, Pagans, atheists, human secularists, and every kind of believer (or nonbeliever) in between can participate. The flip doesn't care if you graduated Summa Cum Laude, got your GED, or dropped out of high school. Race and gender are immaterial. Nationality is moot.

> **The great and glorious masterpiece of humanity is to know how to live with purpose.**
>
> —Montaigne

It matters little if you are an unemployed steel worker, a corporate executive, a sales rep, or a social worker. The flip doesn't take Visa, MasterCard, or American Express. All are welcome to the flip.

There is only one prerequisite—the desire to better yourself and society. That's it! Ah, you say, there must be a catch. Well, yes, there is. Beyond the desire to change—to become a full-fledged Flipster—you must do the work yourself. No one else can live your life. No one else can make your decisions for you. Living in the Right-Side Up world requires being responsible for your actions—all of them. It demands inner work and requires letting go of the need to blame others for your circumstances. The flip may lead to bold actions and even to temporary chaos.

Seems challenging, we know. It is even harder work than it sounds. There is an infinite array of temptations, influences, and distractions to keep you living in the upside-down world. But if you can break free and make the flip, the reward is worth it.

MEET THE FLIPSTERS—
CONVERSATIONS ON THE BRIDGE

We realize that we may have painted an impossible ideal in the eyes of many. Some of you are highly skeptical, jaded even—and ready to heave this book into the trash. Before you rush to judgment, we ask that you listen to some prominent thought leaders, experts on the human mind and the impending flip that is coming at us whether we want it or not.

Between the upside-down world and the Right-Side Up one is the bridge of choice, where people can choose between two ways of living. To help you further understand and integrate the flip, we will meet a variety of leaders who have dedicated their life's work to helping people shift their consciousness and awaken to an enriching and undeniably flipped life. These people on the bridge are true agents of change already engaging in the dynamic, vibrant world of possibility.

First up is Dr. Paul Ray, one of the world's leading authorities on social and cultural trends, who discusses the differences between the fundamentalist and modern movements and how they affect the flip to the next stage of our conscious evolution. Byron Katie, author of *Loving What Is,* gives her view of the flip and how anyone can flip any situation just by changing the way one looks at it. Yolanda King, founder and CEO of Higher Ground and daughter of Martin Luther King, Jr., shows how each of us has our own unique light to shine. We close this important chapter with the inspiring insight and words of wisdom from *New York Times* best-selling author Barbara De Angelis, who discusses how we can find our authentic selves and create lives of happiness and fulfillment.

In the interest of brevity we edited down the "conversations" with the Flipsters. For the complete interviews, and to read interviews of additional Flipsters not in this book, please visit our website at www.theflip.net.

Okay, here we go . . .

A CONVERSATION ON THE
BRIDGE WITH DR. PAUL RAY

Paul Ray, Ph.D. (www.culturalcreatives.org), is coauthor with his wife, Sherry Ruth Anderson, Ph.D., of the best-selling book *Cultural Creatives: How 50 Million People Are Changing the World.* Paul has surveyed and classified more than 100,000 Americans in the past thirteen years, showing how the subcultures of values permeate all aspects of American life. During the time of the research reported in the book, he was executive vice president of American LIVES, Inc., a market-research and opinion-polling firm specializing in surveys and focus groups based on American lifestyles, interests, values, expectations, and symbols. The research projects that led to the discovery of the "Cultural Creatives" include studies of the effects of values on consumer choices and the preferences of Americans for housing, cars, food, recreation, vacation travel, finances, health, political causes (e.g., environment), media use, and altruism. He also leads studies of innovation by consumers and business.

We first asked Paul how a modern person, accustomed to luxuries and conveniences unparalleled in human history, might become aware of how his or her affluent lifestyle deleteriously affects the welfare of the planet as a whole. "Part of what I'm impressed with as a macrosociologist is the persistence of the past to affect people through unconsciousness and habit," Paul comments. "People believe that things should be just as they were when they grew up as a kid. To a lot of people, tradition is nothing more complicated than 'whatever is comfortable for me.' The persistence of habit goes with unconsciousness. So the beginning of change is coming to a conscious awareness that our backs are against a wall as a species, that we really have to make fundamental change to assure the survival of ourselves and our children."

But what can flip people out of their habitual denial and resistance to change? "Just pushing or rebelling against what's happening is only the first step out of unconsciousness," Paul observes. "The moment you start turning your attention toward a more embracing, higher kind of consciousness, and asking how we could create what I call a wisdom culture, then you're taking the next step toward a new level of development.

"Modernism is an evolutionary plateau in the same way that agricultural society was a plateau above hunting and gathering. Modernism is a level above agrarian societies in terms of complexity, sophistication, cultural knowledge, and so on. But modernism has never faced up to the idea that we can consciously invent a better world together."

That idea, Paul asserts, is the underlying motivation of the growing segment of society that he has identified as Cultural Creatives. "These are people—50 million American adults and 80 million European adults—who take the idea of ecology very seriously, and they support slowing business growth in order to save the planet. They also take very seriously women's issues and issues of personal growth and relationships. We found that the typical

Cultural Creative cares intensely about the issues raised by post-World War II social movements. These movements include those focused on civil rights, the environment, women's rights, peace, jobs, social justice, gay and lesbian rights, alternative health care, spirituality, personal growth, and now, of course, stopping corporate globalization. All of those concerns are now converging into a strong concern for the whole planet."

What distinguishes the thinking of a Cultural Creative? "Holistic thinking; that is, thinking in longer time horizons than the next quarter's profits, the next election cycle, or even one's own life span. This means that Cultural Creatives are motivated by concern for all the people of the planet and all the living systems of the planet. The idea of living systems is new to modernism because that perspective looks at how nonliving things are put together or taken apart, which is fundamentally a nineteenth-century idea. This idea is obsolete in every part of contemporary science and technology . . .

"One of the things that dogs our culture now is that we're living in a time when a lot of institutions are starting to fall apart. The falling-apart process has both dangers and opportunities. Modernism falling apart is what will leave enough open space to go to the next level of cultural integration."

> **Hope sees the invisible, feels the intangible, achieves the impossible.**
> —Anonymous

But isn't a time of falling apart also a time of chaos and anarchy? Paul Ray is optimistic. "Rather than seeing this as a time of great fear and potential tragedy, we can see it as our chance to rise above our old ways to become our best selves. If you were to take a 10,000-year perspective on humanity, we've come to the high point of our drama. Artistically, it's a cliffhanger! It's exciting and appealing—the chance to start building and living in the world you want."

A CONVERSATION ON THE BRIDGE WITH BYRON KATIE

Byron Katie (www.thework.com) became severely depressed while in her thirties. Over a ten-year period her depression deepened, and Katie spent almost two years seldom able to leave her bed, obsessing over suicide. Then one morning, from the depths of despair, she experienced a life-changing realization that her illness was based upon her perception. This epiphany flipped her life.

TIME magazine has profiled Katie, calling her "a visionary for the new millennium." In March 2002, Harmony Books published Katie's first book, *Loving What Is: Four Questions That Can Change Your Life,* cowritten with renowned author/translator Stephen Mitchell. *Loving What Is* has been translated into twenty languages. Her second book, *I Need Your Love—Is That True?,* was also a best-seller.

"I was depressed for more than a decade," Katie confesses, "and if I look back on it, probably forty years. My self-esteem was so low that I didn't believe I even deserved a bed to sleep in. So I slept on the floor. One particular morning as I lay on the floor asleep, a cockroach crawled over my foot. I opened my eyes and in place of all that darkness, rage, and confusion I'd known was a joy that I can't describe. What I suddenly understood was this: *When I believe my thoughts I suffer, but when I question my thoughts I don't suffer.* I've come to see that this is true for every human being.

"In that moment, I simply noticed the nature of my thoughts when I no longer believed them. That is a moment of truth—or a moment of clarity, as I call it. And I think we all have them. We all have these moments when we're lucid. We begin to see that the whole world is created through our thoughts, and when we believe our thoughts we literally project them on our material world. Once we begin to question our stressful thoughts, we're on the way to heaven—happiness, that is. Isn't that what everything is for? We want health, balance, and happiness."

Life is a flower of which love is the honey.

—Victor Hugo

Then why is there so much unhappiness in many people's everyday experience? Katie suggests it has less to do with unhappy circumstances than habitual thought patterns. "Suffering is simply believing whatever we think. The mind is prone to think 'life isn't fair' and then not to question that assumption. It immediately begins to only see in tunnel vision, to only see and bring to mind all the proofs, pictures, thoughts, stories—all the other evidence that supports the first assumption: Life is unfair. But by that point, you may not be seeing what's real at all. I use the example of walking through the desert and seeing a snake. You jump back, your heart is racing and you break out into a sweat before you look again and notice there is no snake, just an old rope. How could you have been so silly? Immediately, the fear subsides and the laughter starts. That's an example of what questioning the mind does.

"For me, problems are no longer possible because I see through them. I invite people to understand that every snake is a rope, not just some of them.

There's no exception to that in my life, so I'm open to whatever happens next. For all I know, all hell could break loose. I look forward to it."

We asked Ms. Katie what the average person can do when confronted with their own "snakes." Her process, which she calls The Work, is simple enough. "We need to question what we believe. There are four questions you can ask yourself to investigate a stressful belief. When we think a thought, what should immediately arise along with that thought is the question *Is it true?* The second question is a more thorough version of that: *Can I absolutely know that it's true?* The third question shows cause and effect: *How do I react when I believe that thought?* And the fourth question brings us back to our origin: *Who would I be without that thought?* And then I ask people to turn the thought around. The turnaround is a way of experiencing the opposite of what you believe and seeing that it is at least as true. You'll find these four questions and the turnaround thought quite powerful in changing your perceptions."

A CONVERSATION ON THE BRIDGE WITH YOLANDA KING

Yolanda King (www.yolanda-king.com), founder and CEO of Higher Ground Productions, is an amazing and dynamic voice among twenty-first-century speakers. The first-born daughter of Coretta Scott King and Dr. Martin Luther King, Jr., Yolanda has a mission to encourage personal growth and positive social change through her artistic endeavors, including acting, producing, speaking, and teaching. It is Ms. King's passion for peace and positive change that prompted her vision for founding Higher Ground Productions, an organization dedicated to teaching people to celebrate diversity and embrace unity through the arts.

With her father being one of the major lights of modern civilization, one naturally wonders if Yolanda feels an obligation to extend his legacy. "I have felt a calling for as long as I can remember," she affirms. "When you grow up in an environment where there is a commitment to service, to making a difference and helping others—a commitment that is not only just talked about, but is actually lived in front of you—it naturally takes root in your life. I see it in all my siblings, not just me. We had the opportunity to see that commitment lived so purely and so passionately, both in my father and mother.

"They say the best sermons are the ones that are lived. My father not only talked the talk, and did a really great job of that, he also walked the talk and so did my grandparents, on both sides. So there was this ancestral energy that resulted in my feeling a very strong responsibility. So I've spent a great deal of my life trying to carve out a place for myself in this awesome legacy and make a difference on my own."

Since no one can simply imitate the legacy of their famous forebears, how did Yolanda find her own special means of contributing? "I took the long road to get to where I am," Yolanda reveals. "Interestingly enough, I'm working on a book now that's called *Embracing Your Power in Thirty Days*. But it took me almost thirty years to get there! I'm showing people a process that will minimize their wandering around in the wilderness like I did.

"I've wanted to be an actress since I was eight. That was the first burning desire in my spirit, to perform. And I started doing theater at a very young age. But I got sidetracked because I thought that it was not significant enough. I thought it was a very self-centered profession and I could not see how I could make a difference that way. So I tried to do other things, even though I was acting at the same time. I had a theater company and we ran around the country doing work that was touching the lives of young people. But because I was trying to figure out a way to combine this huge calling to make a difference with this passion to perform, I did a lot of other things trying to find myself. At one time I had three full-time jobs—which is impossible!

"The point is that it took me a while to realize that I could do both— that I could utilize my art and my gift, and that I could use that gift to uplift and to *edutain,* as I call it—blend education and entertainment. I realized that I could be true to this calling. And my gracious, what peace I have had since I've been able to reconcile that within my spirit!"

Yolanda's experience made us wonder which comes first: a personal or social inspiration? "It's really a blending," she says. "I feel strongly that you can't stand up for anything else unless you have learned to stand up for yourself in an honest, authentic way. If you're not true to yourself, if you're not clear about who you are and what your purpose is and what your unique gift is to the planet, then there's only so much that you're going to be able to give to the world. So I try to help people understand that they have a light, that they are significant, that they are a part of this incredible whole. Each and every last one of us has something very special and unique that we bring to the rest of us. It is from that impetus that people begin to look at what's happening in their home, in their workplace, their community, and what's happening on this planet. I believe if you are clear about who you are, you can be a wonderful light for the world. Everywhere you go, that sense of clarity, that sense of conviction, reverberates.

"On the other hand, I think it's pretty difficult to be a true light on this planet and not be engaged in service in some way. Once you have awakened to what your own potential is, I can't imagine that you would not want to share that. It doesn't have to be in the way of conventional activism, like marching and petitioning, even though those methods are incredibly important. Activism can look very different for everyone, but there is no way that you can be in that place of change in your own life and not want to effect change in other places.

"Now, there are those, of course, who are on the high spiritual path, that go to caves and into monasteries, and that's what they do and that's fine. But I can't imagine it. That's not the tradition that I come from. I come from a tradition that's spiritual and visionary, but deeply activist."

What is Yolanda's dream for the evolution of humanity? "My dream would be the worldwide realization that each and every one of us is one. We are so vitally connected that we are like pieces of an incredible puzzle. We are all together, breathing this one breath. My dream is that once we realize that, we would understand that if I hurt or harm you, I'm destroying a piece of myself. I can't do that because it would be like cutting myself off at the knees or tearing out my heart! When we realize that, and I believe that we will, there will be peace. That would be my dream for the evolution of humanity—universal recognition of our oneness."

> **The art of living lies not in eliminating but in growing with troubles.**
> —Bernard M. Baruch

A CONVERSATION ON THE BRIDGE WITH DR. BARBARA DE ANGELIS

Barbara De Angelis, Ph.D. (www.barbaradeangelis.com), is one of the most influential teachers of our time in the field of relationships and personal growth. For the past twenty-five years, she has reached tens of millions of people throughout the world with her positive messages about love, happiness, and the search for meaning in our lives. As a best-selling author, popular television personality, and sought-after motivational speaker, Barbara has been a pioneer in the field of personal transformation, one of the first people to popularize the idea of self-help in the 1980s, and one of the first nationally recognized female motivational teachers on television.

Barbara is the author of fourteen best-selling books which have sold more than eight million copies and been published throughout the world in twenty languages. Her latest book is *How Did I Get Here? Finding Your Way to Renewed Hope and Happiness When Life and Love Take Unexpected Turns*. We asked Barbara about how taking stock of one's place in life can contribute to a flip of perspective. "Asking the question *How did I get here?* can be an amazing moment of awakening because most people don't have the courage to ask such questions. As I wrote in the new book, 'As travelers on life's paths, we are defined by both the questions we ask ourselves and by the ones we avoid asking.' A lot of people spend their life running from questions, and I have spent my life running toward questions. I invite people to ask the kinds of questions that help them awaken and live more conscious lives. Times of deep questioning are not times of weakness or falling apart, but periods of tremendous transformation. You do have to let go of the ego in a sense, and be willing to allow the unraveling of yourself, your beliefs, and your expectations in order to truly flip and make a breakthrough. You can't fly when you're still on the ground. You can't move while you stand still. It can be frightening when you're flailing around and there's nothing to hold onto. That's a very powerful moment of breakthrough. But it requires a sense of truly letting go and trusting that there will be something on the other side of your leap."

In figuring out "how we got here," do we run the risk of becoming absorbed with the past? "Understanding where we came from, what decisions we've made, and how we've limited ourselves is essential for moving forward," says Barbara. "Otherwise we may tell ourselves that we're in the present, but we'll have a trail of ghosts following us. Every time I do a session with someone, I see their ghosts hovering: the ghosts of their former relationships, of their family, their parents, and so on. Until we understand those influences and become free of them, saying 'I'm living in the moment' doesn't mean anything. In the moment doesn't mean anything unless you're in each moment without being in reaction to the moment before, and the moment before, and the moment before. I call that emotional freedom, which means being free of the influences of the past. The more of that freedom we have, the less fear of the future we will have.

"After all, the universe sometimes takes us by surprise. Most people refuse to grow until they are forced to grow. You can choose to grow or you can be forced to grow. Most people on the planet tend to be forced to grow and even then are often resistant because of their fear. And fear makes us inauthentic, not our real selves. There's nothing more exhausting than living without authenticity. People do not realize how much energy it takes to not be who we are. It's unbelievable how draining it is to talk, to act, to love, to be a way that is not authentically you.

"On the other hand, nothing is more exciting than to start to live authentically. You'll feel an enormous power surging through you; again, that's emotional freedom. It's as if we've just had this power turned back on after an outage. As hard as it is to do this, the reward is fantastic. Everything is flowing; you're not blocking the flow of shakti or whatever you want to call it. Most people are walking around cut off from that because they're afraid of the consequences, yet in a sense it's no one's fault because we live in a society where authenticity is not rewarded. What's rewarded is conformity and fitting into an image. As a culture we mistrust things that are too different. So it takes a lot of courage to be authentic in a world where people really value fitting in."

We wondered if it takes a lot of "self-love" to have the courage to flip and become more authentic in everyday life. Barbara got right to the point: "The truth is, everything we do is out of self-love. And I'm always telling people that it's an illusion that we do not love ourselves. Everything we do is ultimately out of self-love and self-preservation; it's impossible for it to be otherwise. Let's say a person has a pattern of choosing unloving partners. We'll tend to think, 'If she loved herself, she would choose better partners.' But what she's actually trying to do is heal a pattern, probably rooted in childhood, of trying to get someone's love, feeling that she must work very hard to earn people's love. And there is love that is behind her choice. She is telling herself, 'Let me do it right. Let me go back to when I was six and this time I'm going to get Daddy's love, I just know I am.' So it's not lack of love that's making her do that, it's just a misunderstanding of the best way to share and realize love. It's the same thing with people who think they need to become more powerful. In fact, we're all equally powerful. It's just that some of us use our power to hold ourselves back, and others to propel ourselves forward. We all have the same manifestation of shakti, chi, and divine energy. We all are *love*. It's just that some of us are using our love in some very twisted, convoluted ways.

"It's a great revelation for people when they understand that they hold

> **Make each day useful and cheerful and prove that you know the worth of time by employing it well. Then youth will be happy, old age without regret, and life a beautiful success.**
>
> —Louisa May Alcott

themselves back not from a lack of self-love, but because they are used to protecting themselves instead of taking chances. Either way, love is the motivation. You can use the same love that keeps you in place, protected from taking chances, to be courageous and become more authentic."

That is a powerful personal flip.

LIFE, LOVE, LAUGHTER

As you can see from these conversations, the flip is happening on societal and individual levels. It happens when you are personally ready; it's a matter of whether you wish to live in pain and frustration in the upside-down world, or prefer to take a chance by making the flip to the Right-Side Up world. But as Barbara De Angelis pointed out, it takes more work to suffer through an inauthentic existence than it does to become who you truly are.

So who are you? Only you can discover that. But it should be a labor of love. The rewards of living an authentic life cannot be measured: unconditional love, joyous laughter, lifelong friendships, golden moments of grace and wonder.

> One must live and create. Live to the point of tears.
> —Albert Camus

By contrast, living in the upside down-world is taxing. It's a toxic mash of misinformation and mayhem, a stew of contradiction and chaos. It is a daily challenge to know who and what to believe. But fortunately that world is falling apart. Millions of people have embraced the flip in their lives. You can too. You don't have to be famous, wealthy, or some kind of genius. You only have to be aware. There isn't one right way or a bunch of wrong roads. Every soul on this planet has the opportunity to flip, indeed is given the signs pointing to one's own need to flip along with clues to what needs flipping. The answers are as individualized as the person. For some, the change may arrive in a flash of life-changing insight; for others there is a cumulative process of unfolding discoveries. One person may realize the need to change upon receiving bad news from the doctor; for another, it may come in the form of a severed relationship; someone else may evolve from an inquisitive curiosity that invites perpetual growth. Though we are all enlightened beings, we are not on the same path. We may live through similar experiences, but we experience their meanings uniquely. It was once said that "there are as many ways to love as there are moments in time," and we think there are as many ways to flip as well. Finding your moment is a matter of your awareness and desire.

Not content to simply describe the flip in general life terms, we shall press on to new chapters which will discuss particular areas of our lives and specific causes, patterns, and decisions that have caused our world to be upside down—and we'll discuss what you can do about it. We close with Mahatma Gandhi's Seven Blunders of the World, which may be used as an indicator of which way our world is turned today.

1. Wealth without work
2. Pleasure without conscience
3. Knowledge without character
4. Commerce without morality
5. Science without humanity
6. Worship without sacrifice
7. Politics without principle

Take a few moments to ask yourself what needs to be flipped in your life. Don't intellectualize your feelings. Listen closely to your heart. When you're ready, we'll meet you in chapter 2.

FLIP TIPS

**Here are a few easy-to-implement suggestions
for beginning your flip:**

- Call a good friend and express gratitude or appreciation for their friendship.
- Take a walk (without your iPod or Walkman).
- Be cognizant and appreciative of the resources you use—water, food, fuel.
- Be mindful about your intake of electronic media—TV, radio, Web.
- Sing out loud—even if you can't hold a note.
- Shake up your routine by doing something completely out of character.
- Spend an entire day in silence.
- Resist the temptation to judge, blame, or criticize.
- Before speaking always ask yourself: Is what I'm about to say true? Is it kind? Is it necessary?
- Do something kind for someone you don't know.

FLIPPING THE MIND

From Fragmented Thought to Whole Thinking

Barry U. is anxious. His grande mocha double espresso supreme with light crème has kicked in. Two hours into his workday, he's still replying to email, despite a strong desire to delete them all. He suspects no one would notice his lack of response. He checks the stock market every fifteen minutes to follow his 401K, even though he won't need the funds for another thirty years. In a midmorning meeting, Barry is jittery as his boss takes credit for his work in a team presentation. To keep from blurting out his resentment, Barry distracts himself by thinking of bills—two car payments, braces for his daughter, mortgage, phone, cell phone, second mortgage, health club which he hasn't gone to in six months, and three credit cards.

> **Very little is needed to make a happy life: It is all within yourself, in your way of thinking.**
>
> —Marcus Aurelius

His blood is boiling now. Barry thinks of the day's news—three people murdered in Virginia, an Amber Alert in Omaha, wildfires in Arizona, a diet guaranteed to help you lose weight, devastating natural disaster in Sri Lanka, and a scientific study that proves global warming is accelerating at an alarming rate. Barry's mind is awash in fragmented thoughts and disjointed information.

The meeting adjourns. Barry's to-do list just got seriously longer. Back at his desk, Barry spends his lunch time surfing the Web, haunting news sites where he soaks up more information he cannot process, does not need, and can do nothing with. He puts off starting the three reports that are due by week's end, not knowing where to begin. He is flustered. Angry. Lost.

His mind is racing, reeling actually. Insecurity has got the better of him. To calm himself, he pops a Valium and swigs it down with a cup of coffee.

He looks forward to the evening when he can plunk down in front of the TV and watch crime-drama reruns while he catches up on paperwork. But before he gets there he has to pick up dinner on the way home. Oh, and the dry cleaning. Oh, oh, and he has to stop at the ATM and get some cash—after he sits in traffic for forty-five minutes or so.

Unfortunately, Barry's day is typical for many of us in the upside-down world. With so much stimulation, it's no wonder we feel harried, stressed, and overwhelmed. The brain, the central processor of all this stimuli, is an incredibly efficient tool. It receives, interprets, and acts upon all the information coming at it from the five senses—and, as if that weren't enough—an average of forty thousand thoughts per day. That's right, forty thousand.

Whew! We're tired just thinking about it.

A three-pound electrochemically activated gray mass of folded tissue, the brain also regulates trillions of cellular interactions in our body daily. To maintain a semblance of sanity, it must make sense of all that it is taking in, monitoring, and responding to. It's a big job running a human being, so the brain filters and compartmentalizes information in its myriad forms into neat little categories. Unless, of course, it is overloaded with sensory input, in which case it is like an entire gallon of juice being poured into an eight-ounce glass. The excess information overflows the receptacle, so to speak, and creates a big mess—in our minds, in our lives, in our upside-down world.

> **All that we are is the result of what we have thought. The mind is everything. What we have thought, we become.**
> —Buddha

The most prevalent manifestation of this self-generated mess shows itself in a range of fear-based emotions—anxiety, insecurity, low self-esteem, jealousy, guilt, blaming of others. You get the picture, and it isn't pretty. There is simply too much to consider and not enough time, leaving us unsure of, well—of everything. This fear-based state overshadows our thinking and darkens our outlook, producing ever more fear and anxiety and disrupting our quality of life.

So why do we keep bombarding our brains with so much clutter, with so much "noise"? (Uh-oh—something else to think about, right?)

A BRAIN TEASER

Now here is an ironic and puzzling fact: the brain is the vehicle for one of the most fascinating and mysterious things we know—the human mind. Yet *one cannot find the mind in the brain.* It just can't be done.

The mind is an invisible force of incomprehensible power. Through the brain the mind has been researched, analyzed, and pondered by the best and brightest in the world. Hundreds of billions of dollars have been spent studying brain chemistry, neuroscience, psychiatry, psychology, human behavior, sociology, and genetics and still very little is actually known about this remarkable vessel of thought, creativity, and spirit.

Sure, scientists can stick an electrode here or a probe there and elicit this emotion or that sensation, and they can describe the electrochemical process behind such phenomena, but they cannot tell you why a particular person thinks, behaves, believes, imagines, or dreams the way she does.

The ancients believed the psyche and the mind were inseparable, one and the same. That is, the mind is the spirit or soul of a person. The mind is the intangible essence that makes each of us unique. What did the ancients know that we have forgotten?

> **The soul contains the event that shall befall it, for the event is only the actualization of its thoughts, and what we pray to ourselves for is always granted.**
> —Ralph Waldo Emerson

Buckminster Fuller, the esteemed inventor, author, and visionary said, "Ninety-nine percent of a person is invisible and untouchable." Indeed, Bucky was onto something. For who can truly know the imperceptible thoughts, feelings, consciousness, awareness, and intuitions of another? Can you? Most of us have a hard enough time understanding our own thoughts and motivations, let alone what's going on inside those around us.

WELCOME TO THE GREAT DIVIDE

An existential chasm exists between the brain and the mind, between the physical and nonphysical, between the material and the spiritual. This is a natural state for spiritual beings having a human experience. We are meant to witness the conflict and contrast; that is, the fundamental duality of our existence.

We cannot exist here on this planet as purely spiritual beings, ignoring the physical attributes and demands of the Earth. Nor can we thrive in strictly physical terms, tending only to our own personal needs, ignoring our higher selves, endlessly fighting others for survival.

That worked tens of thousands of years ago when humans first crawled out of the muck and dragged their hairy knuckles into caves. But not today.

There are too many of us—six billion and counting—and our ability to destroy ourselves and our environment is too ominous. The antiquated reptilian models of "fight or flight" no longer serve humanity.

Yes, there are situations when a healthy dose of fear is warranted. Fear in the right measure at the right moment can avert a tragedy or save a life. But fear should not be one's primary state of mind. Fear is basically a signal from the brain reacting to unfriendly material circumstances. Whereas its emotional opposite, love, flows from the heart-mind.

Yeah, we know. Sounds trite, huh? *Fear is the opposite of love.* You've heard it before. But a truth like this is always worth remembering and repeating. It is this play of opposites that gives life its rich texture. But the opposite ends of anything actually bookend the whole: For example, male and female are opposite genders, hot and cold are opposite temperatures. They are simply different representations of the same thing. One cannot exist without the other. That is the universal interplay of energy. The trouble starts when the opposites become so polarized in people, and collectively in society, that views and positions become intractable, intolerant, and riddled with fear.

We have a choice whether to let our fears overtake us, isolate us from others based on our insecurities, and leave us fundamentally afraid to face the world. Instead, we can embrace life, love others despite their faults (and ours), and let ourselves be loved. Doesn't that sound like an easy and wonderful choice to make?

STRIKING THE BALANCE

Since we live in Oneness masquerading as duality (separation caused by opposites), the key is finding balance between the two states and through this fusion, discovering unity and embracing our connection to the whole. This is no easy task. If one gets too weighted down in the physical realm—the upside-down world—a narcissistic "it's-all-about-me" attitude develops that encourages self-enrichment and destructive behavior at the expense of others. Greed, intolerance, bigotry, war, and a boatload of other nastiness become the rule of society while the greater good of the people becomes subservient to nationalistic fervor and the dictates of powerful institutions.

Look around you. Is the world in balance? Is your life? Chances are high, if you are reading this book, that you suspect something is amiss in your life. In fact, the odds are stacked against us in today's fast-paced, technological, financially driven, marketing-manipulated, fear-based world. We often

teeter-totter between being in and out of balance. We struggle to bring ourselves back to center, to remember the best parts of who we are. And that is
one of life's great lessons.

SOMEHOW WE KNOW

We seem to live alone and separate, yet somehow we know that we are part
of something larger, something greater. We know we are part of the totality of
Creation. But we struggle to voice it. Some call it God; others, the Goddess, a
Higher Power, collective consciousness, the Creator, the unified field, the Great
Pumpkin, the One, the Almighty, Allah. There are many names we humans
have created to explain our connection to the larger whole,
but regardless of its name, most cultures throughout time
have recognized and celebrated this Oneness.

Until now.

In today's society we are inundated with meaningless
information that we cannot process and cannot do anything about. We are fragmented thinkers, frantically trying
to jump from one thing to the next. Our brains are overloaded with inane considerations and purposeless distrac-

**The comic and
the tragic lie
inseparably
close—like light
and shadow.**

—Socrates

tions that make it nearly impossible to think. We collapse exhausted into bed
at the end of the day, wondering where our time and energy went.

The result is a squeezing-out of that which we should be thinking about,
leaving little room for our spirits to shine. We have been successfully—and
intentionally—divorced from our souls. Tricked by our own thoughts (and
aided by mass media) into believing that life in the upside-down world is
"just the way it is" and all we need do is work harder and run faster.

It needn't be this way.

MAKING THE FLIP

Mary R. awakens without the aid of an alarm clock. Her mind and body
are naturally attuned to her circadian rhythms. After quietly performing
some personal hygiene in her tranquil house, Mary meditates. She does so
faithfully every morning. Mary inhales deeply, grateful for the Universe's
blessing. She exhales any negative energy she may have picked up from the
previous day's interactions. Her mind becomes clear, sharp, focused. A calm
energy centers her and allows her to enter the day with mindful anticipation.

Dressing for work, she doesn't turn on the television to view the latest madness and mayhem. She doesn't need its frenetic distractions. She doesn't tune into weather or traffic updates. Instead, she steps out onto her front porch, feels the temperature on her skin, and looks at the sky. She decides to bring a light sweater.

At the office, Mary's mind is uncluttered by useless information. She sees the whole of most situations. Her clear mind enables Mary to view moments and issues as singular situations to be dealt with in their proper context. She doesn't assign unnecessary drama to the problems she must address. Her convivial style makes Mary easy to approach. No one is afraid to bring her a problem to discuss. The work flows efficiently—largely as a result of Mary's positive attitude and commitment to wholehearted living.

Like everyone in the Right-Side Up and upside-down worlds, challenging circumstances still do confront Mary. She is not immune to illness, heartache, family complications, or conflict, but her choice to approach life in a whole-thinking manner allows her to better handle life's inevitable tests. She views these as pop quizzes—life lessons designed to show her how to become an ever-better human being.

I think, therefore I am.

—Descartes

Mary, like all Flipsters, knows that she will never fully master every moment or circumstance. There are no absolute final answers. But Mary and the millions of Flipsters like her know that life is a work in progress. They share one important, commonly known secret—the phrase "perception is reality" is more truism than cliché. Those making the flip have quieted their minds. They have turned off the "noise" of life and instead have plugged into their infinite inner source.

CONVERSATIONS ON THE BRIDGE

Let's hear what our resident experts have to say on the matter of flipping your mind. First, we'll hear from Dianne Collins on the nature of our perceived realities and how these perceptions affect our self-imposed expectations in society. Next we'll spend some time with John Selby and learn the power of mastering your mind to stay in the present. Peter Russell will discuss the evolution of human consciousness, and we'll wrap up with Gary Zukav, the best-selling author who has inspired millions with his visions of a new reality.

A CONVERSATION ON THE BRIDGE WITH DIANNE COLLINS

Dianne Collins is the author of *Do You QuantumThink?* and the creator of QuantumThink (www.quantumthink.com), the groundbreaking new system of thinking that makes cutting-edge science and perennial wisdom instantly accessible and practical in modern daily life. Dianne is CEO and co-owner of Star Group, a consulting firm that presents QuantumThink in corporations, government agencies, and to the worldwide public in entertaining multimedia teleconference and audio programs.

Dianne's work is based upon the well-established field of quantum mechanics, first advanced in the early part of the twentieth century. A hundred years ago, physicists made an amazing discovery that radically changed the science of the day, contradicting the classical worldview of a mechanistic, building-block universe. This discovery established that a subatomic particle could exist in two different states—as a point and/or a wave—depending, in part, on how the particle was observed. This scientific discovery led, in turn, to the concept of the "quantum leap," based on the observation that a subatomic particle could disappear and simultaneously reappear elsewhere.

> **Thought is a kind of opium; it can intoxicate us, while still broad awake; it can make transparent the mountains and everything that exists.**
>
> —Henri Frederick Amiel

"The classical worldview that has shaped our thinking until now consists of analysis and conclusion," says Dianne. "We've always wanted to know the 'how-to.' How did we do it? How did we get there? How is it going to happen? We want to see the pathway before we will commit. However, a quantum leap means that something can go from one place to another, or from one energy state to another, without being able to trace how it got there. There's no 'how-to,' there's no linear pathway; it happens instantaneously.

"Quantum leaps occur based on the intent of the observer," Dianne continues. "This is a completely different reality than the classical worldview. If our thinking allows for the possibility of quantum leaps, that means that we can accomplish things faster and with different dynamics than we ever thought because we are open to results being accomplished in new ways. This is essential now because our high tech world functions beyond the linear limits of time and physical space. Thinking this way eliminates the feeling of being overwhelmed. It means we are in charge of our reality."

That's pretty heady stuff, obviously. One has to wonder just how much impact this new science will ultimately have on our everyday lives. "The old classical worldview conditions our thinking," Dianne points out. "It's important to see how this view of separation, of seeing external circumstances as separate from us, and of seeing things as unchangeable, affects our actions. In a world of so-called absolutes, your options are narrowed down to something being *either* this way *or* that way. This simplistic mentality sets us up to become victims of circumstance. The important thing is to see how this limited classical view of the world as machine has programmed our mode of thinking. When you are reacting to life mechanistically, you are not really choosing. You're unaware that old patterns of thinking are 'choosing' for you.

"In a quantum worldview, you realize we are not victims at all. We are creators of our destiny and of our experience, moment-by-moment. Quantum scientists call this the 'observer effect.' We are the observers shaping what we see. There are distinctions but no actual separations between what we bring and what we get. We are continually making subconscious choices that create our reality. We are not victims at all, unless we choose to be. We are creators of our lives. From the perspective of this new worldview, notions of either/or fall apart."

How is separation-based thinking reflected in our social systems? Dianne observes, "Our systems were created out of our need for logic and organization, which were projected out of a mechanical worldview of either/or, such as our two-party political system or our judicial system based on guilty/not guilty. These deterministic systems force decisions, even everyday business decisions of doing something either 'your way or my way.' The system takes you with it.

"There is no real choice of thinking because you are swept up in the limitations of the given system. It reduces the world to black and white, when it is actually made up of a rich spectrum of color, and especially when it comes to complex social issues—a whole lot of gray. There are so many more intelligent, exciting, workable, profitable possibilities than what we've been able to consider because either/or thinking has automatically limited us to known options. From the perspective of a new worldview, notions of either/or happily fall apart. We enter a grander reality of both/and. The quantum discovery is that infinite possibility is available to us in every moment. When you distinguish where your thinking and approaches are automatic—in that very moment of awakening—you free yourself to choose."

So what would the Right-Side Up world of whole thinking look like?

"We would see a world of vivid interconnections," Dianne suggests. "We would see how the imbalance in our environment causes erratic weather systems, resulting in meteorological catastrophes. When we have disasters, it costs us lots of money, both in individual insurance rates, and in the cost of government-funded relief. In a Right-Side Up world, government and industry would see the interconnectivity and do everything to create environmental balance. Rather than focusing on fixing effects, they would work creatively at the source and from the whole.

"When industry leaders awaken their thinking according to the way reality actually works they would realize they can transform processes without being constrained by fear of loss of revenue or power. Antiquated, dehumanizing, cutthroat tactics that nations have used to dominate one another would fade as leaders discover ways for globalization to benefit all regions. When the media learns the relationship of consciousness to results—that what you focus on expands—they would shift their perspective from extreme negativity to an enlightened viewpoint and still maintain ratings.

We can destroy ourselves by cynicism and disillusion, just as effectively as by bombs.
—Lord Clark

"On an individual level, people would see and feel the interconnectedness and become more mindful, considerate, joyful, and engaged in improving everyone's quality of life—not just amassing as many material items as possible. These things may seem obvious, yet it is one thing to know how we *should* be and quite another to actually be living it. An expansion in thinking can do it. When this happens for people it's awesome."

A CONVERSATION ON THE BRIDGE WITH DR. JOHN SELBY

John Selby (www.johnselby.com) has spent his professional life studying meditation. Growing up in California, he became a student of Krishnamurti. He also studied with a number of other great living teachers and then at Princeton and UC Berkeley turned to an academic exploration of the psychological foundations of spirituality, as well as carrying out mind research for the National Institute of Mental Health. Selby did fieldwork on shamanistic practices with the Hopi Indians and tribes in highland Guatemala. He maintains therapy and training centers in California and Europe, and is the author of more than two dozen successful books, including *Seven Masters, One Path; Kundalini Awakening in Everyday Life; Conscious Healing;* and *Immune System Activation.*

In this section, John discusses how mastering the mind to stay in the present allows us to be receptive to our higher power, our deep intention to achieve a state of whole thinking. "Managing the mind is about learning to choose the focus of attention," John explains. "We mostly focus our attention habitually, without really choosing. One trait of the upside-down world is the addiction to thinking, which is a 'broadcast' function of the mind. Our minds are either in broadcast mode or receiving mode; in receiving mode we are focused on perceiving and intuiting. To shift deliberately from broadcast mode to receiving mode is difficult for many people."

But what's the secret of being in receiving mode? John says, "You need to shift out of cognitive, linear thinking, which either keeps your awareness in the past or projects you into the future. Most people in the upside-down world are stuck in the past/future function of the mind. Cognitive thought is a manipulative function; the receiving mode of intuition and perception is a participatory function. To be in a participatory state, you need to learn to bring your attention to the present moment. The present never repeats itself; the present moment is always new. The key is learning to quiet the mind to experience the present moment."

> **A sub-clerk in the post-office is the equal of a conqueror if consciousness is common to them.**
>
> —Albert Camus

And how is that done? John has discovered through his research that thinking can be effectively stopped by paying attention to two particular stimuli that are always with us. "You can do this now by first becoming aware of your breathing," he suggests. "Say this to yourself as you put your attention on your breathing: 'I feel the air flowing in and out of my nose.' Now you need to put your attention on one more experience to short circuit the mental chatter, so also say to yourself, 'I also feel the movements in my chest and belly as I breathe.' When you feel yourself breathing and your heart beating, you are aware of the present moment. This centers your mind, balances the soul, and creates clarity and calm. Most people desperately need some meditative calm to help them deal with their daily hustle and bustle, the stresses and strains of everyday life.

"Hold the focus on the present moment and act. From our heart we can then know what is right to do. All else flows from there. Anyone can certainly change their world—in every moment—by being present. Begin with oneself; that's a great place to begin the flip."

A Conversation on the Bridge with Dr. Peter Russell

Peter Russell, Ph.D. (www.peterrussell.com), is a fellow of the Institute of Noetic Sciences, The World Business Academy, and The Findhorn Foundation. His consulting clients have included IBM, Apple, Digital, American Express, Barclays Bank, Swedish Telecom, ICI, Shell Oil, and British Petroleum. He is the author of many books, including *The TM Technique, The Upanishads, The Brain Book*, and *From Science to God*. As a revolutionary futurist, Peter Russell has been a keynote speaker at many international conferences. In 1993, the environmental magazine *Buzzworm* voted Peter Russell "Eco-Philosopher Extraordinaire."

Here Peter discusses the ever-evolving consciousness of humankind, deftly explaining how our inner world manifests in a plethora of daunting problems. "As we reflect upon our own consciousness," Peter says, "it seems that there must be an experiencer—an individual self that is having these experiences, making all these decisions, and thinking all these thoughts. But what is this self? What is it really like? What does it consist of? We don't really know. We may be self-aware, but we have not yet discovered the true nature and potential of consciousness. In this respect, our inner evolution has some way to go."

That leads to the obvious question of whether there's any noticeable evolution of consciousness going on today. Peter observes that "throughout history there have been those who have evolved inwardly to higher states of consciousness. They are the saints and mystics who have realized the true nature of the self. Such people are examples of what we each have the potential to become. There is nothing special about them in terms of their biology. They are human beings, just like you and me, with similar bodies and similar nervous systems. The only difference is that they have liberated themselves from a limited, artificially derived sense of identity and discovered a greater peace and security within. In the past, the number of people who made this step was small, but the times we are living through make it imperative that many more of us now complete our inner evolutionary journey into full wakefulness."

We mention to Peter that it seems odd that anyone could achieve an advanced awareness in a culture that seems unconscious of its own destructive nature. His reply: "The many crises that we see around us—global warming, desertification, holes in the ozone layer, disappearing rainforests, polluted rivers, acid rain, dying dolphins, large-scale famine, a widening gap between the 'haves' and the 'have-nots,' nuclear proliferation, overexploitation, and a host of other dangers—all stem in one way or another from human self-centeredness.

"Time and again we find decisions being made not according to the merits of the situation at hand, but according to the needs of individuals or special-interest groups. Governments strive to hold onto power, businesses seek to maximize profit, leaders want to retain their status, and consumers around the world try to satisfy their own needs for identity and security. In the final analysis, it is our need to protect and reinforce an ever-faltering sense of self that leads us to consume more than we need, pollute the world around us, abuse other peoples, and show a careless disregard for the many other species sharing our planetary home. Even now, when we recognize that we are in great danger, we fail to take appropriate remedial action. We continue driving our cars, consuming dwindling resources, and throwing our waste into the sea because to do otherwise would inconvenience ourselves."

> **The golden moments in the stream of life rush past us, and we see nothing but sand; the angels come to visit us, and we only know them when they are gone.**
>
> —George Eliot

Does Peter think that a flip in consciousness is inevitable, or could the upside-down world actually destroy itself? "The global crisis now facing us is, at its root, a crisis of consciousness," Peter concludes. "The essence of any crisis is that an old way of functioning is no longer working. Something new is being called for. In this case the old way that is no longer working is our mode of consciousness. The old mode is destroying the world around us, and threatening the survival of our species. The time has come to evolve into a new mode. We need to wake up to our true identity, to take the step that many saints and mystics have already taken, and discover for ourselves the peace and security that lie at our core."

A CONVERSATION ON THE BRIDGE WITH GARY ZUKAV

Gary Zukav (www.zukav.com) has inspired millions with his books, including the best-selling title *The Dancing Wu Li Masters: An Overview of the New Physics,* which won the American Book Award for Science. *The Seat of the Soul* became a number one *New York Times* best-seller and remained on the best-seller list for three years. He also wrote *Soul Stories* and coauthored with Linda Francis *The Heart of the Soul: Emotional Awareness* and *The Mind of the Soul: Responsible Choice.*

Gary presents an unfolding vision of a planet without conflict, a world that reflects the values of the soul—harmony, cooperation, sharing, and reverence for life. "There is a major transformation in human consciousness now under way," Gary asserts. "And when I say major, I'm not talking about big or bigger than most, I'm talking about something that's unprecedented, except for the very origin of our species.

"This shift in consciousness is affecting millions of people from every culture in both sexes, every race, every economic circumstance, and every religion. It is an expansion of our capability to perceive beyond the reach of the five senses. And this transformation is bringing into focus new values and new perceptions of our reality.

"In the past we saw power as the ability to manipulate and to control; to hire people, fire people, control our children, neighbors, employees, and control voters, markets, and nations. But the power to manipulate and control things that are external is now counterproductive, producing only violence and destruction. In other words, what used to be healthy medicine is now toxic. In its place, people are beginning to understand power in an entirely different way: as the alignment of your personality with your soul. That, to me, is the spiritual path; aligning your personality with your soul to create authentic power."

An obvious question is how this new kind of power feels as we use and apply it. Gary comments: "The experience of authentic power is not otherworldly or mystical. It's more than a feeling, it's the experience of being fully engaged in your life, of being in the present moment, excited about what you're doing, knowing that you're alive for a purpose. You're doing what you were born to do. It feels like living without the consciousness of fear, moving forward in your life without attachment to the consequences. That is authentic power: the key to a life of joy, of meaning, of vitality, of creativity, of health. That is what we are all being called to; now we need to grow spiritually in order to evolve."

Does this mean that there is a new awakening of the soul in human consciousness? "You are not a soul in a body," Gary clarifies. "You are a body in a soul. So it's not the soul that's awakening, it's you that's awakening to your inherent soul. Your soul is always awake in the sense that it comprehends much more than the personality does. It exists in eternity, while we exist in time. So the creation of authentic power requires aligning your personality with your soul.

"Your personality is a mixture of fear and love. People don't usually think of themselves as fragmented, but they are. And they are often experiencing different parts of their personality in conflict. For example, you may walk past a homeless person and have an impulse to give money and at the same time, an impulse to run away, and an impulse to say angrily, 'Get a job!' This is the experience of a splintered personality. To create authentic power requires becoming aware of all the parts of your personality, then healing the frightened parts and cultivating the loving parts. The personality is an energy tool of the soul, a vehicle that the soul has adapted for its own purposes to learn within physicality, within the domain of time and space."

> If water derives lucidity from stillness, how much more the faculties of the mind! The mind of the sage, being in repose, becomes the mirror of the universe, the speculum of all creation.
>
> —Chuang Tzu

How quickly can an individual do the healing that leads to authentic power? "It is possible for consciousness to change in a moment. However, there is a low probability unless you have the discipline to become aware of what you are feeling, and make choices when the unconscious, fear-driven aspects of your personality come to the foreground. You might have an intellectual picture of the world as compassionate and kind, but emotionally you don't feel safe in it and you don't trust it. So, your experiences of fear will show you what you actually believe, and then you can learn to make a different choice.

"This is how we will all shift to a planetary consciousness of 'universal humans'; still a planet of individuals, each of whom reflect the values of the soul instead of the fears of the personality. That is our potential and that is what we are here to create."

IT'S TIME TO CHANGE YOUR MIND

The mind is an invisible force with a magnitude of power and depth that we are only beginning to comprehend. But in today's upside-down world it is awash in stimuli that are overwhelming our ability to cope with daily life. Since our personal reality is based on our perceptions, it is critical that we

WHOLE THINKING EXERCISE

Our brain constructs a static world of separate parts, but, in actuality, everything is interconnected—one infinite web of vibrant, pulsating life. By becoming more aware of your breathing and how you interact with life, you can begin to shift your thinking from dividing the whole into parts to seeing and feeling the whole within everything.

Let's begin . . .

Take a slow deep breath in through your nose.

Feel the vitality of life charging every cell in your body.

Exhale deeply out through your mouth as you feel yourself discharging the old stale energy.

Continue to breathe deeply as you slowly look around.

Notice the seemingly empty space that separates you from the objects in the room.

Continue to breathe and sense that the space all around you is one fluid field of energy.

Begin to feel your interconnectivity.

Notice how things relate to each other—the walls, the windows, the outdoors.

Observe how the light illuminates everything.

Notice the interconnectivity of nature and feel yourself as part of all that is.

Practice this throughout the day. Anytime you feel stressed, alienated, or anxious—take a moment to focus on your breathing and bring your awareness to this unified state of consciousness. You will discover how much more connected you are to the present moment.

reduce the amount of information—and agitation—we are feeding our brains.

The knowledge that each of us creates our own reality gives you tremendous power to take control of your life. It may not seem like it, and you may not believe it just now, but you are the creative force behind all the moments you experience. You are the only one who lives your moments. You decide whether to be lighthearted or serious, to be kind or grumpy.

You are the creator of your world. Is it upside-down or Right-Side Up? So how will you use this newfound power? Your choices and decisions will determine the quality of your life, and the collective fate of humankind. You may scoff at the notion of having that much authority over your destiny. But scientists, psychologists, and spiritualists through the centuries have known this truth. It is only the advent of our 24/7 culture, with its pressure and pace, that we have forgotten who we are. It needn't be this way. Nope. There are volumes of books, CDs, and videos available to help you calm the mind through healthy techniques. We even offer one in this chapter (see sidebar). There are also workshops, seminars, and therapists available to assist in your quest for calm.

When you make the flip, you awaken to your true identity and discover a vibrant awareness and an enveloping sense of peace, security, and love that reside inside you.

The time to make the flip is now. Begin today. Will you remain a victim or take responsibility to live wholly, fully present in your daily activities? Will you join with millions of others in flipping from division thinking to whole thinking?

We hope so.

FLIP TIPS

- Reduce your consumption of news.
- Meditate, pray, or practice yoga daily.
- Find a spiritual practice that feels right to you.
- Meet new friends who have a positive outlook.
- Reduce your daily activities by 10 percent.
- Say "no" once in a while to social engagements.
- Read books that feed your spirit.
- Listen to music that moves your soul.
- Take leisurely walks in a natural setting.
- Resolve not to judge others.

THREE

FLIPPING THE EMOTIONS

From Emotional Resistance to Emotional Flow

Lately, Barry has stopped expressing his feelings. His boss, who regularly takes credit for Barry's work, recently passed him up for promotion. There's no question he deserved the enhanced title, the raise, and perks—he's one of the hardest working, most loyal employees in the firm. Barry feels angry and resentful but doesn't have the courage to confront the situation. Barry's inability to stand up for himself, based on the fear of losing his job, causes him to be viewed with pity and contempt by his fellow workers. Barry knows this. He can feel it in the air, and in his heart.

Consequently, Barry doesn't offer his ideas as freely. People are whispering about his erratic moods. He's on an unfortunate and unnecessary downward emotional spiral. For Barry, trapped in his upside-down world, it is easy to repeat the learned behaviors of his youth. The fear of rejection based on years of hurts, slights, and misunderstanding with his parents, siblings, and friends have left him afraid of intimacy. Barry's parents, lost in their own upside-down world, didn't equip Barry to face his feelings. Men of his parents' generation were tough "kings of the castle" and didn't cry; women dutifully bore their sadness in silence.

> **Our fears are more numerous than our dangers, and we suffer more in our imagination than in reality.**
>
> —Seneca

Things at home aren't much better for Barry. He gazes at a picture of his wife and wonders if she still loves him. Does his daughter respect him? Does anyone even know him? How could they? Since he doesn't share himself, those nearest him must merely guess at his thoughts, beliefs, and emotions. He is simply wrapped too tight for his own good. Barry, once alive with so much promise and wonder, is now outwardly bitter and inwardly numb.

Know anyone like this? Sadly, we all do. Maybe not in these exact terms. But we all know people whose lives seem perpetually upside down, who appear sullen, withdrawn, or depressed. Their anger simmers just below the surface while their eyes reveal a private pain that needs to be heard and understood.

WHO'S IN CHARGE HERE?

Expressing our feelings can be a scary, nearly paralyzing, challenge. Resistance to recognizing and admitting our emotions is rooted in fear. Fear of rejection, of being ridiculed, of being judged—fear of any reciprocal emotion outside our zone of comfort—creates a stern defense that we often don't know we are deploying. So this fear becomes suppressed and is masked within the rational mind; it goes underground. Warranted or not, real or imagined, our fears are relegated to the subconscious and begin to direct our motivation irrationally. This leads us to say and do things that create distance or close us off from others without realizing that we are doing it.

Alone with our fragmented, separated thinking, we begin to wonder if we are in charge of our own lives. Resentments build, habitual animosities arise, and casual comments turn into personal slights. Our relationships begin to crumble. To cope, we may turn to drink, drugs ("I don't have an addiction, it's a prescription!"), or a whole grab bag of behavioral addictions from sex to shopping, and downward we spiral. These days it seems everyone has a symptom, a compulsion, or a disorder to obsess about. It's as though we have created our own snug blanket of neurotic excuses for our behavior and yet refuse to take action on the underlying issue feeding all the pain: fear.

Don't believe us? Try these eye-popping statistics on for size.

- 65 million Web pages based on psychology
- 33 million Web pages featuring self-help
- 2.7 million Web pages related to addiction

This isn't the tip of the proverbial iceberg; this is a snowflake on the tip of the iceberg. Our emotional states are in so much need of repair that we have counselors, therapists, life coaches, psychologists, psychiatrists, past-life regressionists, hypnotists, reiki healers, self-help groups, twelve-step programs, and multibillion-dollar pharmaceutical industries selling us services and products to help us cope. All are trying to help us navigate this complex world of conflicting, contrasting emotion we have created for ourselves.

The Big Secret

Here is one truth that cannot be avoided: No one—and we do mean *no one*—can change you but yourself.

Yes, there are tools and techniques and wonderfully talented professionals available to guide you through the intricate maze of self-absorbed emotions so that you may eventually find your way out of the upside-down world to the Right-Side Up world. But ultimately it's up to you.

Okay, so now you want to slap us upside the head for stating the obvious. But is it obvious that you accept the responsibility for your life? Do you complain about the problems of the world, or do you roll up your sleeves and get involved? Do you tell your lover exactly what you want or are you annoyed that he or she just doesn't know automatically? Do you express your feelings or keep them bottled up until you are ready to explode at a friend, relative, or coworker?

Give these questions serious consideration. Be honest and true. If you're not sure of your emotional honesty, here is one simple question that should clarify everything for you: Generally speaking, are you happy or sad?

Emotionally balanced, expressive people are happy with their lives. Sure, they can have down periods due to a lingering illness, the passing of a loved one, or any number of life's harsh difficulties, but, usually, mentally healthy people spring back from setbacks with aplomb. They recognize the crisis for what it is, deal with it, and return to their authentic self.

> **We must accept finite disappointment, but we must never lose infinite hope.**
> —Martin Luther King, Jr.

Welcome to the Club

If you're not feeling so good about yourself, welcome to the world's largest club. As evidenced by the anecdotal statistics presented earlier, there are legions of people looking for answers to their emotional pain. But what are you truly searching for? Your answer is absolutely specific to you and your perceptions. Chances are, underneath all the complicated reasoning and rationalization, you are looking for a way to genuinely connect to others.

Painful emotions, regardless of their specific causes in your personal history, are all rooted in a sense of separation. This fundamental alienation is a by-product of our dualistic world. The experience of separation begins in childhood and can be devastating. When we are recipients of the harsh words or actions of others, we feel victimized. When young, we have little capacity to understand what is happening to us and express exactly how we feel about it. Our youth is fraught with damaging influences and factors—being chosen last for a neighborhood game, being misunderstood by our parents, teased at school, made to feel stupid by a teacher. These troubling emotions imbed in our memories and even in our bodies at a cellular level. They lie dormant, accumulating an ever higher, ever more dysfunctional emotional charge. Such emotional imprints can set the stage for a lifetime of suffering, conditioning us to expect disappointment and rejection throughout our days.

Be the change you wish to see in the world.
—Gandhi

To muddle matters even further, we are taught the destructive habit of comparison almost from birth. People constantly judge and criticize each other for their looks, their clothes, their cars and homes, and their wealth. We get caught up in fashion, trends, and relative status with no hope of ever winning this megalomaniacal game. This exercise in futility has no good outcome. Because there will always be someone smarter, prettier, nicer, richer, or more something than yourself. So why get hung up on these ego exercises? Why not think, believe, and feel for yourself?

WHAT'S MARY UP TO?

Mary has been working on herself for years. She had a difficult childhood and had to do a lot of soul searching to resolve her emotional traumas. She learned to accept her feelings and not be afraid to express them. When Mary needs to talk to a coworker about something that is bothering her, she schedules time to calmly and directly state how she feels. She doesn't talk behind anyone's back or sabotage relationships.

Mary has learned how to manage her stress by balancing her lifestyle to include healthy outlets for releasing her pent-up feelings. On her commute home from work, she imagines the stress of the day releasing. As mentioned in chapter 2, each morning she spends time quieting her mind and setting her intent for the day.

In her relationship with her boyfriend, she has no resistance to expressing her love, yet keeps an independent life because she enjoys her alone time. She is in no rush to get married but is sensitive to her boyfriend's aspirations to share a home. Because Mary is being true to her heart's desires, she is able to make positive choices without becoming codependent in her romantic relationship.

Her relationships aren't perfect, and Mary is no saint. She gets upset, even angry, at times. But Mary has learned to channel her darker emotions in a way that allows her to communicate without raising her voice. Thanks to a rage-aholic father, she knows firsthand how shouting hinders communication. She simply listens with an open heart and mind, allowing herself to stay centered and ready for a transformation.

GO WITH THE FLOW

When your emotions do not flow with ease, you build up emotional friction. This friction creates tension and resistance. Emotional resistance is similar to swimming against a rushing current. It is an exhausting and ultimately futile exercise. By acknowledging and accepting your emotions, you will flow through life with greater ease. But first you need to get over the fear of drowning; your emotions will not overwhelm you. It is the suppression of emotions that makes them seem so overpowering, but they are not. Emotions only attain the power you give them.

When a feeling arises, you have the chance to notice its nuances. You can observe all the qualities of the feeling. Bringing awareness to the feeling instead of resisting it will dissolve your fear and leave you open to living each moment. When you are fluid with emotional energy, you allow yourself to feel any feeling, knowing that peace is always on the other side. By allowing emotional energy to flow without resistance, you become a more loving person.

A simple equation (from Whole Self Management ©2000) to understand the physics of emotion is:

Resistance = Stress = Breakdown

If you can clear the resistance to feeling an emotion, you can eliminate the stress and breakdown. Breakdown can be reflected in a full spectrum of experiences, ranging from communication failures to serious compromise of your physical and psychological health. Sometimes you will notice unmistakable symbolic signs: your car will break down, your cell phone will stop working, your computer will crash, a favorite memento will break. These signs are all around us all the time if we choose to see. Conversely, positive messages and synchronicities occur when you accept the flow of your feelings. An unexpected letter, information that reinforces something you were working on, a business deal out of the blue, an article seemingly from nowhere that illuminates a problem—all these are signs that you are going with the energetic flow of the universe. Some call it synergy, others call it good luck. In the Eastern philosophies it is called the Tao.

Be open to the messages.

IMAGINE YOUR LIFE

Imagine you had the ability to feel any emotion with ease and grace. What kind of life would you have if you truly experienced emotional freedom? What would you focus on if you were not weighed down with feelings such as guilt, envy, and resentment? How liberating would it feel to live in an expressive rather than repressive mode? How wonderful would it be if you didn't haul around a burden of perpetual stress?

The answers to these questions are available by simply taking a deep breath (inspiration) and letting go of your emotional resistance with the exhalation. Right now. When you live in the moment and allow your feelings to flow, you begin to dissolve the self-constructed barriers of your past. The past is behind you and cannot be undone, so let go of it. The future, always a powerful potential fear-based paralyzer, isn't here yet and almost never materializes the way one thinks. Fear of what might happen—imagining that all our negative what-ifs are coming to pass—is always worse than what actually comes.

For a positive affirmation to heal your perspective on the past, present, and future, try saying this every morning to your God, Self, or higher power: "Thank You for the past as it actually was, the present as it truly is, and the future as it is meant to be."

WHAT'S YOUR PLEASURE?

All pleasurable emotions arise from the feeling of connection. The more we are able to bond through love, the more we are able to trust the dance of life. Love is, after all, what everyone truly wants anyway. Even the most hardened person, who would scoff and dismiss that statement, is masking what he or she really wants and needs: to be loved and accepted as they are.

Love is a feeling of connection to the whole. Fear, on the other hand, reflects our sense of separation. Most of the emotions that have been labeled negative are merely the feeling of separation.

So, again, the choice is yours. Do you want to feel connected to or separate from the world? Do you want a pleasant or a painful existence?

You may be thinking that we've just presented a mighty fine theory, but are rightly wondering what you can do about it.

The answer depends on the depth of the pain and sadness you are carrying. Because of the intense complications of living in this modern upside-down world, nearly everyone (yours truly included) can benefit greatly from a trusted, professional therapist. Seeking guidance from someone experienced in psychology doesn't mean you're crazy. We recommend finding a good therapist, experiencing a session or two, and deciding from there. If you feel you are not in need of therapy or counseling, then consider a life coach. Life coaches often act as a neutral third party who do not possess your natural emotional biases. They are a "forest for the trees" resource, showing you things you fail to recognize yourself.

> **All humanity is passion; without passion, religion, history, novels, art would be ineffectual.**
>
> —Honore De Balzac

While deciding whether you want counseling or coaching, consider the work of Dr. Brian Alman, a noted therapist, author, and lecturer. Dr. Alman says there are four distinct stages for dealing with and ridding yourself of an emotional problem:

1. **Awareness:** No matter what the issue, no matter how difficult or horrible, the first thing you must do is become aware of the problem. As long as you deny the issues affecting you—a bad relationship, a feeling of abandonment, never being able to measure up—you will never take control of your emotions or your life.

2. **Acceptance:** Accepting yourself, even loving yourself, is an essential second step in breaking free of your negative emotions. You have to accept yourself for who you are. When you accept yourself unconditionally, warts and all, then you immediately start to make a change for the better.

   Acceptance is proactive, energizing, and life changing. As soon as you accept yourself as you are, positive changes can begin to happen. Through the power of your own mind, you can access inner resources to accept who you are so that you are able to make the changes required to become the person you wish to be.

3. **Expression:** Expression means taking all the memories, family issues, thoughts, habits, and feelings you've uncovered in the awareness and acceptance phases and releasing them, literally pushing them out, or "expressing" them.

   It was repression—denying these feelings, holding them in, pushing them down into your body—that created problems in the first place. Expression is the opposite of repression, and giving voice to your feelings allows you to let them go.

4. **Resolution:** When your life feels empty, or when you're deeply dissatisfied with yourself or your relationships, you may try to solve the problem with a variety of unproductive behaviors—addictions, vices, overeating, anger at others, intolerance, and on and on. You do these things to fulfill yourself, to satisfy yourself, to comfort yourself, to make yourself feel better, but they are compensations rather than real solutions.

> **There can be no transforming of darkness into light, and of apathy into movement, without emotion.**
>
> —Carl Jung

If you want to get free of your emotional problems, to kick the old habits for good, you need to find new solutions and new understanding. You need to "re-solve" your problems in a way that will work for you—and that will keep on working. To do this you need determination.

Knowing the four stages of dealing with an emotional issue is only the first step. You have to be willing to actually take those steps. If you are struggling, that's when a professional therapist or life coach can be helpful. Friends and relatives can be of benefit, but all but the bravest of us have things inside us that we are unwilling to share with those closest to us for fear of rejection or criticism. If you do seek out the advice of a professional, we suggest that you be discerning in your selection. Finding someone to assist you with understanding and lessening your burdens is like finding an intimate partner. Choose wisely. But do not let the fear of choosing the wrong person keep you from looking.

We can all use help navigating this world. You have nothing to be ashamed of, nothing worth being miserable over. Conquer your emotional fears and discover a welcoming path to the Right-Side Up world.

CONVERSATIONS ON THE BRIDGE

Much has been said and written about emotions. Understanding our feelings has been one of the most perplexing challenges for philosophers, religious thinkers, psychologists, and therapists through history. Some days, life seems so complicated it appears impossible to figure it out. And yet, as you will see from our Flipsters of Emotion, going from emotional resistance to emotional flow may be easier than you think.

We start with parenting expert and author Carista Luminare-Rosen, who discusses how human emotions are influenced while we are still in the womb. Next, psychologist and author Faye Mandell, who shows the critical need to differentiate our feelings from our thoughts so that we may experience our feelings directly. Then we hear from best-selling author and love expert Daphne Rose Kingma, who speaks on the changing nature of relationships from psychological to spiritual—and the impact this transformation is having on the tradition of marriage. Next, famed author and relationship lecturer John Gray weighs in with powerful insights about the compatibilities and conflicts of male and female emotions—and the evolution of gender roles. Dr. Candace Pert, an internationally recognized pharmacologist, reveals that emotions are stored at a cellular level in our bodies, and discusses how the repression of emotions can result in a host of illnesses and disorders. We finish with a powerful interview with social entrepreneur Ayman Sawaf, who discusses the benefits of an emotionally literate society and the positive affect it can have on ourselves and future generations.

A CONVERSATION ON THE BRIDGE WITH DR. CARISTA LUMINARE-ROSEN

Carista Luminare-Rosen, Ph.D., is the founder of the Center for Creative Parenting (www.creativeparenting.com), a holistic preconception, prenatal, and early parenting educational service offering counseling, workshops, trainings, and products for those preparing for parenthood. Her holistic-health perspective offers potential parents the opportunity to create a unique preparation plan, integrating their personal and professional needs, whether they prefer to conceive naturally or with the assistance of medical technology.

She is the author of a comprehensive book, *Parenting Begins Before Conception: A Guide to Preparing Body, Mind, and Spirit—For You and Your*

Future Child, which shows future parents how they can lay the foundations for a healthy and happy life before a child is conceived and born.

When do a person's emotions first begin to be influenced and shaped? Carista responded, "We all know the cumulative effect of childhood experiences on adult lives. Yet some of these effects begin before the child is born. Years ago, after studying many of the great models on human development, I began to realize that something fundamental was missing in the fabric of the family, education, and health care system. Why do so many adults spend the core of their creative life in reaction to the effects of their childhood experiences and traumas? What an inefficient use of adult life—to spend it healing yourself from your childhood pain.

"In the American culture this experience is clearly the norm. What has been profoundly lacking in our social consciousness is a holistic model that can help prevent an incoming child from experiencing unnecessary trauma and can facilitate the awakening and integration of the soul with the human personality.

> **All emotions are pure which gather you and lift you up; that emotion is impure which seizes only one side of your being and so distorts you.**
>
> —Ranier Maria Rilke

"If a child begins life with parents who care for her whole health, she will innately know some of the intrinsic elements for creating a life of well-being. And since each and every human being is conceived and born, this potential crosses all cultural barriers. It is literally the starting point of preventive medicine. I believe it is every child's birthright to have a family and culture that support her essential nature, the true self—body, mind, and soul.

"Prospective parents should ask themselves what they can do to prepare for their child before she is born or even conceived. Unhealthy parenting has such a negative impact on the adult personae; so, conversely, a prebirth holistic model for parenting can produce positive, healthy children. To care for a human life before it has even been created can become a realistic goal of prospective parents and a basic building block to any holistic health care system."

We asked Carista if having a baby at home versus at a hospital might affect the newborn. "Regarding the birth itself, it is a major rite of passage of great complexity for the baby and parents. Yet in the Western world, during the past several decades, technological interventions and advances have placed most births in hospitals focusing exclusively on the physical health of the child, denying the psychological and spiritual aspects of birth. No one was aware of or even cared about your psyche or soul during your birth. This is significant because we all have physical, emotional, mental, and spiritual bodies needing attention during this extraordinary life event.

"Honoring every birth as a rite of passage sets the blueprint for each human being's first experiences of life in this world. It can determine whether he or she feels safe and loved, or frightened and insecure. There is a growing movement of conscious birth educators and assistants who value the first moments of life as the blueprint for a child's first beliefs about life, love, safety, and security."

Does Carista see future generations flipping their approach to parenting? "Most children learn to survive, but the Right-Side Up world of living is about being able to authentically thrive. In the future, Right-Side Up parents will do whatever healing work they need for themselves prior to bringing a child into the world. This preparation and awareness will optimize the full potential and whole health of their child. Consider how remarkable it would be if every child had the opportunity to flourish in a world of consistent love and security from the beginning of life. There is so much a parent can do to nurture and empower the essential self to become a fully realized human being."

A CONVERSATION ON THE BRIDGE WITH DR. FAYE MANDELL

Faye Mandell, Ph.D. (www.namastepublishing.com/mandell.asp), is the author of the groundbreaking book *Self-Powerment: Towards a New Way of Living.* Faye is a psychologist, organizational consultant, and executive coach. Over the years, her studies in quantum physics have led to the conception and development of her watershed Self-Powerment Model. This model marries data from science to human awareness, making practical use of both of them. It provides a link between what is accessible and known only to a few and what is accessible and knowable to everyone.

We asked Faye how feelings control our individual worlds. "First, we have to understand that there is a difference between feelings and feelings of thought," she explains. "What our culture has labeled feelings are not feelings, but rather feelings combined with thought—which are combined with an abstraction.

"As an example, if I'm feeling anxious about a report that's due at three o'clock and it's twelve o'clock and it's not done yet, I might experience anxiety. That's a present moment feeling that allows me to focus to get it done. But when I take that feeling and combine it with a thought which says, 'Oh my God, I'm never gonna get it done and they're gonna fire me and I'm gonna lose my house and my family,' then all of the energy that would be used to focus and be creative to get the report done is instead used in the combining of the feeling and the thought.

"That combination of the feeling and the thought takes one out of the present moment. Combined with anxiety, the feeling takes one into the future; combined with frustration, it takes you to other people and things. When that feeling/thought is combined with disappointment or sadness, it takes one to the past. That is how feelings get connected to abstract thought and poison the capacity of the thought to do what needs to be done."

How might people use that knowledge to flip away from conditioned responses and remain in the present? "The flip is to move from believing in thought as the way to understand the world to direct experience as the way to experience the world. So we learn understanding by experience and then we can choose to think when we need to. If we allow ourselves to experience our feelings, then we will stay in the present moment and we will be self-powered.

"Feelings are indicators that emotional states are out of balance and the feelings then translate simultaneously into an action, because this is an action-orientated model, to keep people clear, focused, and in control. And when you are focused, clear, and in control, you know and can immediately experience the illusory nature of thought."

We pressed for a real-world example. "If I am feeling frustrated because I am in a traffic jam and I am late to an appointment, I could do two things. I could piggyback that onto the anger and I could go, 'That %@$# so and so . . .' and then I would be combining a feeling which is my frustration, with a thought, which would get me so tense and frustrated I might run into the car in front of me. But if I was feeling my frustration and I said, 'Okay, frustration is an indicator that I'm not in control. I can't be in control of the traffic, but what can I be in control of? What can I do with this moment here that's going to keep me clear and in control and focused?' Well, I can muse on something that I need to think about or I can listen to some music. What is self-evident is that I can't control the traffic, but I can control me."

So, how can people separate their feelings from their thoughts? Faye responded, "That pairing of feeling to the thought happens in a nanosecond, so the only way you can separate it is to know where you are in time and space.

You stop listening to the stupid content of the thought and start focusing on where it takes you in time and space. The minute you're in the future you know it must be anxiety that you piggybacked. The minute you focus on other people and things, you know it's frustration that you piggybacked. The minute you focus on the past, you know it's sadness or disappointment—get back and experience the feeling, immediately translate it into an action in your present again.

"Listen to the structure of your thoughts. Listen to the tenses and the pronouns. You want to be present with the feeling of 'I am.' If you're thinking in terms of he, she, they . . . whatever, then you're projecting onto someone or something else in the past, present, or future. 'Am' is a verb. It is the first person present singular of 'be.' So any of the tense verbs—should've, could've, will, might, perhaps, did, didn't, was, wasn't—they're all not 'am' and take you away from experiencing what you're actually feeling. It's so simple. Always return to 'I am.' That is the feeling you must address. 'I am mad; I am hurt,' and so on. And when you feel it you state it aloud. That gives you power over your emotions and your thoughts—'I am.'"

> We know too much and feel too little. At least, we feel too little of those creative emotions from which a good life springs.
>
> —Bertrand Russell

A CONVERSATION ON THE BRIDGE WITH DAPHNE ROSE KINGMA

Daphne Rose Kingma (www.daphnekingma.com) is a widely recognized expert on matters of the heart and the author of ten books on love and relationships, including *The Future of Love: The Power of Soul in Intimate Relationships; True Love; Finding True Love; The Men We Never Knew,* and the classic on the psychological journey of ending a relationship, *Coming Apart.*

Daphne is also a highly esteemed emotional healer. For more than twenty years, she has offered private consultation to clients in Beverly Hills and Santa Barbara, California, as well as by phone to people all over the United States and in Europe, providing insight, transformation, and healing of the heart. Her remarkable gift for sorting out the emotional issues in any life situation, whether in complex corporate environments or the most intimate relationship, has earned her the affectionate title "The Einstein of Emotions."

We decided to test Daphne with a tough question from the start: What is love? She didn't hesitate to answer: "Love is the unmistakable energy in which, for a moment, or a week, or a lifetime we recognize our profound, indissoluble connection to another, to all others, or to the universe. It's that energetic flash or vibration that tells us we are not alone. When we, as electromagnetic bodies, experience love, we're vibrating at that level of connection. And each of us has had moments in which we feel that. Culturally, we have relationships that represent various configurations of connection based on the energy of love, defining how two people stand in relation to one another. Marriage, for example, is a particular configuration of connection that has certain earmarks and traditions. The tricky part about what's happening these days is that we've had a traditional tendency to equate love with marriage and family relationships. We've expected love to look like marriage that inevitably involves a certain kind of domestic life. It must be emotionally exclusive and there aren't going to be other people that are a part of it, except any children that are born of it. And it's going to be lifelong.

"So we've habitually defined love as belonging to that kind of relationship. What's happening now is that traditional relationships are blowing apart and we're learning about the real nature of love. We're learning that it can occur in all sorts of configurations; it can occur in a conventional marriage, or it can occur for five minutes in a powerful conversation in a grocery store. It can occur in a fleeting romance. The flip in our view of love is that we are moving from a narcissistic basis for relationship to a spiritual basis. In terms of marriage, we're moving from the form to the content. We used to be completely focused on the form: 'Are you married? Do you have children? Oh, you got divorced, now you're not married anymore. Oh, you're not married yet? When are you going to get married?' Now we're moving from the form to the essence, the questions become 'Do we love one another? Can we expand our love? Can we continue to love the person we loved in marriage and now love them as a friend? Can we love our enemies and strangers? Can we participate in many forms of relationship and know that each of them can be about love?'"

Does this mean that the tradition of marriage is endangered? "The current national statistic is a little more than one out of two marriages end in divorce," Daphne reveals. "It's been that high for a while, so we are getting used to that figure. But inside we're still having trouble with it. That is, our psyches are still struggling because we cling to the belief that love is exclusive, that it belongs to one person and one relationship, and the relationship has to fulfill everything. So we're still experiencing emotional shattering when marriages end. We think it has to be somebody's fault, instead of thinking: *We went on a journey together. We reached our particular destination and now it's time for something different.* We are flipping from a conventional psychological investment in ourselves and our relationships to a more spiritual perspective. The forms of relationship matter less than what's going on inside them: Are we loving one another? Are we loving one another in marriage? Are we loving one another after marriage? Are we loving one another in friendship? Are we loving one another in the workplace? I know many people who say they love to go to work because they love all the people they work with. They're expressing the fact that those relationships are meaningful and nurturing to them."

What role does Daphne think marriage will play in the future? "Marriage, like any other relationship, is elective. People can say, 'We are going to choose to make a marriage out of this relationship because what we want to do is raise children, and we feel that in terms of society and provision and security for these souls we're bringing into the world, that that will be a better relationship for us.' Other people may decide it isn't necessary to get married. They want to love each other as long as it serves their development and fills their hearts. But they don't need to be married to feel that love, that energy."

> **See that each hour's feelings, and thoughts and actions are pure and true; then your life will be also.**
>
> —Henry Ward Beecher

A Conversation on the Bridge with Dr. John Gray

John Gray, Ph.D. (www.marsvenus.com), is the author of fifteen best-selling books, including *Men Are from Mars, Women Are from Venus*, the number one best-selling book of the last decade. In the past ten years, more than thirty million Mars and Venus books have been sold in more than forty languages throughout the world.

An expert in the field of communication, John Gray focuses on helping men and women understand, respect, and appreciate their differences in both personal and professional relationships. He offers practical tools and insights to effectively manage stress and improve relationships at all stages and ages, based on a clear understanding of the brain chemistry of health, happiness, and lasting romance. We asked him right away for a clue about why men and women handle their emotions so differently. "The major stress hormone for women is oxytocin, which lowers stress in a woman's body," John explains.

"Oxytocin is like a love hormone; it gets generated whenever you give of yourself to somebody. So when women are under stress they tend to start giving, and their stress levels go down. It's so easy for women to do this. Often, women typically give and give until they end up feeling victimized that others haven't given to them.

"On the other hand, oxytocin doesn't lower stress in men. So it's not automatic for men to start giving to other people as a way to combat stress. Women may find that they're giving and giving to their men without a lot of reciprocation, and then they feel very justified in being resentful. The root of the word *resent* is *resentir,* to feel again. In resentment, a person is refeeling her pain and her misery and her victimization: 'See what I've done? I've given and given and given and I haven't gotten anything back.'"

How can men respond effectively to this situation? "Men tend to give in different ways than women, and they're surprised when their gifts seem to go unrecognized," says John. "But what has a powerful effect on women is not big things but little things, like signs of affection, giving her flowers, helping with little errands that stress women out. I often have to explain to men that big stuff like buying cars or paying for vacations, having a big night out, all that stimulates testosterone and testosterone lowers stress in men. But women experience stress reduction by receiving little things that help her have a consistent feeling that *He thinks about me, he cares about me constantly.*"

> When I do good, I feel good. When I do bad, I feel bad. And that is my religion.
> —Abraham Lincoln

Does this mean that men are more resistant to feeling their emotions? John doesn't think so. "I don't see any difference between the genders in terms of being in touch with authentic feelings. Some people are more emotional than others, but the differences are not gender-based. I see women who are just as shut down as men, but women are much more talkative than men. They'll talk about other people and all their problems, but they don't necessarily talk about what their authentic feelings are underneath it all.

"In terms of being articulate and being able to express how they feel, men can be very articulate. But again, men have different chemistry than women. There's strong hormonal feedback for women when they talk about feelings; for men there's not as great a need to talk about the feeling part of himself when his serotonin levels are normal. There is a greater need for a man to raise his testosterone and dopamine levels, and he does this through achieving his goals, overcoming obstacles, meeting challenges, being truthful to what his purpose is in this world."

Apart from gender-based chemical differences, does John see an evolution in male and female cultural roles? "Without a doubt. Men are more interested in developing the nurturing side of themselves, whereas women are more interested in developing the assertive side of who they are, including their leadership roles.

"But there's some fallout when either side goes too far. Women went way over to the masculine world when they tried to carry the banner, We can do whatever men can do and we can do it better. Then they realized that they can do all that, but it's hard to be men and also be happy women. So eventually they find the center, which is the attitude We can do what men *can do and we can do it like women, and we can be happy.* Likewise, men can be sensitive and nurturing, yet still be good providers, strong and confident, at the same time.

"Regardless of biochemical and cultural differences, we can teach men to be more respectful of women and teach women to be more appreciative of men. That's something that culture can educate us all to do."

A CONVERSATION ON THE BRIDGE WITH DR. CANDACE PERT

Dr. Pert (www.candacepert.com) was awarded her Ph.D. in pharmacology, with distinction, from Johns Hopkins University School of Medicine. She has held a variety of research positions with the National Institutes of Health, and until 1987, served as Chief of the Section on Brain Biochemistry of the Clinical Neuroscience Branch of the National Institute of Mental Health. She then founded and directed a private biotech laboratory.

Dr. Pert is the author of *Molecules of Emotion: The Science behind Mindbody Medicine* and an internationally recognized pharmacologist who has published more than 250 scientific articles on peptides and their receptors, focusing on the role of neuropeptides in the immune system. She holds a number of patents for modified peptides in the treatment of psoriasis, Alzheimer's disease, chronic fatigue syndrome, stroke, and head trauma. One of these, peptide T, is currently undergoing research in the United States for the treatment of AIDS and neuroAIDS. We were most interested in Candace's flip from conventional neuroscience to her pioneering work in body-mind medicine.

"When I first started at the National Institutes of Health," Candace recalls, "my emphasis was on drug addiction. I thought my research with opiate receptors and endorphins was going to lead to a new drug to cure addiction, which now seems silly. But my research shifted as I discovered that peptides and other informational substances are the biochemicals of emotion, and their distribution throughout the body's nerves has all kinds of significance. For starters, body and mind are simultaneous. I like to say that the mind is the flow of information as it moves among the cells, organs, and systems of the body. The mind, as we experience it, is immaterial, yet it has a physical substate that is both the body and the brain."

That would mean that emotional traumas are actually stored in the body's cells as information. "Yes, it's stored everywhere," Candace clarifies. "I've been a big promoter of the idea that we shouldn't give too much credit to the brain. The brain is not the mind; we have a body-mind that consists of a vast information network. Information is stored at receptors that are in contact with every cell and they're also in contact with this cellular matrix, which is everywhere.

"I believe that emotions are not fully expressed until they reach consciousness. When I speak of consciousness, I include the entire body. I believe that unexpressed emotions travel up the neural access from the periphery, up the spinal cord, up into the brain. When emotion moves up, it can be expressed. It takes a certain amount of energy from our bodies to keep the emotion unexpressed. There are inhibitory chemicals and impulses that function to keep the emotion and information down. I think unexpressed emotions are literally lodged lower in the body."

Does this mean that unexpressed emotions need to be moved energetically in a cathartic way? "Emotional expression is important, but I'm not recommending that everyone go into primal scream therapy. Emotional blockages are like a kind of cyst, walled off and out of communication. I think it's more important to engage in movement, dance, exercise; expressing things physically rather than making it another head-trip. This is so important because there is overwhelming evidence that unexpressed emotion causes illness. Raw emotion is always wanting to be expressed in the body; it's always moving up the neural access. The need to resist it is coming from the cortex. All the brain's rationalizations are pushing the energy down. The cortical resistance is an attempt to prevent overload; the brain is stingy about what information is allowed up into the cortex. The real, true emotions that need to be expressed are in the body, trying to move up and be expressed and thereby integrated. That's why I believe psychoanalysis by itself doesn't work.

You are spending all your time in your cortex, rather than in your body. You are adding to the resistance."

Where does drug treatment fit into this understanding of emotional expression? "Psychiatry is headed for a major flip," Candace muses, "and I flipped a while ago. All my friends are biological psychiatrists, but many of us are more and more critical of psychiatric drugs. They're really not the answer for many diseases, and in more cases than are recognized, they may do more harm than good. The good therapists are already using leading-edge therapies like eye movement desensitization, plus a number of energetic interventions fused with good psychotherapy."

A CONVERSATION ON THE BRIDGE WITH AYMAN SAWAF

Ayman Sawaf (www.aymansawaf.com) is the founding chairman of the Foundation for Education in Emotional Literacy, a nonprofit organization devoted to the advancement of emotional intelligence in business, education, families, and society. He is also coauthor of the best-selling book *Executive EQ: Emotional Intelligence in Business.*

We first asked Ayman to define "emotional literacy." "We teach all kinds of literacy in our society, like reading literacy and computer literacy, but emotional literacy is absent," observes Ayman. "This is unfortunate because emotional literacy is the ABC of our feelings, the language of all relationships. Emotional literacy is the antidote to a range of social ills—such as violence, disease, and depression—and the key to healthy and vital relationships.

"When we are emotionally illiterate, emotions get stuck within our bodies and our mind and basically short-circuit our biophysical systems. This can trigger all kinds of diseases; mental, emotional, even physical. There's a certain group of ailments, like divorce, drug abuse, dysfunctional family relationships, abuse, and so on that are associated with emotional illiteracy."

> **Feelings are everywhere—be gentle.**
> —J. Masai

Since literacy is usually an educational issue, how does emotional literacy affect our children's development? "We teach what each emotion means," Ayman explains. "To feel it, express it, recognize it, to understand why they are having a particular feeling and what's the information that's behind it. An emotionally literate kid has the ability to be responsible for how she deals with whatever situations she finds herself in, instead of having to react to the environment with anxiety and attempts to control.

"Another way to say it is that an emotionally literate kid will be an empathic kid. An empathic kid cannot hurt somebody else because they know how it feels. Most of the violence in kids, bullying and abuse, comes from shame. A shame-based kid always ends up abusing other kids with no remorse. Emotional literacy will reduce shame, and that reduction of shame will reduce the abuse and violence that is so prevalent."

On the positive side, what feelings will emotional literacy promote? Ayman responds that a major feature of emotional literacy is the effective expression of love. "Love is the highest emotion and most of us grow up not knowing what love is. We're supposed to know what it is, but we don't grow up asking, 'What is love?' So we supposedly learn what love is from our friends in high school, and confuse it with sex. We confuse it with this and that, and literally nobody ever teaches us about love and intimacy. Vulnerability is a major component of intimacy. When people are flowing and they're really comfortable with their emotions and know how to respond to them, the fear of intimacy, the fear of vulnerability disappears. The core of love is intimacy. People want to love so much but they're scared of intimacy."

Does Ayman see the world evolving into a more loving place? "After the Industrial Revolution and the Information Revolution, I'd say we're entering the Emotional Revolution. In a recent USA Today poll, when asked what changes in our school system people would like to see, the majority said they would like to have more school counselors. Thirty-two percent said, 'We want emotional diagnosis for our children before schooling.' Eighteen percent said, 'We want to teach our kids not to hate.' To me, it is obvious what those three things indicate, that parents and educators are saying 'We want emotional literacy,' but they have no name for it."

THE JOURNEY OF A THOUSAND MILES . . .

Your emotional state—whether good or bad, whole or fractured, healthy or in disrepair—is up to you. Yes, you may have suffered slights in the past. Yes, there may have been unfair things done to you, or are continuing to be done to you. Some of them may even be horrible. But you do not have to remain a victim.

As you have seen in the conversations about flipping our emotional habits, great advancements are being made in the understanding of the human mind and heart. The flip is occurring in dynamic and vivid ways throughout our culture. Millions have begun their journey and are hoping you will join them. Millions of kind souls are ready to open their arms and their hearts to assist you along the way. But, like us, they know they can only be supportive of your flip. It is your life.

Is it easy? No. But there are only two choices: the Right-Side Up world of wholeness and connection, or the upside-down world of separation and painful struggle. You will find that once you start taking steps toward a new world, it is not nearly as hard as it seems. It will take work, and it will challenge you. You will move forward and slip backwards sometimes. But keep going! And believe in yourself.

Finding the resolve to make the flip will empower, embolden, and enlighten you. Once you start on the path you will not want to return to the upside-down world. This very minute is a great time to begin your journey. Let's begin, shall we?

FLIP TIPS

- Always keep your word.
- Forgive yourself and others.
- Find a good therapist.
- Tell a dark secret to a true friend.
- Express appreciation a dozen times daily.
- Write letters to those who have hurt you—but don't mail them.
- Write letters of apology to those you have hurt—and mail them.
- Make a list of your faults.
- Live without expectation of reward.
- Go one entire day without criticizing anything.
- Listen more than you speak.
- Let go of your inhibitions—there is no right or wrong.
- Don't judge.
- Practice letting go of your ego.

FOUR

FLIPPING THE CHANNELS

From Mindless Programming
to Mindful Media

Night after night Barry watches TV before falling asleep. He gives his thumb a good workout flipping the remote control, searching for something to lose himself in. He pays more attention to the tube than he does his wife, his child, or the paperwork he promised to catch up on. He scans the spectrum of televised fare, never stopping for more than a few seconds, until he finally settles in for chunks of high-energy, low-substance cable news.

Secretly, Barry is fascinated by the crises du jour. Terrorist bombings, military operations, and natural disasters monopolize his attention. Watching the news reiterates his assumption that the world is a mess, and provides reassurance that his life isn't so bad relative to others. Flicking the channel changer gives him the illusory power of control over his environment and instant gratification. Both are temporary sensations that leave him empty when he comes face to face with real situations and life choices. His false sense of power dissipates quickly when he is not in front of a TV.

> **It is precisely the purpose of the public opinion generated by the press to make the public incapable of judging, to insinuate into it the attitude of someone irresponsible, uninformed.**
>
> —Walter Benjamin

When he gets sick of the news, Barry finds himself watching "reality shows" to see other people suffer some of his same indignities. This indulges his voyeuristic nature, but lately even the reality shows seem contrived, so he moves on in search of action flicks. Barry loves to watch car chases, hit men, and gunplay, the whole range of carnage and mayhem. It feeds his simmering inner rage and the destructive part of his personality. His fragmented, stunted thinking and his emotional insecurities are robustly reinforced.

By the time Barry falls asleep, remote in hand, TV still on, he will have been inundated with more than three thousand marketing messages that day alone. Three thousand a day.

Barry does not suffer a rare addiction. His dazed stupor is not the exception. His hypnotic glaze is the rule, shared by tens of millions of good people looking for their daily media fix.

COCKTAIL ANYONE?

Folks, we are willingly consuming an intoxicating media cocktail of entertainment, information, and advertising. We are subjecting ourselves to a highly effective concoction of these three major diversions used by the mass media to tell us the "Who, What, Where, When, How, and Why" for every aspect of our lives. Entertainment, information, and advertising are purposely intermingled so that we cannot tell when we are being informed, manipulated, marketed to, or misled. No doubt, a reader or two is afire with indignation at this point, thinking, "I have a mind of my own, thank you very much, and I can tell the difference between reality and illusion." However, almost no one in the United States is beyond the reach and power of the media. Only hermits and those living completely off the grid can escape its influence. Please bear with us as we walk with you through the dark shadow side of the upside-down world of addictive programming and see if at the end of the show, you still feel that you're in total charge of your own mind.

> **Cinema, radio, television, magazines are a school of inattention; people look without seeing, listen in without hearing.**
>
> —Robert Bresson, filmmaker

We'd like to state up front that we find much value in the entertainment media—when watched or listened to mindfully. There are many good shows available to entertain, educate, and enlighten. Unfortunately, one must search though a heaping pile of dreck to find the good stuff.

On TV, which is by far by the most pervasive, powerful, and persuasive medium, programs run the gamut: feel-good morning shows, afternoon soap operas, talk shows, game shows, reality shows, comedy sitcoms, hour-long dramas, miniseries and made for TV movies, documentaries, biographies, kids shows, nostalgic reruns, cartoons, religious programming, infomercials posing as TV shows, news, movies, and lots and lots of sports. And it's all 24/7.

THE DARK AGES

Thirty years ago, twenty-four-hour networks were unheard of. How did the ancients of those dark ages ever get along? How did they feed their minds? How could they have functioned? How uninformed they must have been. And then came the cable companies starting in the mid-1970s when the major networks lost their monopolies. By the end of the 1970s there were twenty-eight cable networks (channels) broadcasting to fifteen million homes with cable. By 1989, seventy-four cable networks provided programming for fifty-three million homes. Today there are 104 million U.S. homes receiving cable or satellite programming from more than three hundred networks.

That's a mind-boggling number of programming choices. And a lot of time to fill. So how do all those expensive airwaves get filled?

Here's a nice little interactive exercise, a bit of audience participation. Grab a pen and a piece of paper. We'll wait.

There are two columns below—DARK and LIGHT. To keep your copy of *The Flip* in pristine condition, it is recommended that you write down the list below on a separate piece of paper. Allot ten minutes—and ten minutes only—to watch TV. Take the remote for a spin—up and down the channels—placing check marks in either a Dark or Light column based on the types of images you see. Here are a few examples of the types of scenes and images you might see and which column they fall in. We'll meet you back here in ten minutes.

DARK	LIGHT
Violence	Joy
Angry Characters	Inspiration
Jealousy	Intimacy
Raised Voices	Laughter
War Scenes	Hope
Murder	Healing
Cruelty	Compassion
Deception	Happiness
Despair	Friendship

For those of you who took the time to do it, how did it go? This is truly an eye-popping awareness exercise. Most likely, more than half of what you saw depicted fearful themes, angry people, or terror. Whether it's pundits arguing on news channels, crime scene investigations, or desperate housewives scheming in the neighborhood, there are few opportunities for uplifting entertainment. Even the religious figures preaching about God seem to be yelling at their audience, stirring up the emotions of fear, guilt, or shame.

As much as we all love to sit on our couch and veg out watching TV after a hard day of work, we need to question what we are really subjecting ourselves to.

WHAT'S WRONG WITH THIS PICTURE?

The twenty-four-hour news cycle has created a culture of fast-paced headlines without substance or context. Viewers are fed rapid streams of concurrent data—news, stock market scroll, weather, sports updates, and subhead stories all at the same time—with little opportunity to process it all. Turn on CNN, Fox News, or MSNBC and see for yourself. This barrage of the senses leaves us no ability to validate what was presented, forcing us to accept that the news is true. This is purposeful on the part of the news operations, who function as little more than flacks for corporate and government interests.

> **Media is just a word that has come to mean bad journalism.**
>
> —Graham Greene

Sound radical? Ladies and gentlemen, we present Exhibit 1: The Florida Second District Court of Appeals on February 14, 2003, unanimously agreed that there is no rule against distorting or falsifying news in the United States. In an article by Liane Casten of Chicago Media Watch, FOX News "asserted that there are no written rules against distorting the news in the media. They argued that, under the First Amendment, broadcasters have the right to lie or deliberately distort news on public airwaves." The Florida Appeals Court agreed.

The flip that is occurring here is that people aren't buying the misinformation. The Pew Research Center reports that less than 32 percent of viewers believe the news is accurate; 53 percent say they don't trust the news. Newspapers and national news magazines fare much worse, ranking below 25 percent. Hey, we're not as dumb as they think!

Additional studies reveal that the more televised news one watches, the less informed one becomes. The owners of networks are multibillion-dollar conglomerates with a vested interest in satisfying their corporate advertisers. They have an active interest in compliant citizen-consumers. As such, important issues and news on the environment, corporate malfeasance, and political shenanigans are given short shrift, purposely skewed, ignored, or outright censored. For a great perennial book on the topic, pick up the latest *Project*

Censored published by Sonoma State University (www.projectcensored.com), which details the major news stories the mainstream media did not report in any given year. Prepare to be shocked.

Primarily, television stimulates the limbic system, which sits between the reptilian brain and the neocortex, by stimulating fear responses with a smorgasbord of overhyped news coupled with violent programming. The limbic system controls the emotions, feelings, and moods of the brain. Fear-based television stimulates the reptilian response of "fight or flight," in turn creating a mental state wherein we may overestimate the threat of fear. According to Rocky Mountain Media Watch, a nonprofit organization that has analyzed local U.S. TV newscasts for five years, "Forty to 50 percent of news airtime is devoted to violent topics, irrespective of actual rates of crime. As a result, viewers develop an exaggerated sense of the world as a violent and dangerous place."

Thus the mind begins to believe that the upside-down world is full of murderers on every corner, rapists leering in every alley, and burglars near every window. Parents feel they can't take their eyes off their children for a second for fear of their kid being abducted. This is a form of media-induced paranoia.

Not surprisingly, children have an increased level of anxiety relative to the amount of television they watch, as indicated by a survey by the American Academy of Child Adolescent Psychiatry. Similarly, a survey of parents of children in kindergarten through fourth grade revealed that the amount of television their kids watched was linked to the frequency of sleep disturbances.

Of course, everything on TV is punctuated and paid for by commercial sponsors schlepping automobiles, pharmaceuticals, alcohol, food, snacks, cell phones, offers to join the military, and the latest "can't miss" sales by the major retailers. Sixteen minutes of every hour is spent trying to convince you to buy something. Except for public television, the medium of TV was not designed and cannot support itself without advertisers. True, some cable networks such as HBO, Showtime, and Cinemax don't have ads, but you are paying a fee for the "right" *not* to see commercials.

Here's the skinny on estimated ad spending (not just TV) for 2006, according to the Center for Media Research based on the twenty-ninth annual "Advertising Ratios & Budgets" study performed by Schonfeld & Associates:

Automotive industry	$33.5 billion
Food companies	$28.3 billion
Pharmaceutical industry	$21 billion
Telecommunications	$22.2 billion
Retail and variety stores	$8.5 billion

We're not averse to advertising. No sir, no ma'am. We simply feel that citizen-consumers ought to be aware of the real goals of the media. That is—to sell us stuff. The shows only exist to sell ads. The ads exist to sell us. That's what fuels our economy, that's what drives stock prices.

So, armed with that information, one can now make an informed decision when it comes to the forces trying to influence us. Knowing, for instance, that by the television industry's own estimates, food manufacturers spend $12 billion annually marketing sugary cereals, candy, soda pop, and a grocery aisle full of unhealthy processed foods to children, may provide the incentive to turn off Saturday morning cartoon shows and find a soul-enriching activity to enjoy instead.

OUR CONSTANT COMPANION

The medium of broadcast radio has become our traveling companion in our cars. On the AM dial the stations tend to fall into four general categories: right-wing talk radio, featuring insulting hosts spewing words designed to incite discord; religious programming; news; and sports. There may be an oldies station or two in the mix. The fact is, AM radio is dominated by zealous opinions from the right side of the political spectrum. As we shall see in the upcoming Conversations on the Bridge, speaking the truth about issues and events is not part of their business model.

So why listen? Why fill your head with other people's thoughts? Why subject yourself to the aggravation? There is a theory that perhaps we listen to hear people angrier than ourselves in order to feel good about who we are. You'll have to look inside your own mind for that answer.

The FM stations offer a plethora of musical fare: classical, country, classic rock, alternative, hip hop, jazz, and all genres in between. National Public Radio (NPR) has its presence there and has historically offered a good intellectual slate, although there has been recent criticism that the Bush administration has attempted to move this medium rightward.

Amazingly, a hundred years ago, no one in the world was influenced by this much chatter; these media vehicles simply didn't exist. Today, people can't seem to unplug from the TV or radio. Driving silently in our car on the way to work or running errands seems lonely and empty. Many of us are simply uncomfortable being alone with our thoughts.

This is a result of generations of conditioning and can be easily corrected. All one needs is the desire to turn it off and the will to do so. Try this: drive in your car for an entire week without turning on the radio. No music, no news, no screaming bloviators. Only silence. One person we know tried it and didn't turn the radio on for a year!

LIGHTS! CAMERA! ACTION!

Movies have been a form of comfort and entertainment for decades, amusing billions of people the world over. They hold a special place in the hearts of many. They have the ability to transform and transcend, to evoke laughter or tears, terror or a sense of triumph.

The motion picture industry is a big business. Major releases routinely cost tens of millions of dollars to produce, distribute, and market. A successful movie can make the producers, director, and actors millions of dollars. An unsuccessful movie can result in huge financial loss and damage the reputation (and future earning power) of those involved. Because the rewards of a successful movie are so great, many types of people get into the movie business—some for the right reasons,

Hastiness and superficiality are the psychic diseases of the twentieth century, and more than anywhere else the disease is reflected in the press.

—Alexander Solzhenitsyn

and some for the wrong reasons. The prevailing attitude of those involved in making a particular film is directly reflected in the final product and quality of the movie.

We have all seen great, inspiring films. Nearly all of us have also plunked down good money to watch what turned out to be a stinker. Nearly everyone has seen movies that are direct rip-offs of other movies. While Hollywood is in the business of creating cinematic magic, the truth is there are only seven major plotlines and twelve major film genres to work within, so creating something unique is challenging. Plus, the tremendous pressure to produce a successful product causes studios and investors to rely on "tried-and-true" formulas that work. Hollywood only creates what they think we are willing to pay money to watch. If no one went to slasher films they would quickly stop making them.

An excellent example of the challenges of staying true to your art and making an uplifting film is the experience of noted actor, screenwriter, and director Michael Goorjian. Michael has spent the last four years raising money, putting together the deal, pitching and directing the powerful movie *Illusion* (www.illusionthemovie.com), starring Kirk Douglas. Even though acting is, in his words, "the closest thing to spirituality to me" he still had to work hard to play the game inside the Hollywood system and treat the production of his film as a business, or the movie he believed so fervently in would never have been made. That's just the reality of the industry. Talent, a good storyline, and determination can make for a great film, but it doesn't guarantee success.

One movie that made the flip and shattered the existing paradigm was *What the Bleep Do We Know?*, which sold out movie houses across the country for weeks, despite its independent status and almost no marketing budget. As Betsy Chasse, one of the producers of the film explains, "So many people told us this movie was never going to fly and no one was ever going to see it. But we just knew within ourselves that it was going to succeed. So, we threw out the rulebook and went with what felt right. One of the things *What the Bleep* proved was that there were millions of people interested in this type of spiritual content."

In the old days men had the rack. Now they have the Press.
—Oscar Wilde

While there are examples of films that are meant to inspire and entertain, these days one has to carefully evaluate each movie, as genres are becoming more and more sensationalistic and dark, delving into subject matter and content that is excessive, grotesque, or unnecessarily sexual. Many of the techniques used to titillate and shock in the shadow genres have crossed over and are being deployed across all genres to hold audience interest.

Now, an astute student of the arts would say, "But there has to be an antagonist in order to show the good of the protagonist." True, there has to be a villain for the hero to vanquish. But it is a question of degrees. Look back at movies prior to the 1980s, which entertained and thrilled audiences; they did not have the high levels of destruction and death (not to mention foul language) that exist in today's cultural climate.

We're all guilty of guilty pleasures. No problem there. It's okay to watch a movie that seduces the shadow side of our souls occasionally. But remember, if we are constantly filling our minds with images of war, violence, murder, and gore, we will begin to think in those same dark, negative terms. We become what we feed our head.

HUNGRY FOR SUBSTANCE

Mary grew up watching lots of TV as she happily munched snacks. When she was a child, none of her favorite female TV characters were heavy. Nearly all the commercials featured thin women flaunting their beauty. These role models left Mary feeling inadequate and self-destructive as she dug deeper into her bag of potato chips. As Mary matured into a young woman, her bad habits began to conflict with her desired body image. Eating the same foods her idols did—and wanting desperately to look like them—Mary binged and purged.

In college, every other girlfriend was on a diet trying to secure an idealized weight. Friends and relatives tried to intervene, but their care and concern were no match for the images society had drowned Mary in. She lost weight, then gained it back, and lost it. She was on a roller coaster of emotional distress. Her nerves were a wreck.

Eventually, after she realized she had given herself, and almost her life, over to someone else's false ideals, Mary sought help. She pursued a variety of actions to take charge of her life. In addition to therapy and the help of friends and relatives, Mary unplugged. No longer under the influence of mass media, she began the lifelong process of self-nurturing. She gradually adopted a healthy lifestyle of nutritious food in proper amounts. She minimized her intake of TV and radio. She likes television, but now watches only a few selected shows a week. Her schedule no longer revolves around start times for TV programs. She is less exposed to seductive commercials for bacon double cheeseburgers surrounded by a mountain of French fries, and other gastronomic come-ons.

Instead, Mary hungers for spiritually uplifting entertainment. When she goes to her local Blockbuster, she usually walks away with a low-budget independent film, documentary, or lighthearted romantic comedy. Mary only rents movies that she thinks will inspire, educate, or amuse her. Occasionally she will watch a mystical movie that has violence such as *Lord of the Rings* or *The Matrix,* but she has little interest in spending two hours of her precious time watching negative, pointless violence. Instead, Mary prefers reading books, listening to music, or participating in outdoor activities. With a high thirst for knowledge, Mary uses the Internet and the public library as primary sources of information. She loves to actively research her interests rather than passively watching TV. Mary isn't naïve; she casts a discerning eye on the wealth of information available on the Web and forms her views based on multiple credible sources.

NOWHERE TO GO BUT UP

Based on lower TV ratings, radio listenership, movie ticket sales, and plummeting news ratings, millions of people share Mary's desire for a more fulfilling media experience. The flip is happening as people in droves are turning away from traditional, mainstream vehicles. Networks such as LIME, Current, Free Speech TV, Noggin (for children), Women's Entertainment, Oxygen, The Learning Channel, National Geographic, and others are filling the void with programming that lifts the soul. Their success is a strong indicator that people are seeking a higher ground when it comes to their viewing choices. You'll have to be a discerning viewer to find the right shows for you.

On the movie front, every year there are a handful of wonderful movies produced by the major Hollywood studios and dozens more by independent filmmakers. The majority of the offerings aren't "conscious" yet, but there are positive signs to be seen in the popularity of "art house" movie theaters that function as a haven for independent films such as *What the Bleep Do We Know?, Garden State,* and *Sideways.* In addition, there is a strong film club movement in most American cities where people band together to view independent and foreign films ignored by the major distributors.

As further evidence of burgeoning demand for movies with meaning, DVD clubs such as the Spiritual Cinema Circle feature films that are meant to inspire. For a flat monthly fee you receive four movies that typically never get seen outside of film festivals because the financial model of the motion picture industry does not support smaller films, no matter how worthwhile or important they may be.

The flip is at hand as more and more spiritually uplifting films are being adapted from best-selling books, such as *The Alchemist, The Celestine Prophecy,* and *The Way of the Peaceful Warrior.* Will moviegoers flock to see these movies? Yes, if the films are done well with a good message.

On the radio bandwidth, there is a large media reform movement (www.freepress.net) working hard to force the FCC to return the airwaves to the people. This movement consists of activists from both the left and the right. The rise of low-powered radio stations across the country, championed by the good folks at the Prometheus Radio Project (www.prometheus radio.org), that provide truly local programming and news is further positive evidence of the flip.

Perhaps the most heartening and pronounced flip indicator from addictive programming to conscious entertainment is the Internet. The most revolutionary and empowering tool of the last decade, the Web has given individuals the freedom to search, read, review, and evaluate any information they want from a seemingly endless well of resources. Lee deBoer, cable pioneer and chairman of the mind, body, spirit cable network LIME Media, states that "the amazing adoption rate of the Internet and its technologies has put us in touch with more relevant (and irrelevant) content. The Web has allowed people around the world to get involved in online communities and interest groups that are connecting us in unforeseen and valuable ways. New technologies will accelerate an even faster and deeper experience."

This liberation from the passive, coma-inducing vehicles of TV and radio has given anyone with a PC and a data port real choices for data, news, information, entertainment, and opinion. With email, chat rooms, discussion threads, and blogs, a silenced citizenry can now be heard loud and clear. The Internet has heralded lightning-fast changes in our professional and personal lives, causing a massive paradigm shift in the marketplace.

Alas, it is only a tool. Like other media, the Internet must be used with mindful purpose and proper intent—in moderation. The Web, with its open access to virtually any topic humans find of interest, can open fantastic vistas of new insight and hidden knowledge. But it, too, has a shadow side with its predators and purveyors of questionable products and suspect content. As in all aspects of life in the upside-down world, each of us must be vigilant of our choices.

> **The one function that TV performs very well is that when there is no news we give it to you with the same function as if there were.**
>
> —David Brinkley

CONVERSATIONS ON THE BRIDGE

To continue our journey out of the upside-down world to the Right-Side Up one, let's hear what our Media Flipsters have to say on the bridge between the worlds. We start with producer and screenwriter Barnet Bain, who shows us that Hollywood is a reflection of our conscious and shadow selves—and that even though we may not like what we see, it is who we are. Debbie Levin, president of the Environmental Media Association, tells us about the great work she and many others inside the entertainment industry are doing to raise awareness of environmental issues through all forms of media. Our conversation continues with Sheldon Drobny, cofounder of the Air America Radio Network, who discusses the importance of honest discourse and reporting on our airwaves, as well as the need for diversified ownership of the media. We end our media conversation with John Raatz, who speaks about the exciting creation of a new genre—conscious media.

A CONVERSATION ON THE BRIDGE WITH BARNET BAIN

Barnet is a screenwriter and producer who has earned a reputation for creating innovative projects celebrating the human spirit. He produced and cowrote the screenplay for *The Celestine Prophecy* (www.celestineprophecymovie.com). His production of *What Dreams May Come* garnered two Academy Award nominations, winning the Oscar for Best Visual Effects.

> No form of art goes beyond ordinary consciousness as film does, straight to our emotions, deep into the twilight of the soul.
>
> —Ingrid Bergman

Wisdom Media Group recently presented Barnet with the WISDOM WorldView Award for using media and entertainment to raise spiritual awareness and make a significant contribution to the betterment of humanity. We asked Barnet just how accurately Hollywood mirrors reality. "Hollywood is inside of you and me," says Barnet. "So when we look at entertainment or newscasts, what we see isn't outside of us. It's a reflection of something that's going on inside of us as the observers. And it is an opportunity to look deeper into the self. Whenever one feels an intense reaction to violence, depravity, or irresponsibility in entertainment, it's almost always an indication that it's our own shadow that we are not at peace with.

"However, there's a little distinction that I think is important to make. I am not a fundamentalist Christian, so when *The Passion of the Christ* came out, that was not a film that moved me in my heart in the same way as it would move a believer. But it is symbolic of the same move towards wholeness and connection that is afoot in the world. The search for meaning animates films like *The Passion of the Christ* as well as *The Celestine Prophecy*. It's arising out of the same energetic principle. Viewers are empowered in different ways, but the underlying energy is to empower people. For the tens of millions of people who went to see *The Passion of the Christ,* that was a deeply affecting spiritual experience. But to have a negative reaction to a movie like *The Passion of the Christ*—and many did—provides an opportunity to look at one's own shadow. They don't even have to live through the suffering they're seeing; they just have to say, 'We all have a tremendous amount of suffering in our lives, and we all have created many adaptive psychological structures in order to deny that suffering.' So when we see it come up in the world, or in entertainment, we have lots of judgments about it. There are others who have perhaps a different take on that. I've heard the Dali Lama speak to this quite powerfully, quite beautifully. From the sound of that conversation, he doesn't have the same response out of his own shadow to a movie like *The Passion of the Christ.*"

A CONVERSATION ON THE BRIDGE WITH DEBBIE LEVIN

Debbie Levin (www.ema-online.com) is president of the Environmental Media Association (EMA), which seeks to mobilize the entertainment industry in a global effort to educate people about environmental issues and inspire them to action. Taking over the reins six years ago, Debbie has moved EMA in new directions with a strong emphasis on "young Hollywood." Under her leadership, EMA has emerged as the leading entertainment organization urging the industry to portray, model, and interpret environmental issues and lifestyles in the entertainment media. We were curious to know just how Debbie goes about this kind of work in a daily fashion. "We go to executive producers of television shows and pitch them story lines all year," Debbie explains. "Story lines, character arcs, even product placement, where characters can be shown using hybrid cars or canvas shopping bags, that sort of thing. We encourage entire story lines about major environmental issues. We also use celebrity to role-model behavior; that's a huge influence. We know celebrities who are supportive of us, and we use the paparazzi and the magazines and the entertainment shows to catch them in their daily lives. We love it when the TV shows Alicia Silverstone walking out of the market and getting into her Prius holding canvas shopping bags. We try to get these celebrities to be conscious that what they do in their personal life can be inspirational for their fans.

"In fact, I joke around that we teach celebrities how to shop. Because the reality is that everybody goes out and buys something every day. If they shop at the companies that are green and have an environmental consciousness, and make a show of supporting them, then their viewers and fans may follow suit. The actor Edward Norton and I get celebrities to purchase solar panels for their homes. And for every celebrity that buys solar, we've gotten British Petroleum to donate a system to a house in South Los Angeles. It's a great program."

Does this mean that flipping into an environmental consciousness will actually become hip? "I think that's where we've actually been a big help," Debbie enthuses. "We started trying to attract what we call 'Gen E'— Generation Environment—about five years ago. We're encouraging the sixteen- to thirty-five-year-olds to think that buying environmental stuff is cool. We helped launch the Prius that way, by getting over two hundred celebrities to drive the Prius."

Debbie told us that her organization also gives environmental awards. "The EMA awards are another opportunity for role modeling. It's our fundraiser and it's a way for us to have our corporate supporters get a little attention. But it's also a way for us to highlight the television shows and feature films which incorporate environmental messages. At the event, not only do we have an awards show with clips and information about the different entries, but then the party after is all organic. We've got twelve celebrity chefs cooking all organic food. Our silent auction is all environmentally sensitive, and so on."

Can a green consciousness be spread worldwide this way? Debbie Levin thinks so: "I think it's something that will come back into everybody's ordinary lifestyle. After all, our grandparents ate mostly organic foods. We've been living through a weird blip in history. We mistakenly thought that spraying pesticides on our food was a good thing. We're going to move away from that. The global energy crisis that we're encountering is going to spread the use of renewable forms of energy. So 'being green' isn't something that's going to go away. It's going to be integrated into the mainstream out of necessity."

A CONVERSATION ON THE
BRIDGE WITH SHELDON DROBNY

Sheldon Drobny (www.airamericaradio.com) was the cofounder of Air America Radio. He is also the chairman and managing director of Paradigm Group II, a venture capital firm specializing in socially responsible businesses. Mr. Drobny received a bachelor of science degree in accounting from Roosevelt University in Chicago and is a member of Beta Gamma Sigma, an honorary fraternity recognizing academic achievement in colleges of business administration. We were curious about the inspiration to create Air America. "The inspiration was that no one else was doing anything about media in liberal politics," Sheldon recalls. "Having been involved with the upper echelons of the Democratic Party, I kept telling them that if you don't influence the message that the media is going to disseminate, you're going to lose every time. And I asked, within the Democratic circles, 'Is anybody working on a media project, anywhere?' The answer was no. There were plenty of discussions about the media from an intellectual point of view, but nobody was doing the heavy lifting of starting a new company or taking on a new project from existing companies."

Does Sheldon think that Air America is creating a political shift in the cultural landscape? "The shift has been dramatic but we still have a lot of ground to make up. If you look at the numbers, even with Air America now going, the ratio of political broadcast is extremely distorted toward the conservative. Maybe it's now in the area of twenty conservative stations to one liberal, as opposed to one hundred to one not long ago. We made some significant inroads, but we have a long way to go and plenty of opportunities. We are the fastest-growing market in radio by far. But that's a little distorted because when you go from nothing, growing fast is easy. Still, in many markets Rush Limbaugh is down 30 percent."

> **Why should people pay good money to go out and see bad films when they can stay home and see bad television for nothing?**
> —Samuel Goldwyn

Will satellite radio help deliver more new voices to the airwaves? "Definitely," says Sheldon. "Not only will satellite broaden the available selection, but it will also make terrestrial radio much more conscious of their programming—which only benefits Air America. Radio programmers are not exactly visionaries and what they try to do is stay with the prevailing truths. So, whether it's music or talk radio, they're not the ones who put together new ideas. Radio is now being challenged, so conventional programmers are going to have to be a little bit more careful about what they throw into their broadcasts."

Will more diverse voices on radio help our society get out of the "us versus them" mentality that dominates conservative talk radio? "Telling the truth is one thing and having a point of view about it is another. For example, if you're going to talk about taxation, you can argue for progressive or regressive systems, but you've got to argue with some truth at hand. What conservative talk radio is guilty of, in my opinion, is the same as what the administration is doing; it's sending out stuff that's not truthful. If you make it up as you go along, as conservative talk radio does, then you have people who are polarized. When people start hearing other voices, you'll see a change in the dynamics. It all seems to be happening at once now when you see the failures and disintegration of the current administration. I'm hopeful that the crumbling of this administration won't lead to chaos but, instead, a positive point of view where people can discuss alternative ideas truthfully."

> **In Hollywood, the woods are full of people that learned to write, but evidently can't read. If they could read their stuff, they'd stop writing.**
>
> —Will Rogers

Is Sheldon hopeful about the future of media? "If I didn't have hope, I don't think I could get up in the morning," he replies. "I've seen a very big shift in the way the major media is looking at their dissemination of news as sacred truths. It's a fact that progress, or lack thereof, moves even the multinational media companies. Some media are dying; print and newspaper circulation is decreasing dramatically because they're not appealing to the twenty-five to forty group. And they're not watching network news either. So the audience is literally dying with the baby boomer generation. I think there will also be markets that will be captured by independent companies like Air America as long as they stay independent and are not bought out by another major media company. As a matter of fact, I would rather see media companies be pure. If there is to be some future regulation, there should be a bill submitted to Congress preventing multinational corporations from owning media. These big conglomerates should be forced to divest themselves of media companies because that's not the idea that the framers had about the freedom of speech and freedom of the press."

A Conversation on the Bridge with John Raatz

John Raatz (www.thevisioneeringgroup.com) is a partner in Awakened Media, a company founded to distribute conscious media projects with an emphasis on mind, body, and soul. As founder and president of The Visioneering Group, John is a skilled and experienced communicator, strategist, musician, teacher, and entrepreneur. He has worked with many of today's most popular authors, musicians, and artists. One thread that runs through John's professional life is an abiding commitment to others' excellence and success, and to the unfolding process that lifts all of humanity to a new level of ethical and spiritual expression.

Firmly ensconced in his role at Awakened Media, John told us about the flip he sees in the movie industry. "Film is beginning to demonstrate its powerful potential for transformation and there is a vast audience who wants to support the emergence of film as a vehicle for fostering change. There has been a large, nearly underground, movement of consciousness developing and evolving for decades that has, in recent years, become prominent. People are naturally drawn to the vision, values, and ideas being promoted by this community because they are the ideals of Self with a capital S. We're talking about nothing other than essentially speaking to *who we are.*

"If one looks at media today, there's the corporate media, which has a specific agenda that is driven by corporate, governmental, and other interests. Then there is this new media created to appeal to who we are as human beings. And that media is much more powerful because it is more direct. It touches our hearts. It touches our soul. It speaks to us much more than the evening news. Much more than 99 percent of the programs you will see on television and much more than 99 percent of the films you will see in theaters.

"This is a *Self-created* market sparked by the impulses of consciousness moving through all of us in the media profession who are awake and listening. We are assisting in the manifestation of this new world of media."

We wanted to know if this new media has acquired a name yet. John was forthright: "It's almost impossible to be in this world without some kind of a label. The choiceless awareness in one's personal life can be a lovely experience. But in terms of communicating with other people, we use words, we use expressions, we use ideas, and, in the domain of communication, we need words or expressions in order to be able to communicate with one another and help direct this flow that is happening. Right now we call it conscious/inspirational films. There are other terms being used to describe the genre, which aren't as satisfying or as accurate. We hope that by choosing the right film, music, or book projects that that helps define the genre. There's a natural alignment and resonance that will take place."

We asked John what role authenticity plays in its emergence. "Authenticity is key in the development of the kind of media we're discussing. More and more people want to play in this field and develop projects that reflect these higher considerations, these higher visions, these higher values.

"A distinguishing factor is that much of the media in our community is inwardly directed, even though its expression is outward. Authenticity is a natural expression of inner work. In the Hollywood model there have been many expressions of media that are purely outward-directed and designed to appeal to the senses alone. Projects are starting to manifest that are rooted in consciousness and appeal to our hearts and minds in a more refined manner."

With the rising popularity of this genre, does John see it becoming adversely affected by the inevitable commercialization and big money typically associated with the movie industry? John replied, "We have to continue to explore questions of the integration of art and commerce. It's one of those issues that people perennially debate. The Hollywood system is antiquated and no longer serves the purpose it once did. It is no longer indispensable, but is still needed for certain kinds of films.

> A film is never really any good unless the camera is an eye in the head of a poet.
>
> —Orson Welles

"We have a model that doesn't map to the old movie industry blueprint. For example, a well-known director contacted me recently who has a new project. The nature of the project is such that he believes it requires an $80-million-plus budget. We passed on it even though we loved the content because that isn't the range we participate in. We believe incredible films can be made for one to 15 million dollars. It's sustainable. Profitability is possible and sustainable at that level."

Can this important but fledgling media succeed? "I am overwhelmed and deeply heartened by the response, openness, and willingness of people to participate in giving birth to a new genre of film. What is important is that people who resonate with this idea of media as transformational come together and form an alliance. We have to work together to understand what is being manifested to support one another, to exchange ideas, to exchange resources, to collaborate. The type of media that all of us would like to see requires a collective commitment and effort. There is incredible generosity and willingness on the part of many who want to create new expressions of media that connect us to our most essential nature.

"Media is crossing a threshold from being self-serving and agenda-oriented toward fully presenting us with the immense diversity of the human experience. Whether conscious content expresses itself as a book, a piece of music, or a film, it is the content that inspires us and calls us forth and brings us together. Expression of our authentic creativity is the essence of life."

IS THIS THING ON?

Yes, big changes are occurring in media. The flip has arrived; it isn't out there on a theoretical horizon. The wonders of our technological age bring great promise and great responsibility. Our 24/7 society leaves little room for peace and quiet, for reflection and solitude. To stay centered and fulfilled we need to guard against the mindless, disquieting onslaught of programming, data, and information that does not "fill our well."

In the upside-down world, life is already spinning too fast; people's lives are already out of control. New innovations and incredible choices will be at our disposal. But we don't need more media, more amusements, and more entertainment. We need better choices. Our choices are a reflection of who we are—of both our conscious and our shadow sides. If we are to take charge of our lives, if we are to reconnect with our minds and our feelings, we must take care with regard to what we are putting into our heads. We cannot allow ourselves to be willfully manipulated into being compliant citizen-consumers. We must think and act for ourselves as we look out for each other and the collective good.

Being proactive in our choices, remaining mindful not to substitute the addiction of one type of media for another, enables a rightful return of power to each of us. Today, with the flip increasing its energetic momentum, there is much hope for democracy and freedom for all people in the Right-Side Up world.

FLIP TIPS

- Be aware of how you feel when watching or listening to mass media.

- Get your news from multiple sources.

- Mindfully select your entertainment choices.

- Spend one week without turning on the radio in your car.

- Write the networks and cable channels to voice your preferences.

- Support anticensorship groups, such as the National Coalition Against Censorship (www.ncac.org) and the American Library Association (www.ala.org).

- Read books. Read books. Read books.

- Visit websites that scrutinize the media, such as the Annenberg Public Policy Center (www.annenberg publicpolicycenter.org), Fairness & Accuracy in the Media (www.fair.org), and Media Channels (www.mediachannel.org).

- Join the media reform movement (www.freepress.net).

- Write letters to the editor of your local papers.

- Spend an entire day in silence.

- Start a current events discussion group or salon.

FIVE

FLIPPING BURGERS

From Processed Foods
to Natural Wholesomeness

We've seen how our mind and our emotions are affected by the stimuli we experience. Now let's examine how we are influenced by the food and drink we take into our bodies. As George Harrison once sang in "Savoy Truffle": "You know that what you eat you are." Before we travel into the flipped world of food, we'd like to state unequivocally that we are not the Food Police. It matters not to us whether you eat nothing but red meat, or vegetables, or raw foods. To each one's own.

> **It is a difficult matter to argue with the belly since it has no ears.**
>
> —Cato the Elder

Appetite and diet are highly personal matters, and many people struggle with weight problems. Often, people feel harshly judged for their habits and choices. Diet, and the weight that comes and goes, is a lifelong struggle for most. In our upside-down world, we are all highly susceptible to the massive influences of social conditioning and marketing. What we present here may shock you, anger you, or even elicit a reaction of denial. We are not advocating or criticizing any particular dietary lifestyle, only encouraging people to become aware of what their food choices can lead to.

Barry hits a fast-food drive-thru on the way in to work and scores an omelet sandwich, hash browns, and what he thinks is a healthy carton of orange juice. He gobbles down the breakfast as he drives, navigating to his favorite coffeehouse. Mmm . . . tasty. Barry isn't thinking about low carbs, low-fat, or nonfat when he orders his usual caffeinated beverage—a grande mocha double espresso supreme with light crème. He buys an innocent-looking raspberry scone for later and pays his $5.50. Later comes about sixty seconds after he's back in his car. Dee-licious!

Around ten-thirty, Barry visits the vending machine in the office for a little pick-me-up. He buys a soft drink and a bag of potato chips. For lunch, Barry cruises to a burger joint where he inhales a bacon double cheeseburger, some fries, and a Coke. "Oh, and what the heck, super-size that bad boy, would ya?"

Some afternoons Barry is good and resists the siren call of the vending machine. But usually around three-thirty his cravings rumble pretty hard and he finds himself looking longingly through the glass at the candy bars.

It's Barry's turn to pick up dinner, Italian, and he's got his heart set on spaghetti with meatballs, a dinner salad, and garlic bread. Fantastico! To prove to himself that he's serious about reining in his expanding waistline, Barry doesn't order dessert. That would be just too decadent.

THE DIET AND THE DAMAGE DONE

Let's take a closer look at Barry's average eating day. It's about as pretty as video footage of a quadruple angioplasty.

	Calories	Fat (grams)	Sodium (mg)	Sugar (grams)
Breakfast	1,100	61	483	38
Specialty coffee	840	40	n/a	53
Morning snack	843	46	1,348	39
Lunch	2,050	99	2,620	113
Afternoon snack	420	14	140	69
Dinner	1,530	52	3,345	20
Total Damage	**6,783**	**312**	**7,936**	**332**

In one day, Barry has consumed almost three times the calories, five times the fat, and four and a half times the sodium recommended by the food-industry-friendly USDA—and seven times the amount of sugar recommended by the World Health Organization (amazingly, the USDA hasn't bothered to make a recommendation for daily sugar intake). It's too scary to mention the cholesterol and carbs he's ingested.

But Barry doesn't think about the food he consumes. He eats while he drives, while he works, while he talks on the phone, while he watches TV. He senses no connection between the food he puts in his body and the way he feels. Feeling tired, suffering from acid reflux and daily headaches, which he blames on his stressful job, Barry went for a checkup recently. The physical didn't go too well. The doctor told him his lifestyle puts him at risk for heart disease and type-2 diabetes. In other words, his diet is killing him. The doctor advised him to lay off the caffeine, soda pop, processed foods, and red meat.

Barry listened politely and asked for medication to cure his ailments. The physician raised an eyebrow and wrote Barry three prescriptions as he warned him to take better care of himself. Since then Barry has ignored the advice. It's his life, his body, and he'll live any way he darn well pleases. Barry is proud of his defiance. Nobody is going to tell him what to do.

THANKS FOR THE MEMORIES

Like most Americans, Barry views food in a two-dimensional way: first and foremost for its taste, and occasionally—after he's had to open his belt another notch—for what it does to his weight. If food tastes good, we eat it. If it doesn't, we avoid it. But our relationship with food has always been more complex. Certain aromas and tastes bring forth vivid memories and powerful emotions that anchor us to the past and connect us to friends and family. Just thinking of these foods can spark succulent imagery and a desire to eat: Sunday morning buttery pancakes with syrup and sausage; roasted turkey and dressing with mashed potatoes and gravy; hot cocoa with marshmallows on a cold winter's eve; or a simmering pot of homemade vegetable soup and a loaf of fresh-baked bread.

> **Thou shouldst eat to live, not live to eat.**
> —Cicero

The conversion from nutritious meals at home to food on the run started simply enough. Forty years ago, going out to eat—even to a fast-food joint— was a relatively rare experience to be savored and appreciated. A visit to McDonald's was a treat, maybe even a reward for kids who did their chores. But what was once a reward has become commonplace; we are a Kid's Meal, Value Meal, Happy Meal culture. The meals make us happy, yes, but healthy—not so much. Americans are hooked on fast food and casual dining to the tune of $270 billion a year. Let's represent that a different way— $270,000,000,000 per year. To wash all that food down, we consume in excess of thirteen billion gallons of carbonated soft drinks annually. Burp! Pardon us.

It's convenient, to be sure. No slaving over a hot stove, no table to clear or dishes to wash, and fewer groceries to buy. But that perceived simplicity comes at a price. In our quest to make our lives easier, we have actually speeded up, becoming more harried. How many people can say that their lives are more content and fulfilled than their parents'? We have fooled ourselves into believing that we are in charge of our lives, when in reality, we have simply opened up more time to work and less time to be with our families. Natural goodness and common sense have been sacrificed in the false name of convenience.

Just two generations ago, nearly all meals were eaten together at home around the family table. The food was carefully prepared and leisurely conversation took place. Moments and ideas were shared. No more. These days, one meal a week with the whole family is a rarity—and that's probably at a restaurant.

As our pleasant childhood experiences of home-cooked meals are replaced with nutrient-poor fast food and snacks, our natural relationship with wholesome food is displaced by mass-produced substitutes. In our culture, food has become a commodity to be eaten chiefly for pleasure, or to kill time, or to compensate for troubled emotions. Our soulful connection to food for its nurturing and healing qualities has been severed.

TABLE FOR TWO, DINNER FOR FOUR

Restaurants are waging an ongoing battle for our hard-earned dollars. Remember the burger wars between McDonald's, Burger King, and Wendy's? The cola wars between Coke and Pepsi? What were they fighting over? Us. More accurately, our disposable income. The fast-food chains and manufacturers are fighting for the right to sell us high-fat, high-calorie, low-nutrition, mass-marketed, mass-produced food. As citizen-consumers we are being pounded mercilessly with advertising come-ons to live the good life of gluttony.

> The one way to get thin is to re-establish a purpose in life.
> —Cyril Connolly

Like all rhetorical wars, they can't be won. They are merely part of a sales and marketing strategy to gain consumer loyalty. Their number one weapon? Large portions. No, sorry, that doesn't do it justice—gigantic portions. Triple cheeseburgers, enormous omelets, double chili cheese fries—and now, you can literally buy a tub of soda pop. Gulp! We are being up-sized and super-sized at the expense of our own size.

Not to be outdone, casual dining restaurants are now serving platters with oversized portions, the food hanging off the plate. We don't know about you, but we're usually full after the bread and salad, well before the entrée arrives. Further evidence of the fattening of America comes in the sheer number of all-you-can-eat restaurants and endless buffets.

Here's the deal: The more you eat, the heavier you get. The heavier you get, the more you want to eat. The mind is trained to expect certain stimuli once they are introduced into the body. And food is one of the most potent, hard-to-resist cravings in the world. Eat half a package of Oreos at nine o'clock one night and the very next night you'll want another treat. Maybe not the second half of the Oreos, but something sweet.

FAST-FOOD JUNKIES UNITE!

Twenty years ago, cigarettes, alcohol, and drugs were considered "addictive." No one thought fast food was habit-forming. However, a study by Brookhaven National Laboratory involving brain scans demonstrated that when people saw and smelled their favorite foods, their brains lit up in a manner similar to the reactions exhibited by people addicted to cocaine. When individuals were presented with such favorites as cheeseburgers, pizza, ice cream, and chocolate, brain metabolism increased significantly in those areas of the brain associated with addiction.

Americans are receiving nearly one-third of their calories from junk foods laden with refined sugar, chemicals, and salt. It's no wonder chronic diseases such as diabetes, heart disease, hypertension, and myriad cancers are so prevalent.

It's a simple process. Advertising brings us to the trough. Oversized portions laden with fat and chemicals designed to bond with our taste buds and sense receptors ensure a pleasant experience. The brain, seeking comfort, pleasure, and satisfaction, trains itself to want more of the same. Ever-present advertising reinforces our desires and promises culinary nirvana again and again.

The keen marketing minds in the fast-food industry have learned how to find generations of loyal lifelong consumers by targeting our kids. An example of one of the dozens of food industry marketing programs masquerading as an education initiative is Krispy Kreme's "Good Grades" program, which offers elementary school kids one doughnut for each "A." Shockingly, fast-food chains have moved in to our school cafeterias. According to a 2000 study by the Centers for Disease Control and Prevention, 20 percent of schools sell branded fast foods from companies such as Taco Bell, Pizza Hut,

McDonald's, and Subway. Fortunately, parents and state governments have started to push back. More on that later.

Unfortunately, the results of a sedentary lifestyle coupled with overconsumption as determined in a study by Children's Hospital Boston reveal:

- Two-thirds of U.S. adults are overweight; a full-one third are obese.
- Thirty percent of American children are overweight.
- Childhood obesity has doubled in the last twenty-five years.
- Childhood diabetes has increased tenfold since 1985.

BUT WEIGHT! THERE'S MORE!

Okay, so we've spent pages decrying the state of the American diet and you get it: The more one eats, the more one weighs. That's a personal decision, right? Indeed it is, and if one chooses to live with the consequences, whatever they may be, that is certainly their personal prerogative. Again, we are not advocating or criticizing any particular lifestyle—only that people become aware of what their food choices really mean.

The real problem is, we don't know what we are eating. We have no idea of all the ingredients, little knowledge of the nutritional value, no understanding of when it was prepared, and no relationship to the chef/cook/food preparer/chemist/line worker involved in the mass production of most food products. What is most disturbing is that we have absolutely no clue what additives, preservatives, and chemicals have been put in the food to enhance its flavor or force its "freshness."

With food relegated to a commodity, we do not take it as seriously as we should. We cannot be bothered to understand the chemistry that takes place in our bodies when we eat. Even though we know on a personal basis the general affect that certain foods have on us—symptoms of lactose intolerance, migraines from chocolate, allergic reaction to peanuts, heartburn from spicy dishes—many people do not seem able to relate to the bigger issue: What we put into our bodies on a daily basis has a huge impact on our quality of life.

To these authors, the chemical additives, preservatives, flavor enhancers, and dyes are a much more dangerous and insidious assault on our health than overeating. Why? Because very few food additives have been adequately tested individually, let alone collectively, to study all their possible synergistic interactions.

Artificial sweeteners designed to assist those of us with weight gain issues actually create bigger problems. Acesulfame-K, which is 200 times sweeter than sugar, is used in sugar-free baked goods, chewing gums, gelatins, and soft drinks. The original studies on Acesulfame-K were flawed and more recent research indicates it causes cancer in rats. Aspartame, which goes under the names Equal and NutraSweet in the marketplace, has been the subject of much controversy and conspiratorial cover-up. According to the Center for Science in the Public Interest (www.cspinet.org), aspartame was found to cause brain tumors in rats. However, the FDA persuaded a review panel to reverse its conclusion and declare aspartame safe. Your tax dollars at work!

A large list of food dyes (Blue 1, Blue 2, Citrus Red 2, Green 3, Red 3, Red 40, Yellow 5, Yellow 6, etc.) have been shown in studies to have adverse affects on lab animals and are believed by numerous medical professionals to cause attention deficit disorder (ADD) and other forms of hyperactivity. The website www.diet-studies.com is a treasure trove of scientific studies and medical papers that offer indisputable evidence of the malevolent role food additives play with our health and behavior.

Square meals often make round people.

—E. Joseph Cossman

"Artificial and natural flavors" is a catch-all phrase for a concoction of hundreds of chemicals used to make you think you're tasting a delicious apple or a juicy grape. Rather than take you through a boring recitation of all the junk chemicals—and their nasty side affects—that are in our food supply, we'll amuse you with a short running list much in the same way the food industry crams it all together in fine print on their packaging: brominated vegetable oil (BVO), butylated hydoroxyanisole (BHA), butylated hydroxytoluene (BHT), cochineal extract, sodium casseinate, high-fructose corn syrup, dextrose, heptyl paraben, hydrogenated starch, hydrogenated vegetable oil and partially hydrogenated vegetable oil, lactitol, maltitol, mannitol, the infamous monosodium glutamate (MSG), polysorbate 60, potassium bromate, the bad boys of the preservative class—sodium nitrate and nitrite—sulfites . . . ah, well, we're sure you have the idea by now. An excellent and more extensive read on the topic is *The Hundred Year Lie* by Randall Fitzgerald.

The human body is a finely tuned, intricate organism. At a cellular level, trillions of interactions occur each day. Yet we think nothing of introducing foreign substances into it. The body's natural defenses do not know what these synthetic substances are and react to the best of their ability. In some people the reaction is benign; in others it triggers a range of maladies, illnesses, and symptoms that have traditional medicine confounded. Millions of people are now suffering the ill affects of an upside-down lifestyle. Could fibromyalgia, chronic fatigue syndrome, irritable bowel syndrome, and acid reflux be the result of our chemical-laden, synthetic food supply?

FROM BAD TO WORSE

Hang with us. We only have a little more space dedicated to the bad news of the upside-down world—the flip is on the way. Promise!

Further degradation of the food supply is found in high levels of mercury in tuna and other seafood. The FDA recommends that a woman weighing 130 pounds can safely eat half a can of albacore tuna per week. The Environmental Working Group (www.ewg.org) states that no amount of albacore tuna is safe for a woman of this weight based on the high levels of mercury in tuna fish. Sadly, there are few freshwater or saltwater fish that are safe for human consumption on a regular basis.

> **More die in the U.S. from too much food than too little.**
>
> —John Kenneth Galbraith

Say, here's a fun tip: Did you know that the U.S Environmental Protection Agency (EPA) allows toxic waste to be "recycled" and placed into fertilizer? Yep. Millions of pounds of toxic waste—dioxin, lead, mercury, and other hazardous wastes—are spread on U.S. farmlands as fertilizer every year. Millions more pounds of insecticides, herbicides, and pesticides are sprayed on our crops to accompany the fertilizers. Guess what? It ends up in your fruits and vegetables.

We don't want to leave the carnivores among us feeling slighted, so consider that 50 percent of all pharmaceuticals used in the U.S. are to treat diseases in animals caused by confined conditions on factory farms. Steroids are being used to produce larger and fatter livestock faster. Bovine growth hormone is being injected into dairy cows to induce increased milk production. Along with that production comes increased mastitis and the need for more antibiotics to treat the diseased cows. Of course, if it's in the cow, it's in the milk, so milk drinkers beware.

By now, we've all heard about mad cow disease, salmonella, campylobacter, listeria, and E. coli. According to the Centers for Disease Control and Prevention (www.cdc.gov), food-borne diseases cause seventy-six million illnesses, 325,000 hospitalizations, and five thousand deaths each year in the U.S.

Does this seem like our food supply is healthy and safe? Okay, trick question. Really, we'll be describing the flip shortly, have faith. For now, the point is, that while government agencies such as the USDA, the FDA, and the EPA are made up of good people trying to do good work and keep us safe, the heads of these organizations are political appointees. The party in power is always beholden to the corporate interests who put them there. They install former lobbyists, industry advocates, and former corporate executives to oversee the very agencies that regulate their businesses.

Conflict of interest? You bet. Who benefits? Food manufacturers, fast-food chains, chemical manufacturers, multinational corporations, and politicians.

Who loses? The American people: children, the elderly, your parents, your friends, your neighbors. We all lose in this game of commerce that seeks to push product and profit at the expense of people.

Multinational corporations like Monsanto and Cargill are patenting seeds and creating genetically modified organisms (GMOs)—including new strains of corn, soy, rice, and wheat—to create "Frankenfoods" that could pose staggering health, disease, and lifestyle consequences on a societal and personal level. By 2003, there were 167 million acres of farmland in eighteen countries growing GMO crops.

Opponents of GMOs rightly state that once these new organisms are placed in fields, we lose control of the pollination process, with unpredictable consequences for other species in the plant, animal, and insect kingdoms. Proponents of GMOs state that they are trying to bring food to the world to stamp out hunger. This is a noble cause. However, if the food manufacturers were truly intent on ending starvation, they would arrange for better distribution channels so the ample supplies of food we already have would make it to those who desperately need it. The problem isn't that there isn't enough food, the problem is that it isn't equitably distributed.

The real motivator behind the multinational food conglomerates' creation of GMOs are patents and the monopolistic fortunes they bring. In the summer of 2005, Monsanto filed several patents on the pig—specifically, its gene sequence. It's sheer madness.

A significant symptom of an upside-down world is when millions of people are overfed and simultaneously malnourished. Instead of nutritious food provided by the bounty of the earth, we consume high-calorie food invented in laboratories. But our relationship to food is in the process of a huge flip.

THE MOST NATURAL THING IN THE WORLD

Mary makes herself a hot cup of green tea every morning. The antioxidants in the tea enhance her immune system and give her the comfort of knowing she is taking care of herself. She eats a piece of organic fruit and a bowl of all-natural cereal purchased at her local supermarket. It costs a little more, but she knows that the savings in ill health and medical bills, and the increase in her quality of life, are worth far more.

After a youthful battle with weight and self-esteem issues, Mary has a good relationship with food. Having suffered the binging and purging of trying to have the perfect body during her college years—and seeing her friends struggle with their own forms of weight gain and loss—Mary is positive about her body image. She doesn't worry if she gains a few pounds as long as she is within a reasonable range of what feels comfortable for her.

Mary exercises moderately three times a week, riding her bike or taking long walks on a nature trail. She feels vibrant and alive, ready for life's moments. So many of her friends complain of getting heavier, of feeling run down, of losing their energy. Not Mary.

When she shops for food, she reads the labels. She buys organic produce whenever possible and washes her fruits and vegetables thoroughly. Dining out is a pleasant indulgence for Mary, but she shows self-restraint and only eats out once a week. On workdays, she packs a healthy lunch and eats in a nearby park with coworkers, weather permitting.

Mary will have an occasional piece of free-range chicken or fresh fish, but prefers grains, vegetables, pastas, and soy products. She loves a nice glass of wine and enjoys long dinners of healthy food with friends. She doesn't lecture others on her lifestyle choices, but will gladly tell others what she has discovered if asked.

To Mary, eating wholesome, nutritious food is the easiest, most natural thing in the world. Some of her friends sigh and say it's impossible to change their patterns. They don't believe the processed foods they consume are having a negative affect. Because they feel safe in the false cocoon of the upside-down paradigm, the idea of converting to a healthy lifestyle seems like too much work with too few tasty food choices.

A WORLD OF CHOICES

Here is the grand, obvious secret that everyone who has already flipped to the Right-Side Up world of natural wholesomeness already knows: There are thousands of healthy products available. The intuition that something has gone awry, coupled with the advent of the Information Age, has produced strong interest in nutrition and health. As savvy consumers read labels and distinguish good ingredients from not-so-good ones, they become consumer activists. People are voting their healthy food choices with their pocketbook, purchasing billions of dollars' worth of organic groceries and other natural products. The total size of the marketplace for goods and services focused on natural health, nutrition, the environment, and sustainable living is esti-mated at more than $226 billion annually in the United States. Nearly sixty-three million people from across the American spectrum are active consumers of such products and services. Now, that's a flip!

The success of national natural food retailers—Whole Foods Markets, Wild Oats, and others—are a prominent illustration of the transition to healthier food. Organic milk, dairy, and soy products are now commonplace in the dairy case of local supermarkets. All the major grocery store chains have significant natural foods sections, organic produce, and free-range meats.

We are digging our graves with our teeth.

—Thomas Moffett

People are buying organic products for a number of positive reasons: taste, higher quality, better nutrition, no chemicals, and a desire to protect their children from exposure to dangerous toxins. To a Right-Side Up world, whose residents recognize that we are all connected, all one, the socio-economic reasons are also highly favorable:

- support for people making a living wage, common in the natural products industry
- low impact on the land
- reduction of dangerous chemicals in the land and in water runoff into our rivers, lakes, and streams
- sense of community

Many people are also avid supporters of a movement called Community Supported Agriculture (CSA) that supports locally grown produce. This active movement supports a mutually beneficial relationship between local farmers and community members who pay an annual fee in exchange for weekly shares of each season's harvest. Everyone wins with this arrangement: the farmer is financially stable with a known source of revenue, and the consumer receives fresh produce harvested at its peak, usually without the use of pesticides and other chemicals.

This major shift toward organics and natural products is influencing intelligent food manufacturers to change direction. For example, General Mills decided to switch all of their cereal products to whole grain. Traditional food manufacturers, noticing a sea change in consumer preference and watching a decrease in sales of unhealthy fare, are buying up natural produce companies.

Even the government, despite the political pressure from special interests, doesn't want to be left behind. According to an interview in the Boston Globe with FDA commissioner Lester M. Crawford, the FDA is considering warnings on packages of unhealthy foods. Labeling junk food in a manner similar to that used for cigarettes is certainly a sign of the flip. Imagine seeing a large label on a can of soda stating, "Warning: This product promotes obesity and *diabetes.*"

The aggressive and sophisticated methods of marketing used by food manufacturers and fast-food chains to infiltrate the minds of children have stirred the concern of parents. What can't be stopped on the television can be removed from the cafeterias and hallways of our schools. Parents are leading a backlash against junk food in schools. As this book is being written, the states of Arkansas, California, Maine, and Texas, and cities including Los Angeles, Nashville, Oakland, Philadelphia, New York, San Francisco, and Seattle have expelled junk food from schools. Kentucky, New Jersey, Pennsylvania, the province of Ontario, and others have serious initiatives under way. The Organic Consumers Association (www.organicconsumers.org) is one organization, among many, leading the charge.

In Chicago, the nation's third-largest public school district is replacing soft drinks, candy, and fat-laden snacks with healthier offerings. New York City's largest school district banned soda pop sales. More good flip news comes from The Food Trust, which reports that nine of ten parents want soda pop out of schools.

CONVERSATIONS ON THE BRIDGE

If we haven't ruined your appetite with the bad news of widespread indulgence in junk food, you may want to stick around and have dessert with our Flipsters of Food, as we present our signature dish—Conversations on the Bridge. Relax! Our server will pour you a cup of fresh roasted organic Fair Trade coffee as you enjoy these dialogues.

We begin with John Robbins, heir to the Baskin-Robbins fortune and founder of EarthSave International, who tells us the conscious choice he made to raise awareness of the intimate connection between our food and the environment. Nell Newman, cofounder of Newman's Own Organics, tells what led her to found an organic food company. The father of organic flax seed oil, Udo Erasmus, tells us what led to his discoveries and the very real dangers of cooking oils. And then Vandana Shiva, physicist, activist, and author, tells us how she became involved in the biodiversity movement—and why you should, too! Read on—this is an interesting buffet of Flipster entrées.

A CONVERSATION ON THE BRIDGE WITH JOHN ROBBINS

The only son of the founder of the Baskin-Robbins ice cream empire, John Robbins (www.foodrevolution.org) was groomed to follow in his father's footsteps but chose to walk away from his commercial inheritance to "pursue the deeper American Dream . . . the dream of a society at peace with its conscience because it respects and lives in harmony with all life forms. A dream of a society that is truly healthy, practicing a wise and compassionate stewardship of a balanced ecosystem."

John is the author of *The Food Revolution—How Your Diet Can Help Save Your Life and Our World*. He also wrote the international best-seller *Diet for a New America—How Your Food Choices Affect Your Health, Happiness, and the Future of Life on Earth; The Awakened Heart—Meditations on Finding Harmony in a Changing World;* and the widely acclaimed *Reclaiming Our Health—Exploding the Medical Myth and Embracing the Source of True Healing.*

We were interested in learning from John the deep roots of his courageous flip. "I remember reading Rachel Carson's book *Silent Spring* when it first came out," John recalls. "It was 1962 and I was fourteen. That book had an enormous impact on me. Along with many Americans in the 1960s, I was part of the civil rights movement. I marched and worked with Dr. Martin Luther King, Jr., and I both loved and admired him immensely. When this apostle of peace and love was violently murdered, I felt as though a bullet had gone through my heart, too.

"Along with Dr. King and many other Americans, I abhorred the violence and insanity of the war in Vietnam. Only a few short months after Dr. King was killed, another man who many of us viewed as a bringer of hope, Robert F. Kennedy, Jr., was also assassinated. These were very dark times, and I was filled with despair for our nation and our world. In a world that seemed increasingly adrift in violence, cynicism, hopelessness, and fear, I wanted desperately to find a path toward sanity and love. I wanted to be part of a fundamental global transformation, and although I didn't exactly know how to go about a task so huge and idealistic, I did know that, for me, making and selling ice cream was not part of it."

How did John manage to say no to the considerable Baskin-Robbins legacy? "I did not find it easy to explain my thoughts and feelings to my father, a conservative businessman who was proud of the many things his wealth enabled him to buy. He had come of age during the great depression of the 1930s, while I was becoming an adult in the 1960s. Our lives were shaped by very different times. 'It's a different world now than when you grew up,' I told him. 'The environment is deteriorating rapidly under the impact of human activities. Every two seconds a child somewhere dies of hunger while elsewhere there are abundant resources going to waste. The gap between the rich and the poor is increasing. We live now under a nuclear shadow, and at any moment the unspeakable could happen. Can you see that, under these conditions, inventing a thirty-second flavor would not be an adequate response for my life?'

He that eats until he is sick must fast until he is well.

—Hebrew Proverb

"This was very difficult for my father to hear. Having worked hard his whole life, he had attained an extraordinary level of financial success, and he very much wanted to share his achievements with his only son. He thought I was being hopelessly idealistic, and he warned me sternly that idealists typically end up poor and miserable. But I did not feel drawn to the life he wanted me to follow. Whether it was hopelessly idealistic or not, I wanted to be part of the effort to bring about a more compassionate and healthy world. I felt called to take a stand for a thriving, just, and sustainable way of life for all."

John feels that the future of our food currently hangs in the balance: "It could go either way. Genetic engineering could take over, as Monsanto is hoping. Or organic food and agriculture could prevail and become the standard. We could see a pound of meat continue to sell for only a few dollars, despite requiring astronomical quantities of water, energy, grain, and land for its production. Or we could stop subsidizing polluting industries and begin instituting environmental taxes so that the true ecological costs of production come to be incorporated into the price of all the things we buy and sell.

"We could continue to house animals destined for human consumption in conditions that violate their biological natures and frustrate their every instinct and need. Or we could widen the circle of our compassion to include all creatures who draw breath from the same source we do. We could eat ever-more unnatural food, and watch our rates of obesity, heart disease, cancer, and diabetes skyrocket. Or we could take heed of the evidence and begin to feed ourselves and our children life-giving food with which we and they can build truly healthy and vibrant bodies.

"We could become even more alienated from the natural world as our food becomes even more processed, refined, and adulterated. Or our cities could become full of urban and rooftop gardens, with ever-more people celebrating the pleasures of eating food that is wholesome, fresh, and full of vitality.

"I don't know which way it will go. But I do know the choices we make today will have an enormous impact on the way things are tomorrow, not only for ourselves, but for the future of life on Earth."

A Conversation on the Bridge with Nell Newman

The daughter of actors Paul Newman and Joanne Woodward, Nell Newman (www.newmansownorganics.com) had an early introduction to natural foods at their rural Connecticut home. The family had a garden and Nell was taught to cook by her mother, as well as spending many hours fishing with her father. She was the executive director of the Ventana Wilderness Sanctuary, which worked to reestablish the bald eagle in central California. After two and a half years, she left Ventana Wilderness Sanctuary and began fundraising for the Santa Cruz Predatory Bird Research Group. In 1993, Nell launched Newman's Own Organics: The Second Generation—a division of her father's company, Newman's Own—with business partner Peter Meehan. The company, of which she is now the president, has been independent since 2001.

We were interested to learn how the child of two famous actors managed to avoid the lure of Hollywood and instead focus on environmental health and organic foods. "I was lucky because every other year we lived in Connecticut," Nell remembers, "and the majority of my life was spent growing up on a river with a pack of dogs, fishing. My mother was sort of an early environmentalist. We recycled and raised chickens, so it was a more grounded experience than some kids get. The movie-star thing was always there but certainly not a permanent aspect of my childhood. When I was about eight, I realized that the peregrine falcon, my favorite bird of prey, was almost extinct in the United States due to the use of DDT. The thought of extinction and that it might be occurring in my lifetime was a totally mind-boggling concept. So that was the catalyst for my environmental interest, leading me to become involved with several nonprofits later."

Nell reports that her organic food company was inspired by moving to the beach town of Santa Cruz, California. "I had never seen a farmer's market that was 80 percent organic before then. I was immediately inspired. Then I just had to convince Dad, which was a little more complex. My dad thought 'organic' meant the nut-loaf with yeast gravy that my mother used to make in the seventies. So, our first product was pretzels because it was my dad's favorite snack when I was growing up. I knew he would go for it.

We may find in the long run that tinned food is deadlier than the machine gun.
—George Orwell

"When I first came to the Bay Area, I ate at Chez Panisse, the first five-star organic restaurant in Berkeley. You don't walk out of Chez Panisse saying 'This is the best health-food meal I ever had.' You just walk out saying, 'God, that was the best *food* I've ever had.' And it's because Alice Waters utilizes such incredibly good ingredients. This inspired our motto 'Great tasting products that happen to be organic'—so you don't have to convince your children that our cookie is healthy and whole wheat. Instead you can say it's just like an Oreo but different, wholesome."

And what is Nell's vision of the future of food? "It's a tough question. Despite my pessimism, organic farming has experienced sustained double-digit growth, and so has land farmed organically. It is important that the double-digit growth continues. The standards of organic food were written by the organics industry, so they came from the right intent. We pretty much got what we asked for. We need to be aware that the Bush administration continually tries to dilute them. The challenge is to make sure organic stan-

94

dards are maintained at the highest level. But based on strong consumer demand and the adoption by the large grocery chains, I am hopeful we will continue to move forward in a positive direction."

A CONVERSATION ON THE BRIDGE WITH UDO ERASMUS

Udo Erasmus, Ph.D. (www.udoerasmus.com), introduced to the world the importance of essential fatty acids (EFAs) derived from organic flax seeds. He pioneered methods for producing unrefined oils made with health in mind; these methods are still used today by manufacturers of flax and other oils. His groundbreaking book, *Fats That Heal, Fats That Kill,* became the industry's bible on fats. Udo's contribution to the fields of health and nutrition, along with his pioneering work to establish standards of quality for oil manufacture, will continue to benefit humanity for decades to come.

We wondered how he got his start. "I was trained in biochemistry and genetics," Udo recalls, "but I left genetics when geneticists began to talk about cloning people. Because I am German, I'm allergic to those kinds of ideas. I decided that I didn't want to go in that direction. I got married and had three kids and I took a job as a pesticide sprayer. I knew better, but I was not thinking straight. After three years of doing that, I got poisoned. And the doctors couldn't help me. At that point, I got really focused on restoring my health. I started digging through the research and I got hooked on fats as my first step because I knew that fats and cancer have a relationship; about 60 percent of the pesticides we spray may cause cancer. So I thought I needed to know the connection between fats and cancer, and I started studying fats."

Udo would soon be surprised by two discoveries from his research. "The first was how much damage is done to our oils by the processing that turns what's in the seed into a colorless, odorless, tasteless cooking oil. These oils get processed, then they get treated with Drano (sodium hydroxide), window-washing acid, or phosphoric acid—all very corrosive chemicals. Then they're bleached, which turns them rancid. Then they smell and taste bad, so they're heated in a process called 'de-odorization' to get rid of the rancid odor.

"Along with that, I learned that when you do all that to an oil, anywhere from 0.5 to 1 percent of the molecules are changed from something natural that the body recognizes to something that has never existed in nature—that your digestive system doesn't know what to do with—and that is therefore toxic in the body. In fact, there is an association of processed cooking oils with increased inflammation, increased cardiovascular disease, and increased cancer. Why? I did the math on it and figured out that if an oil is damaged 1 percent, then in one tablespoon of that oil, you will get a million toxic molecules for every one of your body's sixty trillion cells. A million toxic molecules per cell, in just a tablespoon, is a lot. Most people use two or three tablespoons a day. My conclusion was that we ought to be making oils with health rather than shelf life in mind."

By 1983, Udo had devised a method for minimum processing of unrefined oils that allows them to retain their healthy properties. "That's really my claim to fame—figuring out how to protect the oils from light, oxygen, and heat, because those are what damage them most rapidly. We maintain that protection during filtering and filling, and store them refrigerated at the factory and at the stores. We recommend they be refrigerated in the home or frozen for long shelf life, and to use them in all food preparation except frying. You can put them in hot soup, on steamed vegetables, in yogurt and cottage cheese, protein shakes, fruit juice, vegetable juice, mashed potatoes, pasta sauce, and so on, but not for frying. When you put oils in a frying pan, you damage them with light, oxygen, and heat. The light produces free radicals, which produce chain reactions and a lot of molecules get changed. The oxygen makes the oil go rancid, and high temperatures cause a number of damaging effects, including twisting molecules into trans-fatty acids. Heat also multiplies the effect of the destructive reactions caused by light and oxygen.

> Only the pure in heart can make a good soup.
>
> —Ludwig van Beethoven

"When you turn food brown, you've changed molecules. And those molecules have carcinogenic and other toxic effects in the body and increase inflammation. One hundred years ago, a big oil industry did not exist and most people cooked their food in water, so they steamed, poached, boiled, or pressure cooked. Even olive oil, which is now recommended for frying, was not used for frying."

Udo also suggests that people should minimize the use of plastic in their food storage. "Plastic leaches into water," he reveals, "and I found out that oils swell plastics and make that leaching easier. So I get my water in glass and I've thrown all the plastic out of my kitchen. Oils don't swell glass, and glass doesn't leach. We don't know everything that's in plastic; we don't know what it does to the human body. All we know is that plastic is a synthetic material that has never been in the environment."

A CONVERSATION ON THE BRIDGE WITH DR. VANDANA SHIVA

Dr. Vandana Shiva (vshiva.net) is a physicist, ecologist, activist, editor, and author of many books. In India she established Navdanya, a movement for biodiversity conservation and farmers' rights, and she directs the Research Foundation for Science, Technology, and Natural Resource Policy. Her most recent books are *Biopiracy: The Plunder of Nature and Knowledge* and *Stolen Harvest: The Hijacking of the Global Food Supply.*

She relates that she first got involved in ecological issues because of the destruction of the Himalayan forest and the emergence of a movement called Chipko. "The women came out and hugged the trees and said, 'You can't let our trees be destroyed' and 'you've got to kill us before you kill our trees, our forest.' I left university teaching in 1982 and started an independent institute to do research with communities on ecological issues. I was doing that through the early eighties, also movement building and women's support. And then in 1984, there were certain events that forced me to move into agriculture, in spite of being a physicist. The Green Revolution was spreading the use of fertilizers, irrigation, and other factors that poor farmers couldn't afford and may have been ecologically harmful as well, in addition to promoting monocultures and loss of genetic diversity.

"I saw three thousand people die because of a leak from the Union Carbide pesticide plant. This was the Bhopal disaster, the largest man-made environmental disaster in human history. And I had to ask, 'What kind of agriculture is it that must kill so many people?'"

In reaction to that tragedy, Vandana wrote *The Violence of the Green Revolution.* "This helped spark an agriculture debate with the global giants, challenging the idea of owning life through patents. In 1987, when I got exposed to all of this through a United Nations meeting in Geneva, I realized I was going to save seeds for the rest of my life. To save seeds so they could stay free, so nature could evolve freely, farmers could have seed freedom, and people would have decent food. From 1987 onwards, this is all I've done! We've had impact, but we're a small organization that manages to do effective things in the face of all the financial giants of the world. For instance, we're having a positive impact fighting the privatization of water. The other day, I was at the World Bank with Paul Wolfowitz, the new president. I was visiting with the trade unions of the water utility to tell him on behalf of the citizens of Delhi, 'We don't need World Bank loans to run our water systems. We have competence enough to do it. And we definitely will not allow our water to be privatized.'

"I think the biggest impact that we've had is the recognition that nature's tremendous diversity is not there to be restricted. Our duty as humans is to protect it. And I think we have reversed the thinking in agriculture, which was driving toward monocultures. We have changed the paradigm to respect diversity in farming. The fact that the organic movement is growing is good. But the fact that it's being taken over by giant corporations means that the option of rejuvenating agriculture, rural communities, and ecosystems is being forsaken. I believe that an organic movement that is only a consumer movement will never be fully organic. No real change will happen solely through consumerism alone. We have to recover our Earth citizenship, partly by making the extra effort to ensure it's the small farmer who is supported by one's consumption."

Once we open up to the flow of energy within our body, we can also open up to the flow of energy in the universe.
—Wilhelm Reich

Does Vandana feel it's likely we will make the flip to Right-Side Up agriculture and consumerism? "I don't think anything is ever inevitable in human history or in evolution. There are always probabilities and possibilities. Right now there's a probability that the machinery of destruction will continue without enough resistance building in society to shift the direction. On the other hand, I also firmly believe there's a possibility that we will elect an overall shift by making little shifts in our lives, and that we will be able to prevent the extinction of human life on this planet. Human beings will be able to rise in consciousness in collected consciousness as a species, not just as a few with a heightened consciousness. I wouldn't do the work I do if I didn't have that hope and that possibility."

CHECK PLEASE!

Taking charge of your eating habits is not as hard as it sounds. There are thousands of healthy, tasty products on the market. There are millions of people already doing it. Farmers, natural food manufacturers, distribution channels, and retail outlets are already in place. Vast stores of information are available on the Internet, at your local health food store, specialty shops, and even your health care practitioner (be sure to read the next chapter for more on that).

Friend, you don't have to go "cold turkey" and suddenly change your life. If you have a desire to experience life to the fullest, start with simple changes. See the Flip Tips at end of this chapter. Begin at the pace you are comfortable with. Tap into your body's amazing energy store by ridding it of the toxins it has been accidentally fed over the years.

Flipping to proper nutrition and good health is not a progressive or conservative issue; it's not a vegetarian versus omnivore issue. It is not about one way being right and the other way being wrong. It is about the personal choices we make in the nutrients we bring into our bodies. Eat what you wish, with knowledge and wisdom about your choices and their consequences. The flip is in full swing. It isn't hard to land in the Right-Side Up world, to fully enjoy the gracious feast of Mother Earth's natural bounty.

Bon appétit!

FLIP TIPS

- Be aware of what you are putting into your body.

- Read the labels on the foods you buy.

- Plan at least two meals at home per week with family or friends.

- Reduce or eliminate soft drinks from your diet, including diet drinks.

- Whenever possible, purchase organic produce and free-range meats.

- Support your local health-food store.

- If your supermarket doesn't carry natural products, speak with the manager and convince him or her to do so.

- Research your child's school lunch choices.

- Reduce your consumption of fast food.

- Visit some of the websites listed in this chapter for a diverse view of organic and natural foods.

- Enjoy life to its fullest with a pleasurable dining out experience once per week.

- Don't lecture or preach to those on a different path. If someone asks, let them know what you've discovered; do so kindly, without judgment.

- Drink organic milk instead of the regular milk found in the dairy aisle.

- Exercise at least thirty minutes a day, three times a week.

- Reduce or eliminate between-meal snacks.

- Order a split plate with your partner at a restaurant and share the serving.

SIX

FLIPPING PILLS

From Treating Symptoms to Maintaining Health

Most days, Barry drags himself out of bed. Coffee is the vital stimulant that shoves him into his day. It takes all his energy just to shower, get dressed, and head to work. Headaches and acid reflux have become more loyal companions than his dog. He feels lousy most of the time. His doctor warned him about his diet and urged him to exercise, but Barry had other ideas.

Barry hates going to the doctor; he doesn't have the time to waste in the waiting room. Once inside the examination room he is asked to disrobe and wait some more. Then his physician comes in; does some cursory checks of eyes, ears, nose, throat, and chest; asks a few questions; makes a diagnosis; and writes a prescription. Wham! Bam! Thank you, man!

> **Health is the greatest gift, contentment the greatest wealth, faithfulness the best relationship.**
>
> —Buddha

That's just Barry's impression, of course. He's been replaying past experiences in his mind as an excuse to avoid facing his current health predicament. Finally, after several months of vague sickliness and prodding by his wife, Barry goes back to his doctor. After a battery of tests administered by a series of specialists, Barry is told that his immune system is weak. This makes him susceptible to all manner of illnesses. When Barry asks what has caused his weakened immune system the doctor replies, "Stress." But he already knew he was stressed out. What Barry doesn't know is that all his symptoms—his headaches, his acid reflux, his perpetual tiredness—are results of his lifestyle choices.

The doctor gives Barry a pamphlet on stress, again advising Barry to try a healthier diet, to exercise, to learn how to relax. Barry, an incessant TV watcher and commercial connoisseur, asks for Ambien to help him sleep. The doc writes the prescription.

A peek inside Barry's medicine cabinet reveals a minipharmacy: aspirin, acetaminophen, and ibuprofen for headaches; cough suppressants, expectorants, cough drops, inhalers, and antihistamines for colds; expired antibiotics for some malady he can't remember; antacids, Milk of Magnesia, Pepto Bismol, and Protonix for his stomach; Celebrex and mentholated rub for muscle soreness; hemorrhoid ointments, suppositories, and creams; Lipitor for cholesterol; and, finally, a host of codeine-class painkillers for special occasions. There's a drug problem in America all right—brought to you by the pharmaceutical industry, sponsored by the FDA.

Barry is still fuming about his doctor as he gets his latest prescription filled (it doesn't help that his insurance company raised his co-pay). He wonders how he could only be allowed ten minutes with *the* person responsible for his health?

What Barry and many of us fail to realize is that doctors are *not* responsible for our health; we are. Physicians, at best, are assistants in our health. Each and every one of us must be conscious of our life choices. Doctors cannot take the medicine for you, nor can they exercise for you, or be with you 24/7 to regulate what you eat and drink. Doctors are not miracle workers. They simply do the best they can based on their education, skill-set, and expertise amidst the stresses, pressures, and pace of their own lives.

> **Take care of your body with steadfast fidelity. The soul must see through these eyes alone, and if they are dim, the whole world is clouded.**
>
> —Johann Wolfgang Von Goethe

If Barry had seen a doctor with a more holistic approach, there would have been a higher likelihood that he would have been diagnosed with stress a long time ago. Because his primary care physician had so little training in preventive care and so much training in pharmacology, it was natural for him to focus on medication over lifestyle changes.

TWO CAMPS ALONG THE SAME RIVER

Make no mistake: Medicine in the modern age is big business. Hospitals, researchers, drug companies, medical suppliers, health care providers, middlemen, and insurance companies aggressively compete in this industry. Estimates by the 2003 U.S. Census Bureau Survey of Health Care and Social Assistance report industry revenues were—set down your drink, we don't want you blowing fluids out your nose—*$1.3 trillion.* That's a rather large number.

It has been a lucrative trade since the mid-1800s when the American Medical Association (AMA), founded by Nathan Smith Davis, squared off against the American Institute of Homeopathy.

The AMA, an allopathic organization, built their camp on the systems-based, surgery, and drugs side of the river. Based on the state of health care in the United States, strong evidence suggests this camp lies in the upside-down world. Our media, politicians, and other professionals in positions of power and authority like to state that we have the best health care system in the world. Not so. Let's examine a few facts:

- We have the most expensive health care system on the planet, with Americans spending twice as much money on health care as other countries.
- The World Heath Organization (WHO) ranks the U.S. health care system thirty-seventh.
- U.S. women rank nineteenth for life expectancy; men rank twenty-ninth.
- U.S. citizens pay anywhere from two to ten times as much for the same drugs sold in other countries.
- Forty-five percent of all global drug sales ($248 billion) were in North America.

Okay, that's depressing; where's the Paxil? On the other side of the river, in the Right-Side Up world, is the holistic health care camp. This group has its roots in remedies that are thousands of years old. It consists of a custom blend of preventive treatments designed to keep a person well, as opposed to fixing a person after they are afflicted. Holistic health care includes the best of traditional Chinese medicine (TCM), ayurveda, naturopathy, and home-opathy. TCM is a four-thousand-year-old system that integrates herbs, acu-pressure, acupuncture, tai chi, and Eastern philosophy. Ayurveda is the traditional Indian approach to medicine, a five-thousand-year-old "science of life" that places equal emphasis on the body, mind, and spirit in seeking to restore the innate harmony of the individual based on three primary "doshas," or mind-body types. Naturopathy originated in Europe as a system of healing that views disease as an aberration of the body's ability to naturally heal. Homeopathy is a complete system of health founded by German physician Samuel Christian Hahnemann in the early 1800s. It is based on the "principle of similars," which states that a substance given in minuscule doses can cure in a diseased person the symptoms that the same substance at full strength would cause in a healthy person.

AN UGLY BIT OF BUSINESS

As often happens when there is stiff competition around the almighty consumer dollar, it got ugly. Before the turn of the twentieth century, the allopathic and natural health camps waged war. As has often been said, "history is written by the victors" and, in this case, the AMA won. Through a series of heavy-handed tactics, the AMA derided anything outside their allopathic sphere as quackery. Restrictive laws were passed, certifications were withheld, careers were ruined—and patients suffered.

Today, we have a massive—and expensive—health care system that ranks thirty-seventh in the world. Yet most Americans remain oblivious to this fact. We have been programmed into believing we have the best health care on the planet, yet are conditioned to settle for less—much less. We casually accept the highest prescription drug costs in the world. We passively accept the increase in our health insurance premiums and simultaneous reduction in services. We put our faith and trust in the physicians and specialists who treat us, assuming that they are current on the latest techniques and trends for optimal health, and up to date on the latest drug interactions and recalls.

One doesn't have to look far to find a close relative, friend, coworker, or acquaintance struck by a major illness. With more than $1.3 trillion spent annually, shouldn't we all be models of health? Okay, that's unrealistic; but shouldn't most of us feel great, energetic, at the top of our game?

Without thinking about it, quickly ask yourself: Overall, how do you feel? Great? Good? Middling? Lousy? Get me to a hospital? Seriously, with no rationalization, how do you feel? Besides vitamins or natural supplements, how many pills do you take or ointments do you smear on each day? Aspirins and other pain relievers count. So do swigs of Pepto-Bismol, eye drops, and cough drops—anything synthetic you take to calm an irritation. If you are like most of us in the upside-down world, it's quite a few.

THE THREE HORSEMEN OF THE APOTHECARY

As stated earlier, health care is big business. It is made up of three large contingents: health care providers, pharmaceutical manufacturers, and insurance companies. Let's call them the Three Horsemen of the Apothecary as we take a closer look.

First up we have health care providers, which includes doctors, nurses, aids, technicians, support personnel, specialists, clinics, and hospitals. Many who minister to the ill and infirm are caring, wonderful, conscientious people who truly want to help. The key word here is that they are *people*—just like you—influenced by the swirl of life's forces, subject to the same emotions, stresses, and challenging circumstances we all face. So why put them on a pedestal and expect them to be infallible? Putting your complete trust in someone else is an abdication of your personal responsibility. Doctors and other health care professionals are akin to coaches; they can offer a good game plan but they cannot complete the plays. You must do that.

Health care professionals have a tough job. They can only treat you within the perspective of their training. If that training is focused in certain areas such as pharmacology, anatomy, and biochemistry and is insufficient in other areas, such as nutrition and drug interactions, then they will not be capable of treating and advising you adequately. Consider a 2003 survey of 122 medical colleges and nineteen accredited osteopathic colleges that revealed

- only 40 percent of schools required a nutrition course and those that did only required an average of 2.5 hours,
- 13 percent offered nutrition as an elective,
- 24 percent mixed nutrition into other courses,
- 23 percent offered no nutrition-based instruction.

> **To insure good health: eat lightly, breathe deeply, live moderately, cultivate cheerfulness, and maintain an interest in life.**
> —William Londen

These are the results, despite a 1990 congressional nutrition education mandate. In 1994, the National Academy of Sciences called for U.S. medical schools to improve their nutrition curricula. Practicing physicians are in near universal agreement about the need for substantial nutrition education. Every parent knows the importance of proper nutrition for their children's development and ongoing health. Yet the topic remains a low priority in 60 percent of all medical schools. Our heath care professionals are being short-changed and so are we; after all, it's our health that suffers.

Once entering their profession, health care professionals participate in seminars, workshops, and continuing education classes as their hectic schedules permit, but often the primary way they hear of the latest advances (besides trade magazines) is through their friendly drug representatives. Drug companies spend hundreds of millions of dollars schmoozing and influencing doctors to write "scripts" for their drugs instead of their competitors'. As the summer 2005 Vioxx trial showed, the drug manufacturer's sales reps were trained to mislead doctors who asked pointed questions about the drug's side effects. A Texas jury awarded $253 million to the widow of a man who died after having taken the drug for only eight months. It should never have come to death and dollars to do the right thing.

Somewhere back in the 1980s, hospital boards across the land hit upon an epiphany: They could make boatloads of money if they privatized their services and focused on profits over public service. They took to this concept like a heroin addict to a syringe. Nonprofit hospitals went private, patients got turned away, fees rose, and collection agencies were contracted. Today, nearly 50 percent of all personal bankruptcies are the result of mountainous medical bills. Meanwhile, the CEO of HealthSouth (recently under indictment for fraud) took home $267 million for six years' work. That's $44,500,000 a year. It's good work if you can get it. Hippocratic oath be damned, there's money to be made.

But don't reach for the Tylenol just yet; there's good flip news ahead.

BETTER LIVING THROUGH CHEMISTRY

Drugs have dramatically improved the lives of many. In a previous age, diseases that once ravaged humans, such as polio, smallpox, measles, and tetanus, have been reduced or eradicated in societies where vaccines and drugs are made available. Medicine, properly prescribed and taken, provides relief for many of our diseases and symptoms. From providing comfort against the symptoms of flu to fighting off potentially fatal infections, drugs have saved millions of lives and alleviated pain for millions more. Their value cannot be disputed.

> No time for your health today will result in no health for your time tomorrow.
>
> —Irish Proverb

But something has gone awry. During the decades between 1940 and 1980, drugs began to be seen as miracle workers. People trusted the word of the FDA, the drug companies, and the politicians. It seemed that medicine might soon conquer all disease and discomfort. They could see, firsthand, new drugs vanquishing illnesses. Antibiotics gave people a fighting chance against whatever infectious bacteria had invaded their body. Those were heady times. Science was going to conquer all. Medicine would dominate all disease. People increasingly believed nearly everything told them and passively put their entire health in the hands of the Three Horsemen. By the 1990s, drug companies and medical professionals began taking advantage of what they thought was the nearly universal zealous blind faith of the American consumer. Instead of making moderate profits and being content with reaching a benevolent hand to humankind, drug companies decided they wanted more. As a result, the pharmaceutical industry has become one of the most powerful in the world. Here are some facts:

• Drug companies spent $800 million in campaign donations and lobbying Congress and regulators over the last seven years. That's about $1.5 million per member of Congress. What were they buying?

• One-third of the three thousand medical industry lobbyists peddling influence in Congress and the regulatory agencies are former government officials. It's a revolving door between industry and the FDA.

• Fifteen former senators and sixty former members of the House of Representatives are now Big Pharma lobbyists.

Pharmaceutical companies bribe Congress into passing legislation that protects their profits but harms patients. They lobby for and get tax breaks and immunity from prosecution for knowingly selling products that are toxic. Don't believe us? Consider the case of Representative Billy Tauzin of Louisiana. Mr. Tauzin sponsored and shepherded the massively corrupt Medicare bill that was a multibillion-dollar giveaway to the pharmaceutical industry. The bill included legislation forbidding the importation of cheaper drugs from Canada and Mexico (even though made by the same companies) and mandated that the federal government could not negotiate price discounts based on its huge buying power.

Say what? Not allowed to negotiate discounts to lower prescription drug costs? Yep, that's right. So what did Billy Tauzin do after he resigned from Congress, only days after the bill was made into law by one vote in the dark of night under questionable circumstances? He took a $2-million-a-year job as president of the Pharmaceutical Research and Manufacturers of America, the chief lobby for brand-name drug companies. Could be just us, but that doesn't seem right by any standard.

Sadly, such corruption is commonplace. Senator Bill Frist of Tennessee has attempted six times to quietly introduce last-minute riders into legislation, granting immunity to drug manufacturers using Thimerosal, a preservative consisting of 50 percent mercury, in vaccines. Mercury is known to be one of the deadliest substances on the planet and has been linked to an alarming increase in autism in children. The drug industry and the FDA, of course, deny the cause and affect.

We offer one more astonishing and appalling example: A September 2004 article by Shankar Vedantam of the *Washington Post* reported that FDA regulators suppressed negative studies about the effects of antidepressants, and in at least three cases blocked the drug manufacturers from putting the information on drug labels. In one case, the FDA reversed the manufacturer's decision to change its drug label so that parents would know that the drug was associated with increased hostility and suicide among children. The FDA forced the company to remove the cautionary label. This was such absolute insanity that both Republicans and Democrats questioned the actions of the FDA.

Controversy after controversy hits the headlines. The fast-paced twenty-four-hour news cycle makes sure little of it registers in your mind. After all, the drug companies are some of the largest advertisers on TV.

The FDA approves drugs that later turn out to kill thousands of people. It is estimated that 108,000 people annually die from adverse reactions to prescription medication in the United States. That figure doesn't take into account hospitalizations or adverse side affects that go unreported. Guess what? The FDA doesn't perform clinical trials, the drug companies do. The FDA merely reviews the data submitted by drug companies, which pay the FDA $200 million a year to expedite drug approvals.

Get out your Crayola and color us suspicious but with so many billions of dollars at stake, that sounds like a prescription for corruption. Bright-light evidence of this is the fact that most drugs are only recalled after scores of people have died or suffered serious consequences. Think Vioxx, Seldane, Thimerosal, Baycol, Fen Phen, Propulsid, Rezulin, and PPA (phenyl-propanolamine). PPA, remarkably, is still available in over-the-counter diet and cold medications. Buyer beware.

POP QUIZ

Most of us aren't good with statistics, and both sides of any debate can make statistics mean what they want. But in our case, there is a specific mathematical equation that can be used to illustrate the dangers of drug interactions and their potential side effects. For every drug used, here is how it breaks out:

Two drugs:	2x1 = 2 possible interactions
Three drugs:	3x2x1 = 6 possible interactions
Four drugs:	4x3x2x1 = 24 possible interactions
Five drugs:	5x4x3x2x1 = 120 possible interactions
Six drugs:	6x5x4x3x2 = 720 possible interactions
Seven drugs:	7x6x5x4x3x2 = 5,040 possible interactions

As you can see, the risk of adverse interactions if taking multiple drugs increases substantially. And this does not take into account that many drugs have multiple ingredients, so the potential interactions increase dramatically. According to the *New England Journal of Medicine,* there are at least three million severe reactions each year. There must be a better way.

PAYING THE TAB

In an upside-down world in the most affluent country on the planet there are at least forty-three million people without health insurance. A large percentage of the uninsured are gainfully employed but do not make enough to pay for health insurance. As a courtesy to readers, we'll remind you that 50 percent of bankruptcies are caused by an inability to pay medical bills. Congress, the health care industry, and the insurance companies were so worried about this situation that they fought for and won new bankruptcy laws to make it much harder for families and individuals to relieve their financial burdens. Look for more destitute families on a street near you in the future.

> **The human body is the best picture of the human soul.**
>
> —Ludwig Wittgenstein

Health insurance rates have skyrocketed. The average family insurance policy is now more than nine thousand dollars a year. Premiums are increasing 15 to 45 percent a year. Employers are reducing their underwriting, and insurance companies are dramatically raising deductibles and co-pays. Already certain classifications of drugs are no longer covered.

It isn't just the citizen-consumer getting squeezed. Doctor's offices and hospitals are seeing their malpractice insurance rates doubled or even tripled, causing health care costs to rise. One clinic we spoke with saw their malpractice insurance go from $100,000 to $200,000 a year, despite having no claims filed against it. The insurance industry and the current administration say it is the result of frivolous lawsuits, but this is outright deception. Think tanks with a political agenda publish false research that distorts the facts to make their point. But the truth is that profits at the top of the food chain for all three industries—health care providers, drug manufacturers, and insurance companies—are at record levels, in the billions of dollars annually. All one need do is read the annual reports of these public companies to discover that we are being bilked. And they count on us to remain uninformed and inactive.

If the health-insurance industry wanted to decrease costs, they would cover preventive therapies that are proven to keep people in optimal health. Are they simply too slow to adapt or could it be that they, like their other two conspirators, are so entrenched in making huge profits off an aging, broken paradigm that they do not desire a healthy populace?

Their position defies logic. It is apparent that we as a nation are not taking care of ourselves—and each other. The world of health care could not be any more upside down.

Putting the Person Back into Personal Health Care

Years ago, Mary made her first appointment with a holistic doctor. Prior to the visit, she received an extensive questionnaire to complete. The survey covered her medical history, her family's history, dietary preferences, activities she enjoyed, her emotional nature, and much more. She didn't realize it, but she was completing a survey that integrated Western and Eastern methods for optimal health. The exercise caused Mary to consider herself in ways she rarely thought about: her sleep patterns, moods, bowel movements, reactions to stress, fears, weight gain and loss patterns, foods she enjoyed and those she avoided, her skin's reaction to sunlight, alcohol consumption, energy levels, and general outlook on life.

> **Health is a blessing that money cannot buy.**
> —Izaak Walton

Just completing the forms gave Mary a sense of comfort. A new awareness took seed and a feeling of hope watered by insight sprouted. Mary remembers that first visit well: the calming music accompanied by the gently cascading water of a fountain in the waiting area, the video she watched in a patient resource library just before her session with the doctor. And then . . . the two hours the doctor took speaking with her, getting to know to her. She asked questions. He carefully explained the entire philosophy of wellness in terms specific to Mary.

Mary visits her doctor every six to eight weeks for wellness treatments that include massage, acupuncture, energy healing, and chiropractic work. This elevates her immune system, balances her energy, and keeps her body in alignment. Each treatment is tailored to where she is in her life at the time of her appointment. She knows the doctor, his associates, and the people who perform the various treatments.

On her doctor's recommendation, Mary takes a small daily blend of vitamins and supplements to keep her body at peak performance based on her specific needs. Since her discovery of holistic medicine, Mary has been full of energy and has a zest for life. She hasn't had an illness beyond a cold in the last four years. She stays clear of government warnings to get flu shots—she doesn't need them because her immune system is strong—and doesn't get caught up in the fear-based scenarios of disease running rampant through society. Mary looks forward to her visits and doesn't mind paying to keep herself well. For the monthly cost of a nice meal and a night on the town Mary stays healthy. She knows that the money she spends on her wellness is far less than what she'd pay in her deductible and co-pays if she allowed herself to get ill.

Is Mary some kind of new-age health nut? Nope. She is simply an empowered woman taking charge of her life. She is living the flip and loving it.

THE TIMES THEY ARE A CHANGIN'

Quietly, and almost unnoticed, the late 1960s and early 1970s brought about an awareness of natural health and Eastern philosophies through the counterculture. This influx of Eastern practices, such as yoga and meditation, opened the door to the West for Eastern sciences based on holistic health—the approach to caring for body, mind, and spirit. The Three Horsemen of the Apothecary had miscalculated the gullibility of people.

In the early days of the holistic health revolution in the United States, the traditional medical establishment regarded the Eastern arts and other mind-body approaches with suspicion and derision. Anything outside the Western path was called alternative at best, and unreliable at worst. But as large numbers of patients found relief in alternative treatments, revenue flowed into the hands of these healers and the medical establishment began to take notice. Forward-thinking doctors and nurses saw the power and logic of natural treatments and began to study and experiment with new approaches. Soon "alternative" medicine transformed into "complementary" medicine, a term acknowledging that Eastern and Western techniques can be effectively combined.

Recent studies show that 63 percent of adults are dissatisfied with their traditional health care and have sought alternatives to ease chronic illnesses. Today, "integrative medicine" is used to denote the discipline of modern science complemented by the wisdom of ancient healing.

Specifically, integrative physicians apply their skills based on which approach is best for the patient. For example, Western medicine is highly effective for acute illness or sudden injury. If you fall ill or are injured in an accident, the advanced medical technology of a modern hospital may be essential. If a child is rushed to the emergency room with a bad case of croup, she could die without the aid of pharmaceutical interventions and breathing devices. On the other hand, holistic health is focused on the true causes of systemic or chronic illness and supports the body's own natural ability to heal itself rather than forcing a "cure." Thus it is less effective in emergency interventions than Western medicine but delivers a preventive potential that allopathy ignores almost completely.

> The art of medicine consists of amusing the patient while nature cures the disease.
> —Voltaire

Lest you think holistic health care is a lark, please consider that traditional Chinese medicine is used by two billion people globally and is practiced in thirty-eight states in the U.S. by nearly ten thousand board-certified practitioners. Ayurveda, popularized in the West in the late 1980s and early 1990s by Deepak Chopra, M.D., among others, is widely used by practitioners in a number of integrative practices. According to a study released by Ohio State University in 2005, based on research from the University of Michigan and the National Institute on Aging, 71 percent of adults over the age of fifty use alternative therapies, and 62 percent of all adults do.

Medical centers throughout the U.S., Canada, Europe, and Australia have integrative medical clinics. In the United States, integrative medicine is no longer relegated to the fringe; it is practiced not only in San Francisco and Boston, but Bangor, Wichita, Boise, and all points in between.

CONVERSATIONS ON THE BRIDGE

There is a vigorous flip taking place in the world of medicine. As we will hear from our Flipsters of Health, we are making fast progress, moving from treating symptoms to fostering holistic health. It is perhaps the most preva-lent flip taking place today, as evidenced by the large percentage of Americans seeking alternative therapies. Brew yourself some green tea, sit back, and relax as we talk with our favorite experts and discuss some natural remedies to the upside-down world.

We begin with Dr. Christiane Northrup, who speaks about the move-ment to treat women's health issues by honoring and understanding women for the unique beings that they are. Dr. Kenneth Pelletier documents the rapid ascension and acceptance of alternative medicine and its positive impact on health. Then we chat with mind-body pioneer Dr. Carl Simonton, who discusses how the brain, through guided imagery, produces profound results in the healing process. We end with Dolores Krieger, therapeutic touch pioneer, who talks about the wide acceptance of the phenomenal results that occur from touch therapy.

So, come on, let's visit with the Flipsters of Health.

A CONVERSATION ON THE BRIDGE WITH DR. CHRISTIANE NORTHRUP

Christiane Northrup, M.D. (www.drnorthrup.com), an obstetrician and gynecologist, is an internationally known visionary in women's health and well-ness. As a practicing physician for more than twenty years and former assistant clinical professor of ob/gyn at Maine Medical Center, Dr. Northrup is a lead-ing proponent of medicine and healing that acknowledge the unity of the mind and body, as well as the powerful role of the human spirit in creating health. Her pioneering work has shown that conditions such as PMS, endometriosis, breast symptoms, and uterine conditions are the language through which women's bodies speak of the wounding they have experienced in a culture which has been unsupportive to women and to those values we call "womanly." Her years of clinical experience have taught her that life-threatening, chronic, or acute illness is often a catalyst for significant inner growth and change.

We were first curious to know the roots of Christiane's pioneering per-spective. "I grew up in a holistically oriented family," she recalls. "My dad was a dentist who believed that you could tell someone's state of health by looking into their mouth. He used hypnosis way back then. He knew that people hated to have dental work done because the mouth was the center of the personality and they didn't like him rooting around in there. He also believed in organic gardening and living close to the earth. If one of us had a bug in our cereal or a piece of food fell on the ground he'd say, 'Pick it up and let the earth pass through you and then you'll be immune to everything.'

"Around 1982, I joined the board of the American Holistic Medical Association, shortly after getting through my residency. I began to hang out with like-minded colleagues who understood the importance of nutrition and exercise. Also, over the years, I met with a number of different healers. Meanwhile, I had a conventional practice and I saw the efficacy of that approach but without a spiritual component, without understanding vibration or the effects of beliefs and behavior."

Christiane remembers when she began to look differently at the typical health problems of women. "I was seeing all these women with chronic pelvic pain, vaginitis, PMS, or uterine problems. And I would see that these problems were associated with what the women believed about their own bodies, like, 'My period is a pain in the ass' or 'My period is the curse of Eve,' and by gosh, that's exactly what their experience was.

"So, my initial working thesis was that the very common gynecologic problems that I was seeing every day were associated with the wounding of women and the feminine in our culture. All you have to do is look at domestic violence statistics. About 40 percent of women have experienced some kind of domestic violence, one in three will be raped during her lifetime, and so on. I began to put two and two together and ask questions. Soon I had concluded that, indeed, what I thought was going on *was* going on. So I left my conventional practice in 1985 to found Women to Women.

"When I started to talk about these things, I had to close my office door. I was afraid I would lose my license. I was afraid to talk about *nutrition* to women who had cancer, let alone their belief system. That's how bad it was. That's why I decided to start a practice that would honor what it is that I think is really going on. And that's when I began working with some like-minded colleagues, women delivering women's health care to women."

Does Christiane see a flip in women's medical care happening within her lifetime? "I think we're seeing the last gasp of the old order," she muses. "There's no other way to go but toward greater consciousness, individual responsibility, and mind-body medicine. But you don't change a system from inside. You change it from outside and then its internal paradigm shifts gradually. I learned that years ago. It was not obstetricians that offered natural childbirth to women. When I started my career, they were still putting women to sleep to have babies, and it was women themselves who wanted something different. Currently there's a C-section rate of 30 percent. It's insane. No woman would subject herself to that if she understood that there are other choices, or if she believed that her body would know how to give birth.

"Still, we're starting to get it right. Women got the right to vote in 1920; that's not very long ago. I think it'll probably happen in less than a decade."

A CONVERSATION ON THE BRIDGE
WITH DR. KENNETH R. PELLETIER

Kenneth R. Pelletier, Ph.D., M.D.(hc) (www.drpelletier.com), is a clinical professor of medicine at the University of California School of Medicine (USCF) and the University of Arizona School of Medicine. At Arizona, he is director of the Corporate Health Improvement Program (CHIP). Also, he is chairman of the American Health Association and is a vice president with Healthtrac, Incorporated. He was a Woodrow Wilson Fellow, studied at the C. G. Jung Institute in Zurich, Switzerland, and has published more than three hundred professional journal articles in behavioral medicine, disease management, worksite interventions, and alternative/integrative medicine. At the present time, Kenneth is a medical and business consultant to the U.S. Department of Health and Human Services, the World Health Organization (WHO), the National Business Group on Health, and numerous major corporations.

> I am dying from the treatment of too many physicians.
>
> —Alexander the Great

Kenneth recalls that his flip into wellness education began in the 1980s when he realized that he was more interested in helping people maintain their health than in fighting disease. "I began to ask myself, 'Where is there any part of our society, or any part of our scientific world that cares more about health than disease?' A light bulb came on and I saw that it was the private corporate sector. Corporations were paying huge medical bills, so they should be interested in health. So in 1984 we started CHIP, engaging fifteen companies to work together in developing programs at work sites to improve health performance, productivity, and cost effectiveness. Today, at the Arizona School of Medicine, we're running the nation's only training program in integrative medicine. It's a two-year post-doctoral program for physicians who are between five and ten years into their practices out in the world.

They do rotations in clinical practices in herbal medicine, acupuncture, and mind-body medicine. The objective is to train them to feel comfortable with developing and overseeing a clinical staff to deliver these services to the general population.

"I can't think of any major city where these kinds of services are not offered now. In some states or geographic areas it may be more difficult to find, but it's not absent. There are small and single practices everywhere, as well as major institutions like the Cleveland Clinic or the Mayo Clinic. The demand has been almost entirely consumer driven."

But Kenneth thinks there's still a long way to go. "Right now, the United States is one of the most unhealthy nations on the planet. We also happen to be spending the most money per person per year for health care. On all of the World Health Organization benchmarks of a nation's health—health outcome, infant mortality, average life expectancy, cancer incidents, heart disease incidents—the U.S. is among the lowest of the twenty nations against which we measure all of our other quality of life issues. And we have been declining in that rank steadily since 1960. So, we are spending the most and getting the least amount of health care. In the midst of this crisis, you see that consumers are seeking out integrative medicine because they're not getting the kind of health care that they know intuitively they need. The number of individuals accessing integrative medicine is climbing exponentially, whereas the number of visits to primary care physicians is either flat or declining."

They do certainly give very strange, and newfangled, names to diseases.

—Plato

Kenneth notes several other forces driving the trend toward wellness education. "Corporate America, being invested in the health of their workers, their dependents, their retirees, is the second driving force. A third is a growing budget and the excellent research outcomes at the National Center for Complementary and Alternative Medicine. And they're looking at molecular/biological mechanisms responsible for alternative outcome.

"Another force is that pharmaceutical companies are beginning to invest in teaching mind-body techniques to help people use medications more effectively with fewer side effects. For instance, acupuncture can be used to decrease pain levels so that people taking anti-inflammatory drugs can use smaller doses at a higher effectiveness rate and stay on them longer, if necessary.

"And ultimately it is the government of the United States looking around the world and beginning to ask the questions, 'How are all these other countries delivering greater health outcomes at a much reduced cost to large populations?' So there's a lot to be learned just from looking at worldwide health care delivery systems."

We asked Kenneth about the role of scientific research into alternative health approaches, including prayer, energy healing, and therapeutic touch. "There's already some excellent research into these fields," he reveals, "as well as more funding. The Templeton Foundation is focused entirely on the effects of faith and spirituality on health care, for instance. And I recently took note of a Journal of the American Medical Association study showing that when people restructure their beliefs relative to pain, it induces a restructuring of the central nervous system so that other pathways are developed around the neuronal pathways that fire for pain. Now that's an extraordinary finding because it demonstrates that consciousness is a fundamental property of biology. It is a precursor and in inextricable interaction with our biology."

A CONVERSATION ON THE BRIDGE WITH DR. O. CARL SIMONTON

Dr. O. Carl Simonton (www.simontoncenter.com) is an internationally acclaimed oncologist, author, and speaker best known for his pioneering insights and research in the field of psychosocial oncology. After having earned his medical degree from the University of Oregon Medical School, he completed a three-year residency in radiation oncology. It was during this time that Dr. Simonton developed a model of emotional support for the treatment of cancer patients. This approach introduced the concept that one's state of mind could influence one's ability to survive cancer.

As chief of radiation therapy at Travis Air Force Base, Dr. Simonton implemented this model. This was the first systematic emotional intervention used in the treatment of cancer—a program that was approved by the Surgeon General's Office in 1973. While in private practice, Dr. Simonton utilized his unique approach for the treatment of cancer patients. A pilot study he conducted from 1974 to 1981 demonstrated an increase in survival time and improvement in quality of life for the participants. His early research established the foundation for two widely acclaimed books, which he coauthored, *Getting Well Again* and *The Healing Journey.*

We asked Carl how he got his start on a mind-body approach to cancer therapy. "I was in my training as a radiation oncologist, dealing with people with advanced cancer and noticing how hopelessness was interfering in their treatment. I began to study this issue of hopelessness, looking for ways to shift patients to a more cooperative state of mind. I was introduced to work on expectancy and the placebo effect, and after about two years of studying different aspects of these phenomena, I happened onto the work going on in the motivation psychology of business, where imagery was being used to influence the attitudes of people in training. The basic issue was about imagining desired outcomes, which fit together with the placebo effect. With my first patient in 1971, I asked him to imagine a desired outcome; that is, simply to imagine himself getting well. He was supposed to die shortly, and instead he got well pretty quickly and suffered no side effects from high-dose radiation therapy. After that, it was clear that this was going to be my path. When I completed my residency and began as chief of radiation therapy at Travis Air Force Base, I had a brand-new department where I was able to do things as I wanted, so we integrated mind-body work into the oncology work at Travis Air Force Base."

> **An ounce of prevention is worth a pound of cure.**
>
> —English Proverb

That didn't mean that Carl's pioneering work was immediately embraced by his peers. "As early as '71, I was receiving strong support on one hand and very intense criticism on the other, to the point of receiving death threats. Fortunately, that was very short-lived, but that's how intense it got. Any time you develop a concept that challenges the existing philosophical concepts of a major bureaucracy, that bureaucracy will become more polarized and take a conservative stance opposing the new idea. That is still going on to a significant degree in American medicine, and unfortunately the American medical model has become the model for the world. In Japan and China, there was a prevailing holistic perspective until the 1960s, when they started to try to model themselves after Western medicine. And sometimes new converts are more enthusiastic than the originals.

"Of course, there are two different systems at work here. One is public appreciation and the other is academic posture. The academic posture is the same the world over. And so Chinese medicine is not at all being integrated into academic Western medicine. But it is being integrated into public Western medicine, which is consumer driven."

Carl suggests that one way to understand the American health care crisis is to look at the relative well-being of our physicians. "The health of physicians has been much worse than the health of the average person in our culture for a long, long time. That's a terrible model, when your health care providers have poor health themselves. So we're absolutely in crisis, and things will have to shift. We will move in the direction of our nature even though medicine has been moving away from our nature. But Nature is infinitely patient."

A CONVERSATION ON THE
BRIDGE WITH DR. DOLORES KRIEGER

Dolores Krieger, Ph.D., R.N. (www.therapeutictouch.org) is professor emerita of nursing at New York University and the author of five books on noninvasive healing, including the landmark work *Therapeutic Touch: How to Use Your Hands to Help and to Heal.* Following her pioneering studies into therapeutic touch in the 1970s, Dr. Krieger has gone on to teach her innovative methods to more than forty-two thousand health professionals and thousands more laypeople. Dolores recounts realizing thirty-five years ago that there were many more ways for nurses to help patients than conventional hospital care facilitated. "I was aware that we were pretty much a 'no touch' society. And what I began to realize was that just the humanness of one person touching or being close to another person was very helpful in terms of simple presence.

"I did not come upon the idea of therapeutic touch alone. It has been a collaboration with a colleague, Dora Kunz, all these years that really has made therapeutic touch what it is today. Dora had unusual abilities to see vital and very subtle energies. She did some work with religious healers and the 'laying on of hands,' but we came to feel it was not religion specifically that was facilitating the healing process. That was the basis for our development of therapeutic touch, and we began to pursue the potential for it, and what conditions might help facilitate it."

Dolores reports that there has been widespread acceptance of therapeutic touch in the nursing communities and in many hospitals. "Just about every profession within the health field by now has been taught therapeutic touch. In fact, we have taught therapeutic touch in over ninety countries in the world, and in the U.S. and Canada in over sixty medical centers and health agencies. In some hospitals, there are separate facilities for therapeutic touch and in others the practitioner uses therapeutic touch during the course of therapy. We can get a relaxation response two to four minutes into the treatment, which is pretty good. That response helps facilitate treatments and healing, and we have a lot of success in easing pain. We train even dental hygienists, for instance. We work with premature babies and children. Therapeutic touch often precedes and follows surgery of all kinds. And we're increasingly drawing the interest of doctors, anesthesiologists, and other medical professionals besides nurses."

NATURAL, LOGICAL, POWERFUL

The practice of medicine has come a long way. There are practitioners around the globe working tirelessly to deliver holistic health care that respects patients and their needs. The flip from treating symptoms to whole health is clearly happening. Yet today, many of these innovative treatments and therapies, though becoming ever more common, are expensive and remain uncovered by health insurance. But even that is slowly changing.

For you budding Flipsters interested in optimal health, the first task is to find a doctor or clinic that practices holistic, integrative medicine. This will dramatically enhance your chances of staving off diseases and actively promote a lifestyle of wellness. Should you fall ill, depending on the type and severity of the illness, a natural course of treatment should be considered. It is our belief that one should always contemplate a holistic approach to recovery rather than blithely popping pills and playing Russian roulette with the interactions, or opting for invasive surgery. Doesn't it make sense to give the body's own miraculous system a chance to heal itself through natural remedies before ingesting synthetic chemicals or carving into it?

Your holistic doctor will know what combination of Eastern and Western treatments to administer. Herbs, poultices, aromatherapy, acupuncture, and other alternative treatments may not be the answer every time, but they are the place to begin. Isn't it better to discover and treat the cause of a headache (stress, pressure, chemical imbalance) than simply mask it with daily doses of ibuprofen? Would you want to temporarily subdue your headache at the expense of your liver? Most would say not.

Yet almost every drug one takes comes with a list of side effects. Often, these side effects are the result of the drug manufacturing process in which the active ingredients of known organic remedies found in nature are isolated and concentrated in pill or liquid form. By taking Nature out of the equation and placing science (and business) as the go-between, we suffer a major disconnect from who we are—human beings of this Earth composed of entirely natural elements.

Yes, there are times when only surgery or drugs or both will work. And we certainly advocate using conventional medicine when appropriate. But injecting some common-sense sanity into our health choices by following a rational line of defense based on prevention is both logical and powerful.

You are in charge of your health. Your body is an amazing, wondrous vehicle, housing your soul. It is an intricate complex of systems designed to defend its survival. On a cellular level, it processes trillions of interactions each day. As such, it is susceptible to the foreign substances we put in it. Every time we take a pill, smoke a cigarette, drink alcohol (don't forget the food and drink consumed, as well) we are changing our body's delicate balance of natural chemicals, enzymes, and proteins. Be mindful of that on your journey and your body will serve you well.

Please take care of yourself. We'd love to meet you some day in the Right-Side Up world.

FLIP TIPS

- Eat a balanced and nutritious diet.

- Exercise regularly.

- Drink lots of purified water.

- Get a physical once a year.

- Determine your ideal weight and work to stay within a healthy range.

- Become an informed health care consumer—ask questions of your doctor.

- Get a second or third opinion on important medical matters.

- Find a clinic that practices integrative medicine.

- Get a massage every one to two months.

- Look into yoga and meditation.

- Look for natural alternatives, but do not rely exclusively on them, as there may be times when conventional medicine is the best course.

- If you must take prescription drugs or over-the-counter medicines, please carefully read the labels and understand the side effects.

- Look at what addictive habits you might have—alcohol, smoking, snacking, caffeine, soda pop—and work to reduce or eliminate them.

- Be an active participant in your own health.

SEVEN

FLIPPING THE SWITCH

From Nonrenewable to Sustainable Energy

Every morning Barry hops into his SUV, dashes to his favorite fast-food and caffeine joints, and speeds to the freeway to sit in bumper-to-bumper traffic. As he inches forward in his plush SUV, he swigs his java, downs his breakfast sandwich and hash browns, and listens to the latest rendition of startling news from the bloviators on the AM dial. His vehicle slowly moves forward as his anxiety level rises with the traffic, the caffeine in his bloodstream, and the bad news. He hears that gas prices are going up again. Barry gets madder. He hears that gasoline might go as high as five dollars a gallon—and Americans should be grateful for it because Europeans pay even more. He swears at the radio.

Lately, Barry's finances have been taking a beating every time he fills up at the pump. He has begun to call his SUV *The Beast,* because it is impossible to satisfy and seems to require more and more money to keep it running. He bought The Beast for its roominess, higher vantage point, cargo area, and its perceived status. He casually brushed aside low mileage ratings. Now, one year into a five-year loan, he wishes he had been more attentive to details. It is costing him ten dollars a day in gasoline to get back and forth to work.

Barry looks longingly from on high as the light rail system in his city whisks commuters to their destinations in one-third the time for only two bucks a day. But Barry doesn't want to sacrifice his personal space. He's a comfort creature, and even though he feels miserable wasting up to two hours of his life each day sitting in traffic—time he can ill afford to lose and can never get back—in Barry's fragmented mind, at least it is a misery of his own making. Having heard that the government offered generous tax credits on Hummers, Barry entertained the idea of tooling around town in such a unique status symbol. Barry's wife told him in no uncertain terms that it was irresponsible to drive a car of that heft and inefficiency. She sarcastically asked, "How many feet per gallon does that monstrosity get?"

At home, Barry's idea of conserving energy is turning off a light switch when he leaves a room. That sense of conservation doesn't transfer to turning off his computer, the TV, or the radio when he's not present. Barry, like most people, thinks that his screen saver has magically kicked in huge energy savings. With an investment of five minutes, Barry could set his monitor, printer, and computer to "sleep" and then shutdown if not used after a period of whatever duration Barry preferred—ten, twenty, sixty minutes. If Barry went further and purchased Energy Star compliant computers and peripherals, he would save enough electricity over the life of the products to light his home for four years.

> The sun, the moon and the stars would have disappeared long ago had they happened to be within the reach of predatory human hands.
>
> —Havelock Ellis

But Barry is oblivious to the energy—and money—he is wasting. He does not see the connection between his lack of energy conservation, his choice of automotive vehicles, high energy prices, his dwindling checkbook balance, and wars in the Persian Gulf. He'll drive on toward oblivion, complaining all the way.

IS IT HOT IN HERE?

Barry, like all Americans, could significantly reduce his energy consumption, save lots of money, and reduce pollution at the same time. It's an easy choice to make. Unfortunately, most people don't want to make even the slightest sacrifice. In the upside-down world, people do not correlate unbridled consumption of finite resources like coal and oil with personal responsibility. The United States comprises 4 percent of the Earth's population, but we consume more than 25 percent of its energy. We think it is our God-given right to live excessively. Well, it's certainly a choice, but it is not a right.

Upside-down citizen-consumers think there is an endless supply of energy, and if not, we'll find some other technology in the future to supply our needs. But energy supply is only a part of the equation. The burning of fossil fuels, along with other devastating human activities, is causing serious damage to our environment, precipitating global warming on an unprecedented scale. Yes, there are those who deny global warming exists. Guess what? ExxonMobil has spent millions of dollars creating front groups and public relations efforts to instill doubt in the debate. There is no debate. There is only doubt stirred by big-pocket business interests to distract and misinform. The facts have been settled, global warming is real, it's dangerous, and it's cooking a neighborhood near you.

Experts the world over have documented in exacting detail (not guesses or estimates, but actual scientific measurements) shrinking ice shelves, receding mountain glaciers, eroding beaches, rising temperatures, and a dramatic increase in the number, size, and force of natural disasters. In December 2004, a devastating tsunami in the Indian Ocean killed an estimated 283,000 people. Also in 2004, there were fifteen named storms in the Atlantic, seven of them graduating to hurricane status. The year 2005 obliterated all records for named storms with twenty-seven, besting the 1933 record of twenty-one. Fifteen hurricanes in 2005 was three more than the previous record of twelve set in 1969. In addition, there were three category-five hurricanes—Katrina, Rita and Wilma. In early September 2005, Hurricane Katrina leveled New Orleans and the Gulf Coast region of the U.S., with estimates of 1,307 dead, up to one million people homeless, 60 to 80 percent of houses destroyed, and $150 billion in property damage. The horrendous loss of life and property is astonishing. Of course, the displaced lives, the sorrow, and the ongoing hardship for the survivors can never be fully measured.

According to the Union of Concerned Scientists (UCS), there is a link between hurricanes and global warming. Further, nine of the ten hottest years on record have occurred since 1995, according to the U.N.'s World Meteorological Organization. The last four years were among the five hottest; 2005 was the hottest on record dating back to 1861. The UCS website (www.ucsusa.org) also reveals that northern hemispheric temperatures over the last decade are at their highest in the last two thousand years. Upside-downers need to either get out the sun block or build an ark, we're not sure which.

ENERGIZE ME

That a capitalistic powerhouse like the United States needs energy resources to secure and maintain its dominance is easy to grasp. Energy runs our factories, lights our homes, fuels our cars, illuminates our television sets, keeps us warm, and provides a hundred other positive benefits. We are not arguing that energy usage is bad. We are only stating that in the upside-down world, mindless consumption is not only selfish and irresponsible, but dangerous and potentially deadly for our children, grandchildren, and all future generations.

The question is not whether abundant energy is useful; rather, what are the cheapest, most reliable, renewable sources of energy? We are informed that energy production and consumption is a complicated matter that we shouldn't worry our pretty little heads about. The people who control the energy supply profess to be of, by, and for the people, but in fact operate solely in the best interest of their profits. And the profits are huge. Those at the top of the energy food chain do quite well. Let's review another round of fun facts, shall we?

1. Four of the seven most profitable companies in the upside-down world are oil companies—ExxonMobil, Royal Dutch Shell, British Petroleum (BP), and Chevron.

2. For these companies, the 2005 breakdown in profit—not sales, profit—was

   - $31.6 billion for ExxonMobil
   - $25.3 billion for Royal Dutch Shell
   - $21.7 billion for BP
   - $14.1 billion for Chevron

3. Combined, these four oil companies made $92.7 billion in profit in 2005.

4. The total value of these four companies is nearly $1 trillion.

We don't begrudge anyone the right to make a profit. A modest profit seems reasonable, especially if funds are reinvested in research and development for alternative technologies to harness renewable sources. What we find perturbing is the brazen gouging and massive profiteering. Not content with their obscene profits, the oil industry in the aftermath of hurricane Katrina immediately raised gas prices to more than three dollars a gallon—an increase of more than forty-five cents a gallon in two days. The Bush administration used the cover of crisis to suspend environmental laws for refineries and chemical companies so they could "cope" with the economic impact. This was on top of the $14.5 billion worth of tax breaks and incentives given in the industry-friendly energy bill passed in August 2005. Hmm . . .

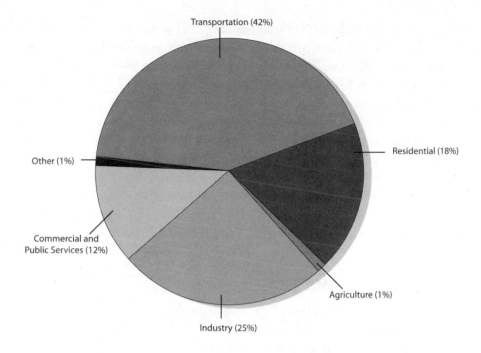

Ladies and gentlemen, in order to break our addiction to fossil fuels, it's important to understand our energy habits. Let's take a graphic look.

As illustrated above, there are four large sectors of energy consumption: transportation, industry, residential, and commercial and public services. The by-product of this usage, based on data from the Lawrence Livermore National Laboratory, is 5,682 million metric tons of carbon dioxide jettisoned into the atmosphere. Stated another way, that is 12,500,000,000,000 pounds of carbon dioxide spewed into the atmosphere per year.

Aren't numbers scary sometimes? They just stare at you, factual, impassive, daring you to think about them—12,500,000,000,000 pounds of carbon dioxide per year.

Not only is the burning of fossil fuels warming the planet at a rate so fast it has normally stoic scientists concerned, but we're breathing this stuff, along with trillions of pounds of other chemicals being released into the air. Oh, and these are just U.S. emissions, not accounting for those in Europe, Latin and South America, India, or the economic behemoths of Asia—China, Japan, and Korea—or lesser-known but sizable capitalistic countries, such as Malaysia, Indonesia, and Vietnam.

Of that 5,682 million metric tons, the big three culprits causing the Earth to go into an asthmatic fit are natural gas, coal, and petroleum. If the numbers aren't enough to sober us up in time to save ourselves, consider this: According to British Petroleum's highly reliable Statistical Review of World Energy 2005, there is enough oil for 40.5 years. In the grand scheme, that's not very long— just enough for our children and grandchildren to inherit the problem. The rate of oil reserve depletion will most certainly accelerate as China and the Asia Pacific economies become dominant manufacturers and their substantial populations become ardent consumers. In fact, Asia Pacific represents 50 percent of global-energy-consumption growth over the last ten years.

It's a safe bet, as we approach the time when the last drops of crude are extracted from the earth, that we will see energy prices become so prohibitive that only the well-to-do will be able to afford gasoline.

NO REST FOR THE WICKED

So what do the illustrious U.S. leaders of the upside-down world do? Industry meets in secret at the behest of Vice President Dick Cheney, and the energy companies write legislation with a laundry list of things they want. They pass a massive energy bill, giving billions in subsidies to the richest companies on the planet. They amend the Safe Drinking Water Act to allow unregulated underground injection of chemicals into the ground. They exempt energy companies from the Clean Water Act for construction activities. They repeal the law to protect consumers from market manipulation, fraud, or abuse in the electricity sector (think Enron and rolling blackouts in California). And they pass a provision that mandates, "A state may not impose a legal requirement relating to fuel economy . . . A state law that seeks to reduce motor vehicle carbon dioxide emissions is both expressly and impliedly preempted."

Thanks to our leaders we are not even permitted to improve fuel efficiency by law. Does that seem upside-down to you? The logic of exploiting finite resources without adequate conservation measures rests on a misguided shortsightedness that will lead to economic and environmental disaster.

MORE ANSWERS THAN QUESTIONS

Mary lives close to her office and carpools most days with a group of friends. When doing errands on the weekend she rides her bike around town. People wave at her. She stops and has conversations. When she has to drive,

Mary sports around in a hybrid car that averages fifty miles per gallon. She is thrilled at the mileage she gets on a tank of gas.

At home, Mary has Energy Star appliances that use 70 percent less energy than standard appliances. She doesn't leave lights or electronic devices on unless she is using them at the time. Her thermostat is set to minimize her draw on the electric grid. A few years ago, Mary read an article about wind farms. Impressed at the ingenuity and light footprint on the earth, she purchases wind energy credits from a co-op, and that allows her to reduce CO_2 emissions.

Fortunately for all of us, the energy flip is well under way. Advanced engine technologies developed by Japanese automakers, Toyota and Honda, have produced hybrid vehicles that are far more fuel-efficient than those with traditional internal combustion engines. Toyota's Prius is so popular that there is a six-month waiting list. Another step toward the Right-Side Up world is the fact that enterprising inventors have taken these hybrids, reworked the design, and achieved 250 miles per gallon, proving that major fuel efficiency can be had if the desire is there.

In the energy sectors beyond transportation—industry, commercial and public, and residential—there are readily available solutions that only require common sense and the will to act. The answer can be summed up in one word: *renewables*.

That's right. Nature provides us a marvelous array of renewable energy sources: sun, wind, water, geothermal, and tides. All of these are viable alternatives being used around the world.

The sun, the most powerful energy source available, shines down on hundreds of millions of rooftops worldwide every day. Collectively, sunshine produces massive amounts of energy and heat. With solar panels, almost every rooftop can become a source of renewable energy and every home self-sufficient. How does it work? Silicon wafers capture photons from sunlight and convert them to DC power, which is then transformed into 120 volt AC power and connected to your existing electrical system and to the local electrical grid. When the sun is shining, you can generate more power than you consume; your meter may actually spin backwards. At night, you'll draw on either a battery array in your basement or utility company power, essentially using the electrical grid as a giant storage battery. Not only could

> **Treat the earth well. It was not given to you by your parents. It is loaned to you by your children.**
>
> —Kenyan Proverb

Americans break their dependency on fossil fuels and clean up the atmosphere, think of the value to those living in third-world nations if they had access to solar panels to produce light, power a water pump, or heat their modest homes.

Royal Dutch Shell and BP, both companies with European origins, lead the oil companies in solar technology. The countries of Germany and Japan lead the world in solar development and implementation. Due to pressure from entrenched energy special interests, America has lagged behind, but that is changing. Thousands of scientists, researchers, inventors, entrepreneurs, policy makers, think tanks, and schools of higher learning are working diligently on renewable resources. Many states offer grants, low-interest loans, and tax credits for conversion to solar energy; the information is available through state offices of the environment, energy, or development.

WINDS OF CHANGE

Wind power is not a new concept. The Babylonians and Chinese used wind power to pump water for irrigating crops four thousand years ago. The first windmills, circa 500 C.E. to 900 C.E., were developed in Persia to automate the tasks of pumping water. Europeans used the power of the wind to grind wheat, which is where the term "windmill" comes from. During the nineteenth century in America, windmills were again developed for pumping water, and to this day the classic Aermotor windmill stands as an icon in the rural landscape.

Today, thirty states have wind-energy projects, generating 9,149 megawatts (mW) of electricity. California alone generates enough electricity to supply a city the size of San Francisco. Wind power is a clean, renewable source of energy, which produces no greenhouse gas emissions or waste products. One modern wind turbine can save more than four thousand tons of CO_2 emissions in comparison to a power station producing the same amount of electricity.

Over the past decade, Europe has taken the lead in the development and promotion of wind power; Germany and Denmark obtain more than 30 percent and 15 percent of their total electricity needs, respectively, from wind power. As technical advances in wind-turbine technology increase their efficiency and

> It is our task in our time and in our generation to hand down undiminished to those who come after us, as was handed down to us by those who went before, the natural wealth and beauty which is ours.
>
> —John F. Kennedy

reduce the cost per kilowatt-hour, the promises of wind power become very attractive. The American Great Plains has enough wind to meet the electricity requirements of the entire country.

The idea that farmers and ranchers can lease their property to wind power companies is starting to catch on. Farmers and ranchers receive an annual payment for providing the land to house wind turbines on their property. This is a significant opportunity for many to boost their income and represents a real solution to help stabilize rural economies by making the wind the next "cash crop."

THE MOST ABUNDANT ELEMENT

Hydrogen is the simplest and most abundant element in the universe. On the Earth, hydrogen does not occur naturally as a gas but rather combines with oxygen to create water (H_2O). When hydrogen is combined with oxygen in a fuel cell, energy in the form of electricity is produced. This electricity can power vehicles, act as a heat source, and provide many other uses. The advantage of using hydrogen as an energy carrier is that when it combines with oxygen the only by-products are water and heat. No greenhouse gasses or other particulates are produced by the use of hydrogen fuel cells.

Hydrogen is produced from various sources, ranging from nonrenewable fossil fuels, such as gas and coal, to biomass. Biomass is a way to tap into the tremendous quantities of hydrogen present in landfills. It is now possible to capture the methane produced from the decomposition of organic waste and strip away the carbon to make pure hydrogen fuel. We can actually turn our waste into energy!

One important wrinkle in the hydrogen solution fabric is that the current energy industry Pooh-Bahs want to develop so-called "black" hydrogen technologies by extracting the gas from fossil fuel sources. But that would further contribute to untenable levels of carbon dioxide in the atmosphere. So why develop black hydrogen and continue to pollute and warm the planet when we don't have to? There are plenty of clean sources of hydrogen that can provide the energy we need without mucking up the planet.

THREE . . . TWO . . . ONE . . . BLAST OFF

The Apollo Alliance (www.apolloalliance.org) is perhaps the best conceived, most far-reaching energy initiative ever envisioned, a true-blue flip. Modeled after the bold mission announced by John F. Kennedy to put a man on the moon, the Apollo Alliance seeks to use the same "can-do" spirit to achieve a secure supply of clean, affordable, and sustainable energy. It seeks to rally the country around a green economy that will create millions of jobs, clean up the environment, and reduce our dependency on foreign oil.

Apollo offers a plan that makes so much sense that only the most jaded and greedy among us in the upside-down world can reject it. It is not based on unreachable pie-in-the-sky dreams but sound, achievable science and technology. We love it! Here is their Ten-Point Plan:

1. Promote advanced technology and hybrid cars.
2. Invest in more efficient factories.
3. Encourage high performance building.
4. Increase use of energy efficient appliances.
5. Modernize electrical infrastructure.
6. Expand renewable energy development.
7. Improve transportation options.
8. Reinvest in smart urban growth.
9. Plan for a hydrogen future (a green one).
10. Strengthen regulatory protections.

In the interest of brevity, we've offered only the main thrust of each point, but the detail required to bring this vision to fruition is already articulated. What might be achieved with the realization of Apollo? Check this out:

Economic Benefits
- Add 3.3 million jobs to the economy.
- Stimulate $1.4 trillion in Gross Domestic Product.
- Stimulate the economy through adding $953 billion in personal income and $323.9 billion in retail sales.
- Offer a 22.3 percent annual rate of return.
- Produce $284 billion in net energy cost savings.

Environmental Benefits
- Reduce national energy consumption by 16 percent.
- Reduce transportation petroleum consumption by 1.25 million barrels per day.
- Place ninety-one million advanced-performance vehicles on the road by 2015.

- Meet 15 percent of electricity demand through renewable resources by 2015, and 20 percent by 2020.
- Reduce sulfur dioxide emissions by 28 percent; reduce carbon dioxide emissions by 23 percent; reduce nitrous oxide emissions by 13 percent.

Other Major Benefits
- Reduce dependence on foreign oil.
- Stabilize natural gas prices through reduced dependence.
- Restore America's withering leadership in technological innovation.
- Reduce our trade deficit.
- Rebuild aging infrastructure.
- Improve social equity for low-income workers by increasing job access and mobility.

How much will it cost, you wisely ask? A modest investment of $300 billion, or less than one year's budget to prosecute the Iraq War. This seems a paltry sum given the opportunity to eliminate the need for such wars to begin with, save our environment, and reduce our energy expenses. In the Right-Side Up world, we'd already be implementing Apollo. So what's the hard part?

First we have to get beyond the staid thinking and status quo investments of the current administration and its energy industry masters. Does that seem too blunt? We suspect that by the time you read these words, you will already be miffed, incensed—fill in the aggravated adjective of your choice here—by gas prices and your home heating and lighting bills. You've probably already experienced a serious crimp in your lifestyle based on profiteering by the energy moguls.

Andrew Bebee, a member of the Apollo Alliance Executive Steering Committee, had this to say about solar power—only one product of the many renewable energy sources—"Just like latent computer power that was sitting on our desktops when we all finally got PCs in the '80s or '90s, we have latent energy power sitting on our roofs, just being turned into heat and waste, essentially by destroying rooftops. The answer is pretty simple, if you can capture that and put it into your house, you might actually be able to power the whole thing."

> **How to be green? Many people have asked us this important question. It's really very simple and requires no expert knowledge or complex skills. Here's the answer. Consume less. Share more. Enjoy life.**
>
> —Derek Wall

Ideas of energy conservation are neither radical nor naïve—they are simply good common sense. A 2005 study by the Pew Research Center for the People & the Press found that seven out of ten people want tax cuts for companies to develop wind, solar, and hydrogen energy. Eight in ten want higher fuel efficiency for cars, trucks, and SUVs. While these trends haven't translated to widespread behavioral changes, clearly we are marching in the direction of the flip to renewable sources.

CONVERSATIONS ON THE BRIDGE

This seems like a good time to visit our Flipsters of Energy to hear what they have to say on the substantial progress being made in sustainable energy development. We begin with accomplished actress and environmentalist Daryl Hannah, who champions the benefits of biodiesel as an alternative fuel already available on the market today. L. Hunter Lovins, president of Natural Capitalist, discusses the unsustainable nature of our current energy consumption paradigm. Philippe Cousteau, president of EarthEcho, reveals how harnessing the ever-present power of the wind, tides, and waves can meet the world's energy needs many times over—while keeping the planet safe for future generations. We finish with popular actor and activist, Ed Begley, Jr., as he shares his personal story of living lightly on the Earth while enjoying a lifestyle of quality and personal integrity.

Please join us for these inspiring conversations.

A CONVERSATION ON THE BRIDGE WITH DARYL HANNAH

Daryl Hannah (www.grassolean.com) is an accomplished actress, with films such as *Splash, Blade Runner, Steel Magnolias,* and *Kill Bill* to her credit. More important to Ms. Hannah is her commitment to the environment. She is a strong advocate for biodiesel, a clean, renewable fuel alternative for cars and other vehicles. In addition to supporting environmental causes and projects, Daryl is a person who has already made the flip, so we asked her how she puts her principles into action. "I drive a 1983 El Camino Diesel, using 100 percent biodiesel. It can run on straight vegetable oil with a small inexpensive modification and it can run on biodiesel, which is thinned with ethanol to be the same viscosity as diesel so that it can run through the engine.

"My car has what is called a closed-carbon loop. The same amount of carbon dioxide emitted from the tail pipe is the same as consumed by plants when they're growing, essentially causing no new greenhouse gases. It's basically lower in every other particulate toxin except for one. It's the cleanest fuel that's available today."

We wouldn't expect a movie star to hold such strong convictions, so naturally we asked what "drove" her to use such an alternative fuel choice. Daryl was direct. "Obviously, we have limited fossil fuel supplies. That's not even negotiable. Why rely on fossil fuels when we have sustainable energy technology and bio-fuels? Plus, bio-fuels are made from oil seed crops like soy, canola, rapeseed, and mustard, so using biodiesel is a way to support American farmers who grow those crops—and support our economy. American farmers have been struggling for a long time, this is a way for them to earn a decent income and help the planet.

"The fact is that we've had the technology and the ability to produce cleaner burning, nontoxic fuel for over 105 years. Yet our kids are still riding on school buses that are completely poisonous. The diesel engine was originally developed to run on vegetable oil. After Rudolph Diesel's mysterious death [he went missing on a business trip to England and was found floating in the English Channel] the diesel engine was converted to run on petroleum-based products rather than vegetable oil. So the car industry went in another direction than the inventor of the diesel engine intended."

> **It isn't pollution that's harming the environment. It's the impurities in our air and water that are doing it.**
>
> —Dan Quayle

Since Daryl is so passionate about the environment, we asked her what she was doing to champion the cause. "I'm doing everything I can to get information out there. I've been doing some green corresponding for *Good Morning America* about different issues like the importance of shopping at local farmers' markets, organics, and the difference between genetically modified foods and conventional and organic products.

"Information is the key. Once people have the information, it empowers them. I think people are hungry for it and are open to it more than ever before. It's not so much the 'crunchy granola hippy thing' associated with self-sufficiency anymore. It boils down to common sense and independence and self-determination.

"More and more people are realizing these things. I was just in the grocery store yesterday and a woman had seen one of the segments that I did on

Good Morning America. She was taking notes and asking me all sorts of questions because she's going to change her house to solar power. She was asking me what kind of car she should buy and stuff like that. It's an example that people are now realizing, 'Oh my god, I have real options.'"

We asked Daryl if the younger generation was open to being socially responsible? "That's something I'm optimistic about. I read some articles that say the youth of today are apathetic, and I beg to differ. The kids that I come across don't even question those kinds of choices, they just make them, because to them it's, 'Why would I do something else? Why wouldn't I try to eat healthy food or drive a fuel-efficient car so I don't get gouged at the pump? Why would I poison the environment?' I meet inspiring kids on a regular basis. They're not even trying to be altruistic; to them it's just straightforward common sense."

Indeed it is.

A Conversation on the Bridge with L. Hunter Lovins

L. Hunter Lovins, Esq. (hunterlovins.com), is the president and founder of Natural Capitalism, Inc. and cocreator of the NC concept. In 1982, she cofounded Rocky Mountain Institute (RMI) and led that organization as its CEO for strategy until 2002. Under her leadership, RMI grew into an internationally recognized research center, widely celebrated for its innovative thinking in energy and resource issues.

Lovins has coauthored nine books and dozens of papers, and was featured in the award-winning film *Lovins on the Soft Path.* Her latest book, *Natural Capitalism,* coauthored with Amory Lovins and business author Paul Hawken, has been translated into a dozen languages. In 2000, she was named a "Hero for the Planet" by *TIME* magazine, and received the Loyola University award for Outstanding Community Service. In 2001, she received the Leadership in Business Award and shared the Shingo Prize for Manufacturing Research.

Hunter told us that environmental activism seemed to be in her genes: "Growing up in my family, it was simply assumed around the house that one would spend one's life making things better. It was what you did. My father helped mentor Cesar Chavez, my mother worked for the coal miners. So I'm not sure I had a whole lot of choice. After college, I helped start Tree People in California. I took up with Amory Lovins and became the policy advisor for Friends of the Earth for Dave Brower and did that until we created Rocky Mountain Institute in 1982."

In alternative energy development, Hunter feels that bio-fuels offer more potential than hydrogen at present. "There remain some real technical challenges around hydrogen, including the question of where we get it. Right now, most hydrogen comes from natural gas. And I think it's a good thing to be pursuing. The folks at Shell Hydrogen are not stupid, neither are the people at BP. China is looking at hydrogen in a very big way because they have serious concerns about giving land competitively for bio-fuels instead of food. China is going to have a very hard time feeding itself. I think the much bigger question about energy sources per se is how do we put forth a whole systems-sustainable strategy for the world that makes sense?

"For example, if China continues to grow economically at the rate that it has been, and uses resources as inefficiently as the West now does, then by 2030 China will be demanding something like ninety billion barrels of oil a day. The world now lifts something like eighty billion, and can probably never lift more. You start to damage the fields if you pull oil out of it faster."

So how do we meet the needs of the world, particularly the developing world, in ways that don't crash the planet for everyone? "One strategy is to have developing nations grow oil crops, that is, feedstock for biodiesels, and then the developed West can buy biodiesel from these nations. This is a strategy that seems to make eminently good sense. So one of the things that I did when I went over to Afghanistan was to carry a how-to biodiesel manual describing how to make small-scale homemade biodiesel production units. Kabul has open sewers. A John Todd-style eco machine that takes advantage of local energy sources and works with the dynamics of the local ecosystem would make much better sense there than trying to put in a less-efficient, conventional-quarrying, break-point sewage treatment facility. That's last century's technology, and we have this century's technologies that do a better job, are appropriately scaled to the task, and are sustainable."

Hunter thinks there's no guarantee that humanity will survive its own poor housekeeping habits, given some recent cultural trends. "There is a very serious threat from fundamentalist Christians who believe we are witnessing the beginning of the end of time. If you listen to some of the people in Congress, some of the people advising the president and the other senior officials, they flat out say, 'Environmental destruction? We really don't care.' And they see being rich as a sign that you are blessed by the Lord. Getting yours is a sign that you're somehow favored.

"I think we want to believe there is this emerging global consciousness. I think we're in a horse race with a very different kind of consciousness, that is, *Me first, I really don't care about you, and as long as I'm taken care of and my folk are taken care of, that's fine. The rest of you can, frankly, drown in a toxic soup.*

"We probably will not survive if we don't make the flip. There's nothing that says that humankind has to survive. Nature runs a very rigorous testing laboratory in which products that don't work get recalled by the manufacturer. That's a cautionary tale for a young species like ours. We will figure out what is appropriate for our environment or we will cease to exist. Nature really won't shed a tear; she'll try something different."

Is there any hope for us? "Right now, we have all of the technologies that we need to create the kind of society that works for everyone. Many of the technologies that are under research will be even cooler. I'm working with a guy in California who has a new way of manufacturing solar cells, which he reckons to prove out in two to four years. He's just gotten his financing, and if he's right, he will be able to produce solar electricity for three cents per kilowatt hour. Right now, you'll pay seven to eight cents a kilowatt hour from conventional sources. This is a very big 'WOW!'"

> **That which is not good for the beehive cannot be good for the bees.**
>
> —Marcus Aurelius

What's next? What are the technologies that will underpin a prosperous economy? "I think it's what we've been talking about: energy efficiency, resource productivity, green chemistry, bio-mimicry, the whole range of sustainable technologies. The companies that can put this together will deliver the future. These are the billionaires of tomorrow."

A Conversation on the Bridge with Philippe Cousteau

Philippe Cousteau (www.earthecho.net) is the third generation of his family to dedicate his life to exploring and explaining the natural world. Philippe continues the work of his late father, Philippe Sr., and grandfather, Jacques-Yves, by working to unite the pursuit of science, the conservation of nature, and education of the public at large. He founded EarthEcho International with his sister and his mother, Jan Cousteau, to work toward these goals, with a particular focus on young people as the future caretakers of the planet. He serves as president of EarthEcho and is responsible for directing and managing its extensive worldwide operations.

He has some very provocative ideas about a clean energy source that most people don't think about: the oceans.* "The oceans are a tremendous resource," he says. "One ocean alternative is wind power, which is better off-shore than on land because wind is more reliable out in the ocean. It has no impediment to its progress. It's just whipping along the surface of the ocean where it can build up speed, as opposed to land where there are trees and mountains. Ocean wind turbines are built on platforms, sometimes several hundred feet tall with very large blades that slowly rotate. Although there are several of these wind turbines in Western Europe and they're very effective, we don't have any in the U.S. yet. There's a controversy around the effort to develop this country's first offshore wind platforms in Nantucket Sound, called the Cape Wind project. The problem is that people living at the coast don't want to be able to see the turbines. They don't want them ruining their beautiful view of the bay—and these are very wealthy individuals. They're different from the underprivileged classes who will have to live in underprivileged neighborhoods where conventional sources for power will be located if this wind power plant or turbine field is not developed in the bay."

Another technology Philippe has been pursuing is tidal power. "That means putting power plants with turbines in coastal areas. As the tide goes in and goes out, it flows to these power plants and causes the generators to turn and it creates energy. But there's also the potential of wave power. Research indicates that just 1/10 of 1 percent of the energy in ocean waves would be able to supply the world's energy supply five times over. Then there's Ocean Thermal Energy Conversion (OTEC), where the temperature difference between warm surface water and cold, deep water is used to pump the cold water up and use that to produce electric power. Every day the ocean absorbs enough heat in thermal energy to equate to something like 250 billion barrels of oil. We have the technology to tap into these clean energy sources; we just lack the will. There's too much vested interest in conventional energy and now a renewed interest in nuclear energy. When we have the technology to develop renewable energy that has no negative output, why aren't we?"

---

*This publication and the appearance or statements herein of Philippe Cousteau are not related in any way to the work or marks of The Cousteau Society, nor is any endorsement implied.

Does Philippe think we'll wise up and make the right energy choices in the long run? "The choices will be made for us if we do not make them ourselves. If we do not begin to temper our greed and our short-sightedness with a more wholesome perspective, then something else will. It will be famine; it will be hunger; it will be lack of fresh water supplies, wars fought over those resources, and disease. Something will temper our growth and our narrow-mindedness somewhere along the way if we don't do it ourselves. We certainly have the potential to do so. We've gone to the bottom of the ocean and to the moon. We just need to acknowledge that our relationship with the world, the stewardship of our planet and ourselves, is a priority. We can do that. I have a vision that this century will mark the next step in human evolution. We've had women's suffrage, civil rights, and certainly those are issues that we're still dealing with. But the twenty-first century will see the predominance of our relationship with the environment—and a more wholesome perspective on the future."

A CONVERSATION ON THE BRIDGE WITH ED BEGLEY, JR.

Inspired by the work of his Academy Award-winning father, Ed Begley, Jr. (www.edbegley.com) became an actor. He first came to audiences' attention for his portrayal of Dr. Victor Ehrlich on the long-running hit television series *St. Elsewhere*, for which he received six Emmy nominations. Since then, Begley has moved easily among feature, television, and theater projects.

Turning up at Hollywood events on his bicycle, Ed has been considered an environmental leader in the Hollywood community for many years. He has served as chairman of the Environmental Media Association, and the Santa Monica Mountains Conservancy. He still serves on those boards, as well as the Thoreau Institute, the Earth Communications Office, Tree People, Friends of the Earth, and many others.

His work in the environmental community has earned him a number of awards from some of the most prestigious environmental groups in the nation, including the California League of Conservation Voters, the Natural Resources Defense Council, the Coalition for Clean Air, Heal the Bay, and the Santa Monica Baykeeper.

Not surprisingly, Ed's flip into an eco-friendly lifestyle began years ago, when the summers he spent as a youth in Los Angeles brought the problem of air pollution up close and personal. "My father had a house in the San Fernando Valley and the smog was horrible. There was choking smog in the '50s, '60s, and through much of the '70s. It just got worse every year. You could not run a half block as a young person without wheezing and having to catch your breath. By 1970, I'd had a bellyful. I decided I didn't want to be part of the problem anymore. So I bought my first electric car in 1970, I started recycling in 1970, I started using biodegradable soaps and detergents, I started reading David Brower's works, and soon encountered 'crackpot' theories about global climate change and ozone depletion that few people took seriously at the time."

We wondered if Ed's success in entertainment made it difficult to keep his lifestyle ecologically sound. "Let me say the smartest thing I ever did with my career had nothing to do with my acting or anything I've done since *St. Elsewhere*. It's the lifestyle choice that I made to live simply. That is to say, I don't need a lot of money to support some big mansion on a hill somewhere. I live in a 1,700-square-foot house, about the same size house that I was raised in. So I can always pay those bills, and keep in mind, I don't have a lot of bills. I don't have an electric bill to speak of because I have solar panels on my roof. Robin Leach of *Lifestyles of the Rich and Famous* called me and said 'Ed, it's Robin Leach. I want to come and do a bit on your home.'

> **We are the first nation in the history of the world to go to the poorhouse in an automobile.**
> —Will Rogers

"I said, 'Robin, I live in a 1,700-square-foot home in Studio City. I know you don't want to come here and film this. It's got a little tiny front yard, a little tiny back yard.' He said, 'That's exactly what I want to come and film.' He wanted to film my solar panels, my compact fluorescent bulbs, my bicycle that I rode to generate power for the battery system that ran the house, all these crazy things. He wasn't looking for any huge spas or vaulted ceilings.

"As I get to be older, I don't work as much as I did in the *St. Elsewhere* days. When you're in your forties you work less than in your thirties, in your fifties you work less than in your forties. That's just the way it is in any business. But I work enough to make ends meet and the point I'm making is, it doesn't take a lot to make those ends meet. There's not a lot of coal required to shove in the boiler for the S.S. Begley. Indeed, it's quite literally wind-powered; I own a wind turbine. It's part of an investment in a wind farm in the California desert. I get money from that every year, certainly enough to pay my property taxes. That's an investment I made in the '80s instead of buying Exxon stock. I really didn't think it would be such a good investment financially."

Does Ed think we'll make it, ecologically speaking? "I'm very hopeful on every front; I really am. I think that most people get it. Why do I think that? Because I see a six-month waiting list for the Prius that has been in effect for years now. People do get the connection between 9/11 and our consumption of oil. When you remember that fifteen of the nineteen hijackers had Saudi passports, you just have to follow the money. Where does that money come from if fifteen hijackers had Saudi passports? Well, it comes from oil!"

WE HAVE THE POWER!

Viable, real-world technologies based on renewal energy sources are now common. Consumer demand drives the price and adoption rate of these critical innovations. Other countries have faced the future and have invested in renewable sources of energy. The U.S., led astray by Big Oil, is being left in the dust. If we do not act now, we will pay a huge price in the near future.

We have the power to move from our current upside-down policies and bad consumer habits to ones that make sense. There is much that each of us can and should do to further the flip of energy from an upside-down world of overconsumption to one that insists on renewable and sustainable energy. And soon we may not have any other choice. As the world's energy demands rise with population growth and continued economic development, global energy consumption may double or triple.

Teach your children what we have taught our children, that the earth is our mother. Whatever befalls the earth befalls the sons of the earth. If men spit upon the ground, they spit upon themselves.

—Chief Seattle

We need an Apollo program to ramp up the production of clean and green technology. We cannot allow government officials and industry leaders to play dice with the atmosphere of our planet. We envision the day when you can harness the sun's inextinguishable power to generate electricity from your own rooftop or turn your garbage into hydrogen fuel right in your garage. Imagine being that self-sufficient. Imagine a secure nation with no pipelines and power stations for terrorists to target. Imagine no more wars for oil. Imagine your children growing up playing under blue skies, drinking clean water. Imagine taking a deep refreshing breath, filling your lungs with the life force, feeling invigorated. Can you see it?

In the Right-Side Up world, it is as clear as a crisp autumn day.

FOURTEEN STEPS TO REDUCE YOUR ENERGY FOOTPRINT

1. Maintain a steady speed while driving.

2. Don't idle for more than thirty seconds; turn your vehicle off.

3. Keep your tires inflated at the proper pressure.

4. Don't use chemical pesticides or fertilizers—they are a source of nitrous oxide, a greenhouse gas.

5. Use your dishwasher's no-heat or air-drying cycle.

6. Avoid overdrying your clothes.

7. Keep your air conditioner set no lower than seventy-five degrees during summer—each degree cooler uses 3 to 5 percent more energy.

8. Use ceiling fans to cut down on summer heat.

9. Close your blinds and curtains during hot summer days to keep the home cooler.

10. Save energy and reduce heat by turning off lights, appliances, and electrical equipment.

11. Turn off the pilot light in your gas furnace during summer months.

12. Insulate your hot water heater and hot water pipes.

13. Install energy-efficient light bulbs.

14. Don't keep water running when brushing your teeth or shaving.

FLIP TIPS

- Turn off your computer equipment at night.

- Purchase only Energy Star-compliant products.

- Reduce your errands by planning multiple stops.

- Carpool whenever possible; you just might make some new friends.

- Write your congressmen and encourage them to adapt sound energy policies.

- Visit the Apollo Institute online (www.apolloinstitute.org).

- If purchasing a new car, consider a hybrid.

- Be a good steward of energy resources at work.

- Be vigilant in your locale regarding the policies and regulations your politicians and public servants are implementing.

- Don't expect everyone else to be responsible first—it starts with you.

- Don't lecture others; they'll find their way in their own space and time.

- Lead by example, living true to an eco-friendly lifestyle and not being shy when someone asks why.

- Join the Green Co-op for products and services that are Earth Friendly.

- Stay in "Green Hotels" (www.greenhotels.org) that are committed to energy conservation.

- Write letters to the editor about sound conservation practices.

EIGHT

FLIPPING THE COIN

From Scarcity to Abundance

Barry is heavily invested in the American Dream. Physically, emotionally, financially, and spiritually, Barry is bought in. For years he has worked arduously to climb his way up to material nirvana. Yet his ascent is slowed by mountainous credit card debt, first and second mortgages, impulse buys of things unneeded, irrational spending on status items, and bills, bills, bills.

> **Wealth shines in giving rather than hoarding, for the miser is hated whereas the generous man is applauded.**
>
> —Boethius

Barry feels trapped by the possessions he now has to work so hard to pay for and has so little time to enjoy. Despite a decent salary, money is a constant concern. He sometimes wakes up sweating in the middle of the night, his heart pounding, as he wonders if he remembered to pay a particular credit card on time. Enticed and seduced by offers of 0 percent interest, Barry gambled on the balance transfer game. He was two days late on a payment once and his rate skyrocketed to 30.99 percent for the life of the balance. To compound difficulties, he recently saw his minimum payment due doubled thanks to the infamous 2005 Bankruptcy Act. Barry feels betrayed.

Yes, he made the bad decisions that got him into this mess. Yes, he believes in fulfilling his obligations. After he was drilled with late charges and a staggering interest rate, Barry went back and read the fine print on his contract. And what fine print it is: legalese in three-point type, so complex Alan Greenspan would scratch his noggin in bafflement. Barry now realizes the deck was stacked against him. He's been had by the moneymen.

Remarkably, even though Barry is over his head in debt and racked with anxiety, he continues to live beyond his means. He continues to work the credit card offers. He and his family are in denial, preferring not to face their precarious financial circumstances. On those nights when Barry wakes up anxious, he usually pops an Ambien and drifts back to sleep. Problem solved.

During the day, when he is not under the influence of mood-improving drugs, Barry frets over layoffs, budget cuts, and reduced benefits at work. His health care plan gets more expensive each year, irrespective of reductions in coverage and increases in deductibles and out-of-pocket expenses.

Barry sees his life spinning into chaos. But he dare not voice his anxiety. He is experiencing a quadruple whammy: increased health care costs, higher energy prices, out-of-control finance charges, and higher local taxes that far exceed his meager federal tax cut. Surprisingly, Barry cannot seem to stop himself from spending. Like an emotionally distressed person who overeats for comfort, Barry finds temporary pleasure in deluding himself that he is a man of means. He spends, his wife spends. They indulge their daughter's material desires. The more he has, the more he wants—and the more he needs to distract himself from the truth. At his core, however, Barry feels empty and he knows that his false "damn the torpedoes" bravado is fast accelerating his day of financial reckoning.

DO YOU COME HERE OFTEN?

Like millions of Americans, Barry needs to change his relationship to money. In the upside-down world, most of us fret over the state of our finances. Only the most balanced and confident among us have a healthy view of money. It isn't money that's the problem; it's our individual and collective view of money that's the problem.

> **The contented man is never poor; the discontented never rich.**
> —George Eliot

Money in and of itself is neither a good nor a bad thing. It is simply a medium for facilitating the exchange of goods and services. How we use money to fulfill our needs, wants, and desires determines whether we have a healthy or detrimental relationship to money. In terms of Maslow's widely accepted Hierarchy of Need (see next page), money can satisfy our physiological needs: food, water, clothing, shelter. It can serve some of our safety and social needs as well. Wealth can even help us achieve success in the upper ranges of Maslow's pyramid. A normal human being in a Right-Side Up world would first satisfy his needs at the physiological level, then graduate to covering the need for safety and security, and move to ever-higher levels as the needs are met.

In the upside-down world, these human needs are preyed upon and

turned upside-down, perverting our natural value system. The pursuit of wealth becomes a substitute for our actual needs. This distortion of "what really matters" is driven and reinforced by the economic powerhouses of marketing, advertising, and public relations. Examples of skewed values include: the pricing of fashionable gym shoes at $150 after they have been produced in foreign sweatshops, under horrid conditions, for two dollars; athletes making more in one year than teachers, firemen, and police officers do in a lifetime; tickets to professional sporting events that cost more than it would to feed one hundred of the hungry and homeless. How we spend our money does matter.

In the upside-down world, it is almost impossible to escape the influential reach of advertising media seeking to persuade and manipulate us into purchasing unnecessary items and participating in events of transient gratification. The average citizen-consumer sees three thousand marketing messages per day, calling, cajoling, and tempting everyone to buy what we do not need—often with money we do not have. That's 1,095,000 marketing messages a year. Each of us sees more ads in one year than the average person fifty years ago saw in an entire lifetime. This incessant barrage of pitches dramatically alters what we think we need in order to be happy and fulfilled.

THE FINER THINGS IN LIFE

We have absolutely nothing against people seeking the finer things in life. Life is enough of a struggle to get through and everyone deserves reward. We do think it's an urgent priority for everyone to understand the consequences of the perpetual pursuit of More.

We live in a culture that defines our worth in terms of scarcity. That may sound counter-intuitive, but here's how it works: We are programmed through advertising and marketing to feel "less than" others if we do not have this car, or live in that neighborhood, and dress in the right designer labels. We are conditioned not to be content, and always to want more. We compare ourselves with others, see that we don't possess the same prized objects, and come to believe that we have a need, indeed a right, to own them. They used to call this syndrome "keeping up with the Joneses." These days it could be called "keeping up with the Trumps."

But how much is enough? Business guru David Batstone's weekly business letter, WAG (rightreality.com/wag), reports that wealthy individuals state they need the following net worth to stop worrying:

- current net worth of $1 million, but need $2.4 million
- current net worth of $5 million, but need $10 million
- current net worth of $10 million, but need $18.1 million

And so it goes. Our perceived need for financial security soars ever higher with the more we possess. Is there ever enough? Not really. Only the super-rich must be able to attain total security, right? But we suspect that their vast wealth is accompanied by another set of problems, namely, the ever-vigilant protection of their assets and lifestyle. And wealth is certainly no measure of happiness or contentment.

Again, we don't begrudge anyone the right to accumulate wealth. We love money, too. We're hoping to make some dough from sales of this book. People who work hard should be rewarded for their labors. That's America! But something has gone awry. America has always been a land of opportunity and affluence. There have always been the wealthy, the middle class, and the poor. However, the last twenty-five years have seen a progression toward a dramatic separation of the classes. America is now divided into the super-haves, the haves, and the have-nots. Among the upper classes, ostentatious living and conspicuous consumption have become in vogue. A dismissive "I got mine, go get your own" attitude permeates all three classes of our society.

An elite class manipulates the system, rewrites the laws in its favor, and calls it the free market.

There is nothing free or fair about it. People from all over the socio-political spectrum are warning that the rules have been dramatically altered to favor the rich at the expense of the middle class and poor. The widening gap between the top and bottom of our society is a predictable disaster in the making. If the present course of shredding the social safety net is pursued, we foresee that the middle class of America will be deci-mated. Poverty, currently afflicting thirty-seven million Americans—most of whom have jobs—has risen each of the last four years, and will inflict its pain on millions more. Perhaps by the time this book hits the market, or shortly thereafter, the economy may implode and millions of middle-class Americans, numb and awash in insurmountable debt, will awaken and ask what happened.

> **I am not against wealth; I am against wealth that enslaves.**
>
> —Mahatma Gandhi

DAD, CAN I BORROW A TRILLION BUCKS?

We are not Chicken Little alarmists trying to scare you that the world is coming to an end. This is a book about the flip, after all, so positive alternatives are in the offing. Stay with us. First, we have to slog through the rest of the upside-down world's dilemma. Here's a glimpse of the national debt on February 5, 2006, at 2:00 P.M. EST. Drum roll, please: $8,207,224,873,545.45. Your personal share of the debt is $27,499.96. If you have a partner, his or her share is another $27,499.96. Kids? Tack on another $27,499.96 apiece.

Bummer, huh?

Our founding fathers, including Thomas Jefferson, warned us of the risks of the banking system: "I sincerely believe . . . the banking establish-ments are more dangerous than standing armies," said Jefferson. John Quincy Adams opined, "Every bank of discount by which interest is to be paid or profit of any kind made by the lender is a downright corruption. It is taxation of the public for the benefit and profit of individuals."

Andrew Jackson dissolved the Second Bank of the United States, the equivalent of a central bank, on the grounds that it was unconstitutional, call-ing it "a curse," and further stating that if people understood how banks oper-ated "there would a revolution before morning." Today we have the Federal Reserve, which was created after years of protest (and some behind-the-scenes shenanigans) on December 23, 1913, just in time for Christmas, when no one was paying attention. Congressman Charles Lindbergh, the famous aviator's father, warned of the adverse consequences of the Federal Reserve: "When the President signs this act, the invisible government by the money power . . . will be legitimized. The new law will create inflation whenever the trusts want inflation. From now on, depressions will be scientifically calculated."

Contrary to popular belief, the Federal Reserve is actually owned by the banks. Chase and Citibank own 53 percent of the Federal Reserve. If they want higher interest rates, they go up. If they want lower rates, they go down. In essence, they dictate their profit margins to the government—at our expense. We the people are not in charge of our money or our own economy. It may seem that all this is quite esoteric and there is little we can do to alter this reality. But we can understand the nature of the beast and protect ourselves against its more nefarious actions.

WHAT ARE THEY UP TO?

Our current global monetary system is centralizing political and economic power with the ability to destroy everything we've worked to achieve. The Earth's natural resources, which sustain us, are in jeopardy as well. Looking back, we can see that bankers have helped to foment war, then financed both sides of the conflict. Nearly every Western war for the last three hundred years has been for the sake of increasing the wealth of financiers. Mayer Rothschild (1744–1812), head of the wealthiest, most secretive, and powerful family in the world, said, "Permit me to control the money of a nation and I care not who makes its laws."

That's because if one controls the money, one makes the laws. It isn't hard to convince politicians of either party to forget their principles and pass legislation that favors special interests. All it takes is cash. According to the Center for Responsive Politics (www.opensecrets.org), the financial and credit industries have contributed $42,116,068 to our elected officials since 1990. That's a wad of dough! Astonishingly, that amazing amount of money ranked them only forty-ninth in overall contributions to our illustrious leaders. What did that money buy?

PUT IT ON MY TAB

For one thing, it bought the Bankruptcy Abuse Prevention and Consumer Protection Act of 2005, which makes it harder for the average citizen-consumer to declare bankruptcy or get debt relief—and does nothing to protect consumers.

The credit industry argued the law was needed due to the increasing number of personal bankruptcies, which was eating into their profits. But while it's true bankruptcies increased, it is also true that credit card industry profits more than tripled, from $12.9 billion in 1995 to $31.6 billion in 2004.

We've all received aggressive offers by credit card companies luring us into credit deals whose cost balloons with the least infractions, such as being a day late on a payment. There is also the issue of predatory lending practices, with heavy-handed marketing of high-interest credit cards to low-income citizen-consumers. So, while we believe people should be responsible for their actions and decisions, so should the corporations who tempt us with offers that are too good to be true.

But who are the credit-hungry deadbeats who are milking the system and cheating the bankers? Actually they are not deadbeats after all, but your neighbors, your friends, your relatives—people who have faced real hardship only to be fleeced by the banking industry, the health care industry, and the federal government. The average person filing for bankruptcy holds a job but earns just $22,000 per year. Eighty-five percent of elderly debtors file due to medical or job-related problems. The Consumers Union states that single moms trying to make ends meet make up a large portion of bankruptcies. A Harvard study showed that 50 percent of bankruptcies were the result of uninsured medical expenses. Have we become so jaded, so enamored by profit that we have lost our compassion and forsaken the less fortunate?

> **This country cannot afford to be materially rich and spiritually poor.**
> —John F. Kennedy

Now, back to our forefathers who strongly voiced their opposition to a central bank and the introduction of interest. What were they afraid of? Simply this: that borrowing with interest would create a debtor class that would be forever enslaved by paying off interest. They had the foresight to know that the average person or family would become so indebted that people would have to work continuously to pay off their debts. Those enslaved to their wages would be distracted from fully participating in a democratic society, further allowing business and politicians to reduce our liberties. Their insight was uncanny, their fears well founded. This is where we are today: upside-down in a land of plenty, exhausting ourselves to make ends meet.

All That Glitters Is Not Gold

Mary's identity comes from her soul. It is her spirit that guides her as she navigates back and forth between the Right-Side Up and upside-down worlds. While she likes and appreciates nice things, Mary finds joy in simple gifts—time spent with loved ones, handwritten note cards, homemade cookies given out of love. Yes, she occasionally splurges on things she likes, but only after careful consideration of her finances. She is not cheap or miserly; rather, she simply has never bought into the concept that happiness comes from possessions.

When Mary thinks of her most treasured things, those items she values most, those things dearest to her, they are usually not expensive items. She does love her bicycle, which gives her both utility and pleasure. She loves her computer, which allows her to stay in touch with the world. And she loves the appliances and utensils in her kitchen, which allow her to make wholesome meals for herself and guests. But there is no flat screen TV in the living room and no luxury car in the garage.

Mary enjoys earning money, but harbors no illusion of being a millionaire. What for? She has all that she wants in the here and now. Her gold standard is her relationships and the moments shared. No amount of money will make those experiences any richer or any more meaningful.

For Mary, shopping is an exercise in social awareness. She loves sexy clothes and beautiful home furnishings and believes she has a right to enjoy these things. She shops mindfully, aware that each dollar she spends is a vote in the marketplace. Whenever possible, she buys organic products. While not fanatical about it, Mary does make conscious choices to support companies that share her values.

Mary invests in a socially responsible mutual fund that only buys stock in companies with strong corporate stewardship and a stated purpose of economic sustainability. No oil companies, no defense manufacturers, no tobacco or alcohol, no sweatshop labor. Her friends think it's impossible to be that responsible, but Mary knows there are several dozen socially responsible investment (SRI) funds that fit the bill. It isn't hard at all to be a good citizen of the world. Mary is thrilled to align her actions with the well-being of the planet. It gives her a warm sense of belonging, of oneness.

She also deposits money in a savings account and donates to causes that she deems important. She pays her taxes on time and doesn't attempt to finagle the numbers to cheat the IRS. While not rich, she is comfortable—and happy. She measures her wealth primarily by her inner peace.

A FORTUITOUS FLIP OF FORTUNE

The flip from scarcity to abundance is happening all around you. The great news is that all it takes to participate is desire and discipline. Consumers in the Right-Side Up world have an amazing array of choices. They've made the flip and are participating in a growing sector of the economy, currently estimated at $226 billion annually. Those in the Right-Side Up world buy natural and organic products at their local health-food store or in the natural products section of their supermarket. They eat organic dairy and produce whenever possible. If they eat meat, they prefer naturally raised beef and free range poultry. In the flipped world, people have insulated their homes and conserve energy and water resources as much as possible. They drive hybrid vehicles or cars with high MPG ratings and use mass transit where available. They read books and magazines and visit websites that feed their soul and honor their spirit. They are selective about the media that feeds their head, mindful that they needn't overstimulate their brains with detrimental, chaotic information.

Yes, in the Right-Side Up world, every dollar spent matters. Flipsters know that corporations consider every dollar spent as either approval or ignorance of their business practices. They have a practical understanding of the intimate connection between cause and effect. Flipsters know that investing in right living today keeps them from being buried by overwhelming problems tomorrow. And they do it quietly, without judgment of others. They live their lives, love their loves, enjoy their pleasure, and have their health.

> **Although they possess enough, and more than enough, still they want more.**
>
> —Ovid

You can, too.

Examples of the flip taking place around the world are abundant. The growing Fair Trade movement (see www.globalexchange.org or www.trans fairusa.org) links consumers who want to purchase products such as coffee, tea, chocolate, rice, and bananas to companies who pay their workers a living wage, promote health and safety, and adhere to sound environmental and conservation principles.

There is a long and growing list of companies which manufacture, distribute, and sell eco-friendly fabrics and clothing. These organic clothes are soft, comfortable, strong, and grown without toxins from pesticides. One excellent source of information for all aspects of the money flip is Co-op America (www.coopamerica.org), which functions as a clearinghouse for all things green. This site has a wealth of information and lists resources for anything from organic products to cosmetics to socially responsible mutual funds.

Looking for somewhere to invest for retirement that has you and the best interest of the planet in mind? Socially responsible investing (SRI) is a rapidly growing industry that allows the investor to integrate personal values and societal concerns with investment decisions. Besides individuals, social investors include corporations, universities, hospitals, foundations, insurance companies, pension funds, nonprofit organizations, churches, and synagogues.

> **Such a simple thing as the giving of yourself—giving thoughtfulness, time, help, or understanding —will trigger the cycle of abundance.**
>
> —Norman Vincent Peale

Socially responsible investment funds typically incorporate three key elements: screening, shareholder advocacy, and community investment. There are hundreds of socially responsible funds available. The Social Investment Forum (www.socialinvest.org) offers detailed data, portfolio make-up, and performance of each fund. This is a great way to put your money where your heart is. Many of these funds regularly outperform traditional mutual funds.

Here are a few other resources you can tap. While we aren't making specific recommendations, investigating these sources of socially responsible investing will certainly put you—and the Earth—on a more harmonious path.

• Social Funds—www.socialfunds.com
• Natural Capital Institute—www.responsibleinvesting.org
• Green Money Journal—www.greenmoneyjournal.com

There are a number of community-centered banks and credit unions that believe in personal service and investing in local communities. You can visit the Credit Union National Association (www.cuna.org) for a review of the benefits and a list of local credit unions.

One of the more successful examples of the flip is in the development of alternative currencies based on local markets or groups with similar interests. Local Exchange Trading Systems (LETS) are now in place in thousands of communities worldwide. Born in Canada, LETS create a local system of trade in which monetary values are assigned to various items—flowers, meals at restaurants, dry cleaning, groceries, etc. It is based on a barter system of goods and services that people in the community have to offer each other. A value is agreed upon for each product and service. A Currency Network Office keeps track of all transactions and their relative price on any given day or week. Individuals have a running balance of credits based on what they've put in or traded for, which can be used at businesses around town and augmented with national currency, like dollars, if necessary. This isn't a theoretical concept—towns in the U.S., Canada, Britain, Ireland, Australia, and New Zealand have adopted their own versions of LETS and local currencies.

The most inspiring story of the economic flip began many years ago in Bangladesh and illustrates how refusing to operate in the outmoded paradigm led to a new way of transacting business.

In 1974, Professor Muhammad Yunus, a Bangladeshi economist from Chittagong University, learned that a woman who made bamboo stools in one of the poorest villages had to borrow the equivalent of fifteen pence to buy raw bamboo for each stool made. Because of the high interest rates, she made only one penny in profit and therefore lived below subsistence level.

Yunus realized that there must be a better way and took matters into his own hands. He lent the equivalent of seventeen pounds to forty-two basket-weavers. He found this tiny amount not only made it possible for them to survive but created the spark of personal initiative and enterprise necessary for them to pull themselves out of poverty.

Yunus continued to give out these "micro-loans," and in 1983, he formed the Grameen Bank (grameen means village), which was founded on principles of trust and solidarity. In Bangladesh today, Grameen has 1,084 branches, which collect an average of $1.5 million in weekly installments. Ninety-four percent of the borrowers are women, and more than 98 percent of the loans are paid back—a recovery rate higher than that in any other banking system.

Muhamad Yunus is a shining example of how one person's vision can create a flip. Today, his micro-credit concept, which blew away the idea of scarcity, has been responsible for more than five million loans. The many lives that have been positively impacted is immeasurable.

Many people are now challenging the seriously dated model of interest being charged for the use of money. James Robertson, Associate Fellow of the Oxford Centre for Environment, Ethics, and Society, and former director of the Inter-Bank Research Organization during the 1960s and 1970s, suggests that interest-bearing business loans should be discouraged and replaced with risk-sharing relationships with banks. This reduces the adversarial role banks play in financing and reduces the desire to force bankruptcy by calling loans due at challenging moments in a company's growth.

Mr. Robertson also believes we should rethink the role of banks in issuing currency and instead make that the province of governments. He recommends that governments issue new money as payment for public spending programs or as part of citizen income. This idea would reduce the undue influence of lending institutions with a vested "interest" in large government debt and return some rational oversight to our national debt.

Bernard Lietaer, one of the architects of the Euro, offers this take on money: "Most people view money as a neutral, passive medium of exchange. It is anything but that. The money system is the meta-system, the one that affects all the others—the economic system, the medical system, the educational system, the production system, even the religious systems. All of them are actually predetermined by the money system. We are blind to this issue."

Mr. Lietaer believes we are in a transition period. "It is an interval of great risk. The risks are not only financial. Some of the emerging money technologies could create a society more repressive than anyone of us thought possible. More importantly, major opportunities are also becoming available: now more than ever it has become possible to address some of the most critical issues of our times, such as enabling more meaningful work, fostering cooperation and community, even realigning long-term sustainability with financial interests. None of this is theory. Real-life implementations have pragmatically demonstrated such results. Combining these innovations can make available a world of sustainable abundance within one generation."

> Money makes a good servant but a bad master.
> —Francis Bacon

Mr. Lietaer is but one of many brilliant minds working on changing the way money works. People in countries around the world are working to ensure that money benefits rather than enslaves. Good, earnest folks are implementing innovative and creative ways of transacting commerce—with integrity and trust and mutual benefit in mind. And that is truly a flip from the upside-down world's status quo.

CONVERSATIONS ON THE BRIDGE

So, that's our two cents. Now let's hear from our Flipsters, who have their own views on how we can go from scarcity to abundance. This chapter's conversations feature Stu Zimmerman on cultivating inner wealth; Dr. Hazel Henderson on the corporate responsibility movement; Danah Zohar on the subject of spiritual capital; and we wrap up with Lynn Twist, who talks about the soul of money and the joy of a life dedicated to service.

A Conversation on the Bridge with Stu Zimmerman

Stu Zimmerman (www.insidewealth.net) founded his own investment firm, Zimco Advisors, a registered investment advisor firm through which he managed more than $30 million in the stock market for high-net-worth individuals and small institutions. At the height of his personal and professional success, Stu realized that true security and wealth are not measured in dollars. Moved by new priorities for his life, he liquidated his business to pursue a purpose beyond financial wealth.

In fall 2002, Stu founded Inner Securities, Inc., based on the principles outlined in the landmark book he coauthored. He is the host of a weekly radio program called "Inside Wealth," aired in the San Francisco Bay area, addressing issues of wealth creation and personal transformation. Stu reveals that his economic flip was initiated by a health crisis in his family. "My wife was diagnosed with cancer at the peak of my financial success. I was living a dream that I had had since I was a teen, of owning my own firm and managing money for wealthy individuals. After twenty years of being in the game, I was achieving my professional goals. All of a sudden, my wife was diagnosed with cancer and I felt like I was getting all the toys but couldn't play with any of them. And so that led me into an inquiry about what the true nature of security and wealth is—because it wasn't what I had bought into. I had bought into the American Dream of playing by the rules of the game to make money, which buys you things, and freedom, and a supposedly wonderful life."

Stu's predicament afforded him a new view of what security really means. "If you get right down to it, any security outside of yourself is an illusion. The only real security comes from within. Having enough money to pay for food, clothing, and shelter: that's necessary. There is a certain amount of money that we all need to subsist and get by. If you buy into the rest of the materialistic culture, it's only as real as you allow it to be. But if we stopped misusing money as individuals, trying to make it deliver what it cannot, then we could begin to transform the world's relationship to money. There's enough money out there in the world right now for a huge shift to occur. If the power brokers and the financial moguls were able to 'get it,' and come from a place of abundance by offering people opportunities and making investments, a global transformation will occur. There's huge global demand for peace, better health, greater education, easing poverty—all of that. There are a lot of investments that can be made by people of very high net worth, who can invest in a world that is more whole, more value-based and filled with virtue."

We asked Stu for an example of such a flipped investment. "A good start would be to get people of affluence to make an investment in media projects that open hearts and minds. People love to be entertained. A lot of the stuff being produced for television, radio, and the movies doesn't fill the real need that's there. The demand is there, so money can flow into that so that people's values get reinforced. Companies can make significant money by finding and filling that demand.

"The imbalance of financial wealth in this world is unsustainable. Something's gotta give. Either the imbalance will be corrected, or the whole capitalist system as we know it will just collapse upon itself. Adjustments need to be made sooner than later to allow for greater opportunity for all the have-nots to bring their standards of living up, beyond survival levels, so that people don't feel like they need to strap bombs to their back to enforce justice. I'm hopeful and optimistic that we'll go into this transformation, this flip, most gracefully. My guess is there's going to be a couple of contractions and some painful moments along the way."

A Conversation on the Bridge with Dr. Hazel Henderson

Dr. Hazel Henderson (www.hazelhenderson.com) is a world-renowned futurist, evolutionary economist, a worldwide syndicated columnist, consultant on sustainable development, and the author of *Beyond Globalization* and seven other books. Her editorials appear in twenty-seven languages and more than four hundred newspapers syndicated by InterPress Service.

She told us that her alternative view of economics was rooted in her childhood environment: "I grew up in the English countryside, which could make any kid fall in love with Nature. I also grew up in a way that was very unusual in this age, in that my mother grew all of our own food in a plot of about an acre. It had everything—fruit trees and berry bushes, corn and asparagus, tomatoes, peas, potatoes, everything you could imagine. That made me realize early on that Nature is our prime source of sustenance."

Living as an adult in New York City, Hazel became politically active out of a concern for her own daughter's health. "I started a group in 1964 called Citizens for Clean Air because I had just had a baby and I was really worried about my little girl getting sick from breathing the air. I began to ask why corporations were getting away with pollution. So I started reading books on business and economics, and began to figure out what was wrong with corporate law. I wrote my first article and sent it almost as a joke to the *Harvard Business Review,* to the only woman on the masthead, with quite a belligerent letter saying I was a citizen activist and we were getting laws passed in New York City about not burning trash, and incinerators, and so on. About three weeks later, I got a call from the managing editor of the *Harvard Business Review,* saying they were going to publish it. I literally rolled on the floor laughing! I never went to college.

"Things evolved for me from there. And I'm thrilled to see corporate responsibility evolving as well, with full-time corporate responsibility positions in some of the largest companies. As we've moved to 24/7 worldwide electronic markets, companies realize their stock price can be broken instantly by making ethical mistakes that can ruin their precious brand."

> **He that is of the opinion that money will do everything may well be suspected of doing everything for money.**
>
> —Ben Franklin

We asked Hazel if she thinks short-term thinking is a flaw inherent to our economic system. "I was on the advisory council to the U.S. Congress Office of Technology from 1974 to 1980. We knew all about global warming back then and I used to say, 'well why can't we get ahead of this?' The problem is politicians who are trying to override the public's common sense. When I started Citizens for Clean Air, I used to go on radio and TV shows to debate economists from energy companies. They would say, 'Oh no, we can't really afford to do any of the things that this nice lady wants us to do. She's a very nice lady, but she doesn't understand economics.'

And I always answered, 'Look, I don't care how many of these theoretical arguments you put out to me, you cannot override the senses and common sense of ordinary people who smell the polluted air, who can see the dirty water. You can't override people's direct experience.'

"There are other problems with our economic assumptions, of course. For one thing, I came to realize how false the Gross National Product (GNP) model of progress really was. It considered education as money thrown down the rat hole instead of the most basic investment we make in our human capital. It carried human beings at the value of zero, the environment at zero, and there was overvalue given to bombs and bullets. It was so completely off the wall. So I devised an alternative set of indicators, which I first published in *Paradigms in Progress* in 1991. Basically, these social-value indicators have to be multidisciplinary. You cannot turn everything into economics. If you're trying to measure environmental pollution or air quality, you don't use money coefficients, you use parts per million of junk in the air.

"I traveled all over the world, and I would see in other countries evidence of progress that had nothing to do with GNP growth. For instance, the streets of Tokyo were spotless and there was no crime. I remember being on a subway in Tokyo and leaving my purse; when I was walking out of the station this little lady runs up to me, puffing, with my purse. How do you measure these things? Those wonderful trains, a 98 percent literacy rate, and none of that would figure into our GNP."

When money speaks the truth is silent.

—Russian Proverb

Does Hazel see a hope for the economic flip? "Well, I see all kinds of signs of hope. For example, for the first time governments are realizing that poverty gaps have to be closed. There's no doubt now in the minds of most people who are governing societies that a global economy cannot be floating an affluent group in a sea of misery.

"The way we lose the game is by concentrating on military power and weapons. We don't realize that the game has changed and that it's all about information and values now. I think the U.S. as a global empire is probably going to be the shortest run of any empire in human history

"For example, the city of Detroit can't rely on the U.S. automobile industry now; the Japanese are running rings around them. But here's the most interesting thing: the Chinese are developing their own automobile industry using all of the European emission standards. They have partnerships now with Daimler-Chrysler to produce fuel-cell automobiles. And U.S. cars will not be sold in China because they don't meet Chinese emission controls. So you see how we shoot ourselves in the foot over and over again.

"What I'm trying to do is get the most leverage that I possibly can. The way you get the most leverage on social change is to alter the 'source code' that's running the country. As I say, we have a malfunctioning economic source code. Once you expose that and help people to understand why it's driving them over the cliff, then it's much easier to get a conversation going."

A Conversation on the
Bridge with Dr. Danah Zohar

Danah Zohar (www.dzohar.com) studied physics and philosophy at MIT and completed her postgraduate work in philosophy, religion, and psychology at Harvard University. She is the author of *SQ: Spiritual Intelligence, the Ultimate Intelligence* and best-sellers *The Quantum Self* and *The Quantum Society*, books that extend the language and principles of quantum physics into a new understanding of human consciousness, psychology, and social organization. Danah Zohar lectures widely throughout the world at conferences organized by such bodies as UNESCO, The European Cultural Foundation, The World Economic Forum, The World Business Academy, YPO, IFTDO (International Federation of Training and Development Organizations), the Swedish National Parliament, Japan's Council for the Growth of Future Generations, and the Australian National Government.

One of her most intriguing notions is the idea of spiritual capital. "Spiritual capital is a whole new philosophy for business and corporate governance in which the basis of your business changes from a focus on the bottom line to a focus on 'how do we get to the bottom line and what do we do with that bottom line when we have got to it.' That means being driven by a deeper vision and a deeper set of values, which takes into account the contribution you make to your own workforce's well-being, to the community's well-being, and to the planet's well-being. If you don't get that right, then you're not going to be sustainable because you're going to lose the morale of your people and you're going to start losing money. Most Fortune 500 companies exist for five years or less. The Quaker companies founded at the turn of the last century go on and on.

"The challenge of shifting corporate culture is to get it into the positive motivation range where the first four motivations are exploration, cooperation, integrity, and power over oneself. Then you can achieve power or mastery over the situation at hand. What if we could build a sort of Knights Templar in the corporate world; comprised of men and women who are effective members of the world, not just wooly-minded idealists, but tough business people who could serve whatever they hold most sacred, most beneficial in their own value system, and lead their companies from that level? The leadership role of these knights would be to nurture and build the spiritual capital of their companies, thereby raising the motivation of the people in their companies.

"There's a bit of this built into the core of European thinking, a concern that the whole of society be involved in the wealth of society. So there is more openness to this spiritual approach to business in Europe, as long as you stress that *spiritual* doesn't mean *religious*. It's more about values and vision and our fundamental purpose."

Danah believes that this shift toward a spiritual economics is necessary to our survival as a species. "Either make this shift in consciousness or we're going to destroy our culture completely. I don't know if we're going to destroy life on Earth like the real pessimists say, but I think we are going to destroy at least what we take for granted: our high-tech, wealthy lifestyle. We're just going to destroy ourselves. For my part, I've just founded a 'total intelligence' company that will take the next step beyond spiritual capital. Total intelligence is a concept of emergent consciousness that arises from the meeting place of mental intelligence, emotional intelligence, and spiritual intelligence. Total intelligence is greater than the sum of the other three parts, an explosion into a whole new way of being."

A CONVERSATION ON THE BRIDGE WITH LYNNE TWIST

Lynne Twist (www.soulofmoney.org) is a global activist, fundraiser, speaker, author, teacher, mentor, and counselor who has devoted her life to service in support of global sustainability and security, human rights, economic integrity, and spiritual authenticity. Lynne has trained other fundraisers to be more effective in their work and raised millions of dollars for organizations that serve the best instincts of all of us—to end world hunger, empower women, nurture children and youth, and preserve the natural heritage of our planet.

Ms. Twist, an original staff member of The Hunger Project in 1977, served as a leader of that international initiative for twenty years, and was responsible for raising the money necessary to support it and its programs. In that capacity, Lynne traveled the world, developing a keen understanding of the relationship of people to money, the psychology of scarcity, and the psychology of sufficiency. Lynne Twist shares compelling stories and insights from those experiences in *The Soul of Money: Transforming Your Relationship with Money and Life.*

We asked Lynne what inspired her to a life of service? "In the seventies I was fortunate to connect with Buckminster Fuller, the great architect, designer, humanist, and futurist. In a speech he made in 1976, he asserted that humanity had passed a threshold and that we now live in a world where it's clear there's enough for everyone, everywhere to have a healthy and productive life with no one left out. He said that humanity had been living in a you-or-me paradigm, a paradigm of separation, where either you make it at my expense or I make it at your expense because there's not enough for both of us.

"Fuller said our structures and systems are all rooted in that belief in scarcity. That really hit me. He was right. I started to see a world where there's enough. I believe that scarcity is a product of a whole bed of unexamined, unconscious beliefs. The condition of scarcity is a lie, an unfortunately deep lie in the culture, and the lightning rod for that lie is money. We've built a financial system, economic system, and a money system that deepens and firms that lie of scarcity that there's not enough to go around, and you've got to get more than you need to protect yourself from being one of the people who gets left out because someone somewhere is always going to be left out."

> The day, water, sun, moon, night—I do not have to purchase these things with money.
>
> —Titus Maccius Plautus

So how can we move beyond current thinking and dispel the illusion? Lynn replied, "It all comes from 'we're not whole'—you're not okay the way you are, you've got to accumulate and acquire more. And that is a tyranny; it's not just a misunderstanding, it's a tyranny that rules right now and I think you can free yourself from it. The radical truth is there is enough right now, right this minute, but you have to let go of trying to get more to see 'enough.' When you let go of trying to get more of what you don't really need, which is what most of us are scrambling to get more of, it frees up oceans of energy to pay attention to and make a difference with what you already have.

"When the bowl of life starts to overflow and dribble over the edge, so to speak, then you move into the experience of thanksgiving and you're grateful that there's another that you can serve or contribute or thank or share.

"I have worked on hunger and poverty, so I know there's not enough food in Ethiopia for people. I've been in refugee camps in Mozambique and Bangladesh where I've held dying children in my arms. I know there are places where there's not enough to go around. But it's a function of the beliefs in scarcity rather than that it's a self-fulfilling prophecy.

"Even those people in those circumstances have taught me the power of sufficiency, of seeing the power of enough and that exquisite experience of having your needs met and realizing that's the moment of fulfillment. Not in getting more. The moment of fulfillment and prosperity that we're all looking for is already there, but we don't have our focus on it. We have our attention on getting more.

"So, it's an instant transformation opportunity that we all have, no matter what our financial circumstances are. Even in situations of what some call poverty, I've seen people living in such satisfaction and joy it just staggers me. The experience of fulfillment and prosperity is available now to every human being at every moment. But it's not available through the doorway of more. That will only lead you to an experience of lack, which is then followed by an obsession for more—which leads you to lack. The only doorway to real fulfillment and prosperity is the doorway of enough or sufficiency."

To find that doorway, we asked Lynn how we can transform our relationship with money. "We've made money more important than human life, the natural world, or God. We've given it more meaning than the most important things that there are. And we're confused because money is our invention. We just made it up. It doesn't have more meaning than human life, the natural world, or God, yet that's one of the lies that we tell, and we even allow ourselves to be called consumers instead of citizens.

"We can actually reinvent money as an instrument or tool, allow it to flow, know that it's part of the commons, that it doesn't belong to any of us, that it flows through every life, and that it is a carrier and a conduit and a currency or a current, and that it carries the energy of him or her who passes it along."

TRY THIS AT HOME

As we have seen, there are amazing flips taking place in all aspects of money. From how we understand and use money, to the connection our purchases have in validating or repudiating business practices, to the rapidly changing role we all play in charting our own financial destinies; it all comes back to our own self-worth and how much we value, or devalue, our fellow human beings.

Changing your view of money is one of the most important things you can do to dramatically improve the quality of your life. Most of us know people of meager means who enjoy their days with seemingly not a care in the world. Conversely, we also know someone affluent who is mean-spirited and miserable. Money and possessions only have the power we give them; scarcity exists in the mind.

Breaking our addiction to material worth is not all that challenging. As we said earlier in this chapter, all it requires is desire and discipline. You don't have to become a dour penny-pincher, dining on cat food and soda crackers. You can enjoy a lifestyle that is more enriching, rewarding, and empowering than your current one simply by honoring that which is dearest to you. Being honest about your habits and traits is an important first step. You must learn to be authentic. Begin avoiding anything that smacks of superficiality. Don't buy into the marketing hype. To borrow a trite phrase from the Reagan years, "just say no" to excess.

A great exercise is to look around your house—at your clothes, your gadgets, your knick-knacks, the stuff you "had to have" that you never use—and take a mental inventory. Most of us have thousands of dollars' worth of "stuff" that we wasted our money on. See the pattern of your behavior and keep it in mind during future shopping excursions.

> **The price we have to pay for money is sometimes liberty.**
> —Robert Louis Stevenson

Could someone else use what you cannot? Certainly. Donate your excess to a charity like Goodwill, the Salvation Army, or the Disabled American Veterans. Not in the mindset to donate? Hold a yard sale. The point is to immediately unburden yourself from possessions you don't need. Seek simplicity. Reduce your economic footprint.

Another great idea is to divest yourself of all but one credit card. You heard us. Don't pretend you didn't. Reduce the temptation to spend money you don't have by eliminating the source of the seduction: those alluring pieces of plastic in your wallet or purse.

The move toward the flip can be rapidly attained if we stop distorting each individual's Hierarchy of Need as defined by Maslow. If, instead, we honored and cultivated these needs during childhood development and on through the education process, we would build a more enlightened society that fully acknowledges the value of each and every human being. Here are some universal ideas to instill in the hearts and minds of everyone:

- Teach awareness of one's inner self.
- Teach people to transcend cultural conditioning and be true citizens of the world.
- Learn to accept yourself and others as they are.
- Ensure the basic needs of all individuals are met.
- Learn to make good choices by teaching critical thinking.
- Rise above life's little problems and focus on fixing the source of the major ones, such as injustice, violence, suffering, greed, and low self-esteem.

If we learn to value ourselves and others, if we can accept people for who they are, if we summon the love and courage necessary to fully respect the needs of our fellow human beings, we will indeed all soon be living in a Right-Side Up world where money is not the primary motivator and corruptor of human behavior but a vehicle to higher human potential and genuine happiness.

FLIP TIPS

- Review your actual household expenses and create a monthly budget.

- Ask yourself how much of your identity is attached to status and owning nice things.

- Consider how to reduce or eliminate expenses that are excessive.

- Don't overindulge your children with gifts; they'll love you anyway.

- Give gifts that are homemade or from the heart.

- Don't buy into the hyper holiday buying mania—instead create holiday traditions that truly honor the spirit of the season.

- Remember that your dollar reflects your social views.

- Subscribe to a socially responsible investment newsletter.

- Reduce the number of times you dine out each week.

- Pool your errands so you make fewer trips, saving gas.

- If you don't need it, don't buy it.

- Make sure you are conserving energy, thereby saving money.

- Donate time, money, or both to a nonprofit organization working to better the quality of life in your community. Contact your local Community Shares (www.communitysharesusa.org) or United Way for assistance.

- **Join an online community dedicated to simple living (www.simpleliving.net).**

- **Stay away from get-rich-quick schemes—if it sounds too good to be true, it is.**

NINE

FLIPPING THE CORPORATION

From Pirates to Stewards

After working for USW Incorporated for three years, Barry feels nervously fortunate. Prior to USW, he was laid off without notice when his employer moved operations offshore. Now USW, citing market forces and competitive threats, is shuttering its manufacturing plants in favor of outsourcing to the lowest bidder in the Pacific Rim.

Despite assurances that the management, sales, and service departments are secure, the lingering anxiety from Barry's previous experience weighs heavily on his mind.

Other signs at USW aren't so positive either. Benefit cuts, increases in health insurance premiums, and wage freezes have created an atmosphere of paranoia. Cancellation of the company picnic has the rumor mill churning overtime. Meanwhile, the board of directors has authorized executive bonuses and compensation for senior management in the tens of millions. Barry doesn't belong to that exclusive club, so he doesn't share in the spoils.

> **Capitalism as such is not evil; it is its wrong use that is evil.**
>
> —Mahatma Gandhi

Welcome to the global economy of an upside-down world, where the bottom line takes precedence over people.

Like many USW employees, Barry puts on a brave face, works long hours, and suffers through meeting after redundant meeting whose principal goals are to increase revenues and slash costs. Barry associates much of his identity with his job. Even with an "Employee of the Year" plaque on his wall, Barry is insecure. His self-esteem is in the toilet. His fear of losing his job reinforces his diminished self-worth, which in turn causes him to make decisions that further degrade his quality of life—to work even harder, to cancel family plans, and treat his coworkers with suspicion. Life for Barry in the upside-down world sucks. Big time.

YOU ARE NOT ALONE

Are you happy in your job? If you are, congratulations! Most people aren't.

A recent survey showed 75 percent of all employees were looking for a new job. With American productivity at its highest level in history, shouldn't people be feeling great about their accomplishments and themselves? Sorry, in the upside-down world doing a good job doesn't count for much anymore. Gone are the days of a worker staying at the same company his or her entire career. Employer-employee loyalty based on an honest day's wage for an honest day's work has largely died out. Trust in corporations has turned to mistrust.

We want to state upfront that not all corporations are bad or are committing piracy. Corporations are critical to the function of society. Well run, they offer products and services that benefit many. But the ship of commerce is under attack in the upside-down world. Some captains of industry are looting and pillaging at will. We've all read the headlines: Massive fraud in the accounting, energy, telecommunications, insurance and health care industries. Wall Street scandals. Products put on the market with harmful defects kept from the public. Untold devastation of the environment. Avaricious executives raking in hundreds of millions as their firms sink. Predatory lending practices.

The ship is taking on water. It's enough to make you want to jump over the side. How did we end up here?

CORPORATIONS ARE PEOPLE, TOO

Originally, a corporation was defined as a group of people legally bound together to form a business enterprise. It was an artificial entity created by the granting of a charter by government and treated by law as an individual entity. In 1886, an obscure but now infamous Supreme Court ruling stated that corporations had the same constitutional rights as people. Some believe this act precipitated the grant of too much power to corporations.

But the Supreme Court, unwittingly and by sheer accident, was not too far off. Like people, there are all different types of corporations—public and private, large and small, well-intentioned and not so well-intentioned.

Just as a newborn inherits the traits and characteristics of its parents based on genetics, environment, and guidance, so does a company take on the traits and characteristics of its founders. This is its corporate soul: an invisible, self-organizing field that permeates all aspects of the firm, drawing together what it needs to achieve its destiny. This purpose may not be visible to those looking in from the outside, but all companies are imprinted with the corporate DNA of their founders.

If a corporation was formed with greedy, malevolent goals, it will take on those characteristics. Similarly, if a company was created to bring products and services of value to humankind, the organization will have a benevolent persona. This is an obvious oversimplification of business dynamics, but the principle is generally reliable.

A company also has a corporate culture defined by the attitudes and actions of its current leaders. In an organization, each individual is like a cell in the human body. It may be specialized, but it must also carry the DNA of the whole. If the leaders of a corporation are engaged in disintegrative business practices and deceptive motives, the bad energy spreads like cancer throughout the body of the organization. If an accounting department cooks the books, a fraudulent cancer will spread to other departments. A department is like an organ inside the organizational body; it serves a primary function that regulates the health and life of the company. If a major organ is diseased, the whole organism becomes ill and may die.

> **Every person's work, whether it be literature, or music or pictures or architecture or anything else, is always a portrait of oneself.**
>
> —Samuel Butler

Beneath the leaders are the employees who give the company its life force. Each person in a company is a human being, complete with his or her own spirit, intent, personality, skills, experiences, and needs. The collective energy and disposition of the workers creates the personality of the company. People need to feel as though their contributions matter. Further, on a soul level, they need to be in harmony with the direction of the company or they will feel disgruntled and disenfranchised. If enough people in enough companies feel the trust between corporations and people has been violated, then the whole of society suffers.

This is the plight of corporate business in the upside-down world.

A Delicate Balance

In American business, there has always been a delicate balancing act between pursuing profit for its own sake and serving the public good. Corporations exist to make money, no doubt about it. Who is to say how much is enough or not enough? Would you want someone telling you how much you were allowed to earn? Of course not.

But most people regulate their wants and desires and settle for a comfortable balance. Unfortunately, there are those whose appetite for success and status is endless. These people are driven by personal ambition and tend to rise to the top of corporate ladders. Once at the top, they are able to dictate the corporate culture and alter its personality, for better or worse. Once at the top, they can still choose to be pirates or stewards.

A major shift has occurred over the last twenty-five years as companies have become more brazen in their lust for profit. There seems to be no way to satisfy the immense hunger companies have for unlimited profit. Why is this?

> **We have too many people who live without working, and we have altogether too many who work without living.**
>
> —Charles R. Brown

Legalized Gambling

Imagine a form of legalized gambling in which billions of dollars exchange hands daily, a betting system that rewards only the acquisition of wealth and nothing else. Now, let's say your company made $1 billion in profit last year. One billion. That's a lot of dough. This year the company makes another billion. Not too shabby, right? Wrong. The investors in the gambling syndicate aren't pleased because the company didn't grow at the rate of return that they bet on. Even though the company made a billion two years in a row, its profits were considered flat. Because it only made a billion and not say, 1.2 billion, the company and its leadership are punished. Perhaps the CEO is sacked, or its units are sold off to achieve better performance. Does that sound unreal, or insane, or faintly criminal?

Friends, that system is the stock market.

Remember how corporations are said to be people? Now imagine that as a healthy, mature person you grew at a rate of 10 percent per year. Take your current weight, add 10 percent, then add 10 percent more, and do it again. Do so for five years, then ten. It doesn't take a mathematician or a dietician to see that gaining that much weight, growing that much, is extremely unhealthy. You'd be obese, immobile, have serious health implications, and would probably endanger your life. It's unnatural to grow at such rates beyond the natural stage of youth.

Because a company's stock price is based on its financial performance, there is incredible pressure put on executives to perform. "Grow by 10 percent and we'll give you five million dollars; miss your forecast and you're fired." Which option do you think you'd have to choose if you wanted to prolong your career?

We are allowing Wall Street, based on its legalized gambling scheme, to determine the most important measures of our economy. But we are looking at the wrong measure—we are looking at quantity over quality. We should be pursuing both and striking an equitable balance.

MAKING THE FLIP

Mary works in the natural products industry. Her company pays a living wage, which is considerably higher than the national minimum. She and her coworkers participate in a profit-sharing plan that gives everyone an equal opportunity in the company's success. Mary is proud of the company's policy of buying only from firms that adhere to sustainable business practices.

Mary and her friends can't wait to get to work; they love their jobs. Their employee productivity surpasses that of many larger companies with more resources. Their customer satisfaction rating is outstanding and customer loyalty is the envy of similar companies operating in the upside-down world.

Making the flip to Mary's world is easier than you think. Millions of people have already done so—with more ready to flip when the moment is right. As previously noted, there is a $226 billion marketplace in the United States for goods and services focused on natural health, the environment, social justice, personal development, and sustainable living.

People who work for or buy products from companies dedicated to a lifestyle of health and sustainability share concerns about the environment, health, and human rights. More and more people share a holistic worldview that recognizes the interconnections between global economies, cultures, environments, and political systems. Increasingly, they feel the need for authentic self-expression in their business dealings—and thus the need for a flip becomes evident. Out of all the institutions that contribute to our societal structure, the corporation is in the midst of the greatest flip because it represents the biggest arena for transformation.

Corporations have the power to address and radically transform humanity's most pressing challenges. They possess the resources to rebuild trust through humane and sustainable business practices. Many corporations are beginning to answer this clarion call to mature their business practices and redefine their organizational values. Through the new movement toward corporate social responsibility, the first steps are being taken to instill the social values that have gone neglected too long in American business.

NOT A SINGLE, NOT A DOUBLE, BUT A TRIPLE BOTTOM LINE

To ascend to the next stage of our social evolution, corporations must look at more than the conventional bottom line. The great news is that many businesses and nongovernmental organizations have already embraced a concept called Triple Bottom Line, which measures a company's worth by its social, environmental, *and* economic value. This shifts emphasis from profit-making for its own sake to a balanced value system of business success, environmental impact, and social good. It's a win-win-win paradigm.

Triple Bottom Line can change the whole ballgame on Wall Street. No longer will the economic health of the nation be measured only by the single standard of profits, without regard to social and environmental concerns.

When corporate leaders recognize that everything is interconnected and financial gain that disregards social and planetary health is a lose/lose proposition, they will shift from being pirates and become stewards. This isn't merely the hoped-for vision of a distant future. The Right-Side Up world is happening right now. Social venture networks, the natural products industry, the burgeoning sustainable development movement, green building, and growing numbers of social entrepreneurs represent this dynamic flip in progress. They bode well for a bright future for us all.

CONVERSATIONS ON THE BRIDGE

Let's meet some Flipsters of Business. They each embody a vision of transformation rooted in a working knowledge of how to implement these ideals into a living reality. First, Patricia Aburdene identifies the latest "megatrend" toward a redeeming spirituality in business. Ray Anderson, founder and chief executive officer of Interface, discusses how his company completely reshaped

SHOPPING WITH STEWARDS EXERCISE

Companies exist to make money. That money comes from consumers. This gives you incredible individual power to influence the behavior of companies by voicing your views with your pocketbook.

Look around your home and identify five products you use regularly (food, shoes, soap, magazines)

Ask yourself if you need the product.

If no, stop buying the product or service.

If yes, research the Triple Bottom Line practices of the company and its products—it's easy to do via the web:

> **www.essential.org**
>
> **www.ecomall.com**
>
> **www.sustainablebusiness.com**
>
> **www.coopamerica.org/pubs/greenpages**
>
> **www.greenbusiness.net**

Are they leaving a small footprint?

Do they treat their employees well?

Are they environmentally conscious?

Do they give back to the community?

Do they have numerous offshore tax shelters?

Are there alternative products made by more responsible companies where your money is better spent?

We're not suggesting you become a radical activist, rather a mindful consumer who walks lightly on the Earth. There are many fine organizations and websites to make this exercise easy, exciting, and fun. You'll be amazed at what you discover.

its business to be environmentally and socially responsible. Corporate expert Marilyn Tam gives us a global glimpse of how people on the other side of the planet benefit from the socially responsible practices of some U.S.-based corporations. MIT lecturer Peter Senge reveals how we can "grow companies by growing people," and socially responsible investing expert Terry Mollner concludes this section with a prediction about the advent of the "relationship corporation."

A CONVERSATION ON THE BRIDGE
WITH PATRICIA ABURDENE

Patricia Aburdene (www.patriciaaburdene.com) is a world-renowned author, speaker, and social forecaster. She is the coauthor of the number one *New York Times* best-seller *Megatrends 2000*, the best-seller *Re-inventing the Corporation*, and *Megatrends for Women*. In 2005, she authored *Megatrends 2010*.

> **Alone we can do so little; together we can do so much.**
>
> —Helen Keller

Our conversation with Ms. Aburdene centered on the spiritual transformation of the corporation as she took us through the patterns, trends, and megatrends affecting business, corporate culture, and capitalism. First, we were curious to know just what a "megatrend" is.

"A megatrend is a direction in society that is so overarching that it remains for at least a decade," Patricia explains. "The major megatrend we are experiencing today is the governmental and corporate manipulation of fear associated with issues of security, from terrorism to Social Security. Some governmental agencies and corporations have exploited prominent national issues for a fear-based campaign to manipulate people to act against their own interests."

Since color-coded terror alerts and Social Security reforms don't really address our fundamental sense of security, Patricia feels we are compelled to look inside ourselves for better answers. "We live in an era of moral crisis, but also of great opportunity," she observes. "The moral crisis has triggered a revival of values and meaning in business, which leads us to the next big megatrend—in this case, the spiritual transformation of the corporation."

That sounds like a wonderful ideal, but how and where is it really taking place? "This change is happening from the top down, bottom up, inside-out, and outside-in. From the top down, wise CEOs are recognizing that the greatest assets and resources of any company are its people. Leaders who empower employees by encouraging self-mastery—and who lead by example from a deeper sense of spiritual truth—see huge dividends in terms of productivity and customer satisfaction. From the bottom up, people are investing in their own search for meaning and commitment to their whole selves. Look at the interest in yoga. Over eighteen million people are taking yoga classes; some of these people are managers, secretaries, laborers, etc. They bring this balanced spiritual energy back into their places of work and influence it. From the inside out, there is a growing emphasis on corporate social responsibility and ethics, as well as shareholder activism. From the outside in, issues such as accounting scandals, geopolitical uncertainty, and the threat of cyber terrorism are forcing us to look at the structures of business."

Does all this mean that capitalism itself can be transformed by corporations who flip? Patricia observes: "Capitalism as we know it is based on a fundamentalism of greed: *Thou shalt increase earnings by fair means or foul.* What the corporate social responsibility and socially responsible investment sectors are showing us is how false the 'lean and mean' myth of effective business is. What we are learning is that money, morals, and meaning are enormously compatible. That's why the new trend is toward the Triple Bottom Line."

A CONVERSATION ON THE BRIDGE WITH RAY ANDERSON

Ray Anderson is the founder and CEO of Interface, Inc. (www.interfaceinc.com), the world leader in the design and production of modular carpet. Ray has embarked on a corporate mission to "be the first company that, by its deeds, shows the entire industrial world what sustainability is in all its dimensions: people, process, product, place, and profits—by 2020—and in doing so, to become restorative through the power of influence." He's leading a worldwide effort to pioneer the processes of sustainable development.

Today, Ray is recognized as one of the world's most environmentally progressive chief executives, having served as cochairman of the President's Council on Sustainable Development during the Clinton administration; and was recognized by Mikhail Gorbachev with a Millennium Award from Global Green in 1996. We asked if there was a personal catalyst that caused Ray to transform his company to a model of corporate stewardship.

"There probably was a lurking sense of legacy in my subconscious. I was sixty years old. The company had succeeded beyond anybody's wildest dreams. The next generation of management was on board and battle tested and it was a time when my thoughts might have turned to retirement to the mountains or the seashore. At the same time, I was searching myself to see if I had a continuing role in the company I had founded. And then we began to hear this question from our customers, 'What's your company doing for the environment?'

"I was not aware of any egregious things that we were doing to the environment. We were in compliance and that, to me, was sufficient at that point. But the questions kept coming, and then this guy in California named John Picard, who was an environmental consultant, left a book on my desk called *The Ecology of Commerce* by Paul Hawken. It was a propitious moment because I had to make a speech I didn't want to make and I didn't have a clue what to say. I could not get beyond 'we obey the law and company bylaws,' which was not sufficient and not what people were looking for. I was in a frustrated mood. I picked the book up with no idea what it was about and just started thumbing, and I came to a chapter "The Death of Birth," and it hit me right between the eyes. It was an epiphany experience. And my epiphany was that I was a plunderer. I was a part of this problem. I realized that this company that I'm so proud of, that had succeeded on so many levels, had missed a key measurement of success all along. It totally eluded us. I felt this sense of legacy, which was 'what's this thing, this child prodigy of mine, going to grow up to be?'"

Curious, we asked Ray what happened after his epiphany. "Well, I needed to voice what I'd realized. And I made a speech to a task force that had been assembled from our businesses around the world, and I used Hawken's material and had that little group of people in tears because I was in tears.

"From there we defined this challenge as a mountain to climb, a mountain taller than Everest that we've got to figure out. It took us two years to understand there were seven faces to the mountain. So how do you climb that mountain? You climb every face and you meet at the top. That summit represents zero footprint on the environment. That was the challenge.

"So the first thing was to send a task force back to their businesses to begin to sensitize their associates and their individual businesses to get something going. And it became a journey of a thousand miles with one little step at a time, and we finally figured out if you do something, you feel really good about that, then you go do something else, and then it builds on itself.

"We had a thousand things to do. The first face of the mountain is eliminating waste. We had four hundred teams working all through our company on waste elimination—many, many hundreds of projects. And we realized early on that the way we'll pay for this whole mountain-climbing adventure was by the cost avoidance we were able to create through waste elimination.

"As we identified the other faces of the mountain, we realized almost every one of them was a technological challenge. Eliminating harmful emissions means re-engineering the processes. If you're going to go to renewable energy, the cheapest energy there is, it's a real challenge. You have to become energy efficient to reduce energy usage. These successes built upon themselves."

Impressed by the progress of Ray and his team, we asked where businesses of the future are headed: "I think with any paradigm shift, the early movers win. You always have the early movers, then you have the fast followers, then at the other end you have the never-followers, and that's who the regulatory system is for, to push them along to catch up.

"Then you have the vast middle ground of people who eventually move, too, when they see it's the thing to do. This is the way it happens in any paradigm shift. We consider ourselves among the earliest of the early movers and we're benefiting enormously from it. The goodwill of the marketplace is unbelievable. Our costs are down, not up, disproving the myth that sustainability is a costly thing to do. If you take an industrial enterprise like ours and approach it in the round as a total system, you find that savings here can fund improvements there, and, overall, you optimize the total system as opposed to optimizing a component of the system.

> **We are not here to merely make a living. We are here to enrich the world, and we impoverish ourselves if we forget this errand.**
>
> —Woodrow T. Wilson

"We've approached it in the round with the idea of optimizing the total system, which means we're not sucking every drop of blood out of waste savings, we're reinvesting some of it into renewable energy and recycling technologies. In my view, the triple bottom line all comes together in one superior financial bottom line if you do it right. And that is what will attract other industries.

"Customers ultimately determine your success, and this is a way to engage customers on a different level. Your people make a difference. This is the way to galvanize people around a higher purpose. Your products can be better because the whole sustainability approach opens up undreamed of sources of inspiration. This is a better way to make a bigger profit. And all the rest, the other two bottom lines fall into place as means to an end, and the end is to show a truly better industrial model.

"This is the flip you're talking about in this book. And believe me, it will happen because the marketplace will make it happen."

A Conversation on the Bridge with Marilyn Tam

Marilyn Tam's (www.howtousewhatyouvegot.com) distinguished background includes prominent executive roles at numerous world-class companies, including CEO of Aveda, president of Reebok Apparel and Retail Group, and vice president of Nike. Ms. Tam is the cofounder and executive director of the Us Foundation, whose mission is to facilitate global action plans and dialogue to address social, economic, and environmental issues. In the following remarks, Ms. Tam discusses the impact of U.S. multinationals' globalization efforts on other countries, while offering an inspiring example of how to conduct global commerce with mindfulness of the needs and rights of the local population.

"Anti-American sentiment and misperceptions about American culture have escalated in every region of the world," Marilyn reports, "and that threatens the business of multinational corporations. There is a widespread need for more awareness, appreciation and sensitivity to other cultures in the domestic U.S. market." Marilyn cites a Roper study, which found that citizens in foreign countries regard American brands as harmful because:

1. American brands have a corrupting influence in changing their culture through aggressive marketing and advertising of nonlocal traditions and a push for hyper-consumerism.
2. The receiving country has an unfavorable perception of American values.
3. The receiving country believes that Americans have a low regard for their country and their values; they are insensitive and arrogant.
4. The receiving country perceives it is being exploited and persecuted for profit.

"These perceptions are causing the multinationals to take notice because it is hurting their business," Marilyn comments. "Whether one agrees with globalization or not, we can't turn back time. Globalization is a fact. Trade, communication, and travel have reduced the barriers and opened up isolated cultures. We are living in a global society, and what each individual, company, and country does affects the whole world. We expect the world to do business with us, but surprisingly, only 18 percent of Americans have passports. Americans have a limited and often unfavorable understanding of other cultures based on ignorance. The famous one-hundred-year-old quote by Ambrose Bierce, 'War is God's way of teaching Americans geography' is still, unfortunately, astonishingly accurate. In the age of a global economy, it is economically unsound, dangerous, and unhealthy to have so little understanding and appreciation for our neighbors."

We asked Marilyn for a specific example of how she's helped a company flip their values. "When I was at Reebok, we explored the production of soccer balls. Before initiating the manufacture of these balls in Pakistan, which is where most soccer balls are made by child laborers, we ascertained what an equitable living wage was in that country. We also found out which factories didn't have ventilation. However, convincing the factory owners that implementing policies of decent wages and better working conditions would actually result in better profit margins was not an easy sell. Getting the factory owners on board proved to be only the first giant step of larger, systemic reform that took Reebok out of the factories altogether and into the business of knowledge.

> **No business is successful, even if it flourishes, in a society that does not care for or about its people.**
> —Eugene C. Dorsey

"In order to ensure that Pakistani parents didn't just send their unemployed children down to the brick quarry, and that the kids got access to an education instead of a hazardous occupation, Reebok committed to a long-term quest for improved life in the region. The process took three years. Reebok first went to the community leaders with the question, 'If we fix our system, will you let the kids go to school?' 'Sure,' was the response, 'if we had schools.'

"Here we are living in America with conveniences that the rest of the world can only dream about. We assume others have adequate lighting, access to education, books—and they have none of these things. Reebok's task was not only to fund and build the classrooms and to train the teachers, but to justify this incredible leap off the business plan to bottom-line-oriented shareholders.

"But we did it, and it was very rewarding for Reebok, but most importantly it positively influenced and bettered the lives of many workers and their families."

Does Marilyn think that more companies are willing to make the investment of time and money required for the flip of business values? "Most companies are realizing that they have to change," Marilyn concludes. "The Earth is running out of resources and market conditions are forcing companies to change. The companies that don't change won't survive. Consumers are waking up to their power. So I think this flip is both necessary and inevitable."

A Conversation on the Bridge with Dr. Peter Senge

Peter Senge, Ph.D. (www.solonline.org), is a senior lecturer at the Massachusetts Institute of Technology. He is also founding chair of the Society for Organizational Learning (SoL), a global community of corporations, researchers, and consultants committed to increasing our capacity to collectively realize our highest aspirations through the mutual development of people and institutions.

> **Treat employees like partners, and they act like partners.**
>
> —Fred A. Allen

Mr. Senge is the author of several books, including the widely acclaimed *The Fifth Discipline: The Art and Practice of the Learning Organization* (1990). This book, which provides the knowledge for organizations to transform rigid hierarchies into more fluid and responsive systems, is widely credited with creating a revolution in the business world. Since its publication, more than a million copies have been sold, and in 1997, *Harvard Business Review* identified it as one of the seminal management books of the past seventy-five years.

We first asked Peter about how major organizations have made the transition from a traditional paradigm to a whole-system perspective. "It comes about, usually, in one of a couple of different ways," Peter observes. "A lot of people come to this perspective more from an internal viewpoint. They just believe there's got to be a better way to manage and lead. Typically, for example, maybe somebody was part of a very innovative team or organization setting early in their career but then found that most of the rest of the bosses were Attila the Hun; you know, people who just slammed their fist on the table and demanded results and really didn't give a damn what effect it had on people. The contrast to those two perspectives often leaves a lot of people going 'I know there's a better way.' I know there's a better way to both achieve results and do it in a way that people really grow. I think that's one of the core premises that we find again and again—that you can grow a business through growing people, and the two are not at odds with one another. So that's what I would characterize as sort of an internal perspective.

"Increasingly, there's also an external perspective. People are looking at the impact of a business on communities in larger living systems and saying, 'This can't continue.' Basically, most of the whole Industrial Age has been about harvesting natural and social capital in order to produce financial capital. We can't do that forever. Years ago people had to live on our energy income, not our energy capital. Today, we're digging up stuff that was put down under the earth hundreds of millions of years ago. We can't keep that up. So there's also an external perspective that says that we have to find a different way of running businesses that produces social and environmental well-being as well as economic well-being, not just destroys those in order to make a buck."

Does Peter believe that our primary traditional institutions are poised for a breakdown? "I think you can see all of these changes as basically arising from a kind of progressive breakdown in the traditional order of things. Dee Hock, who was the founding CEO of Visa and our advisor in creating SoL, says we live in 'an era of massive institutional failure.' It's hard to find any institutions, whether they're in business or education, social services, government, that are really performing well. You could say the healthiest institution is hardly healthy if you look at the well-being of most of its members.

"But even if you take this idea of massive institutional breakdown seriously, it's not like everyone wakes up one morning and says, 'Ah, we've got it all wrong. We need to change.' Quite the opposite. What you see is most of the resources of these institutions, most of the resources of society, desperately trying to preserve the status quo. In a time of breakdown, it's a time of great fear. And in this state of fear, people revert to what's most habitual. That's a basic human instinct, wired into our neuro-anatomy and psychology.

"On the other hand, there are also innovators who say, 'Ah, this is a great space to create something new.' So in times of great change, you see cross currents and a clash of forces, and I don't expect that to get any easier.

"Just look at the behavior of our own country. It's extraordinarily hard for Americans to wake up and realize that we live in a very different world today. The twenty-first century is probably going to be the Chinese century, not the American century. Rapid shifts are occurring around the world in power and influence, and yet we're still acting like everybody wants to be an American, and we have the answer to all the world's problems, and all we have to do is help those poor people do it like we do it.

"That's a classic response to these kinds of cross currents. In a state of fear, just as individuals revert to what's most habitual, societies try to go back to their core traditions, and so what you see everywhere around the world is a turn to fundamentalism—people who have *the* answer and *the* answer is the old way, whether its Christian fundamentalism, Islamic fundamentalism, or U.S. democratic fundamentalism.

"You see fundamentalists within business just as you see fundamentalists within societies, who say that the old way is the right way and we're going to seize power and keep power and traditional ways of doing things. While most businesses cannot deny that their markets are changing, they may still try to cope by reasserting top-down control."

Have Europeans been more open to a more holistic model of business?

What helps people, helps business.

—Leo Burnett

"It depends on the particular issue that you look at. For example, on environmental issues, there has long been a much greater sensitivity in the European societies and the European-based businesses. People who live in relatively small countries have had to deal a long time with the fact that there's no place to put all the junk. If we pollute our river, it flows into your country.

"So today, the European Union (EU) is leading the world in a whole host of new kinds of mandates for business. For example, if you sell an automobile in Europe today, the manufacturer is responsible for taking that automobile back at the end of its lifetime. You can't just dump it in a hole someplace. This law, in fact, was the result, in part, of a few European companies, particularly BMW, doing pioneering work about fifteen years ago designing cars for what's called remanufacture and recycle. There are a lot of valuable components in the car, why don't you design the car so when it has completed its use, you bring it back and reuse them. There's actually a strong economic case that can be made for that, if you design the car with that in mind.

"However, you have to invest in building the expertise. You have to invest in developing a different approach to manufacturing. You have to invest in developing a very different relationship with your suppliers so they can work together with you to design a car that can be taken apart at the end of its lifetime.

"The same is true in many consumer electronics. Most consumer electronics, particularly the bigger items in Europe today, must be taken back by the producer at the end of the product's use.

"The EU is also starting to get on top of the toxins in products. It's not bad luck that so many of us have friends who have cancers in their thirties and forties that nobody ever used to get until they were seventy years old. Undoubtedly, the two primary causes are our food and our manufactured products. Toxins in our personal computers, or in the dyes in our clothes, or in our children's plastic toys get there because manufacturers traditionally haven't really paid much attention to these matters. They use materials based on cost and functionality. If the chemicals that were in your kid's plastic toys or in textile dyes were put into a drug, they would be regulated. But, by and large, if you put it into a toy or a dye for a sweater, nobody regulates it. The EU is starting to change all of that.

"The companies who will excel in the transition to a new kind of business will be ones that can tap the imagination, spirit, and capability to innovate their people. That's what I mean by learning to grow an enterprise by growing the people."

A CONVERSATION ON THE BRIDGE WITH TERRY MOLLNER

Terry Mollner, Ed.D. (www.calvertfoundation.org), is one of the earliest pioneers of modern socially responsible investing. Since the 1970s, he has helped the industry grow from nothing to the fastest-growing asset class of the professional investment community, with more than $2 trillion in investment in the U.S., 15 percent of mutual fund assets, and a growing presence in investment communities around the world.

Terry is the founder, chair, and executive director of Trusteeship Institute, Inc., a think tank and consulting firm founded in 1973 that focuses on the development of socially responsible businesses, employee-owned cooperatives, and spiritually based enterprises. He is also a founder and member of the board of trustees of the Calvert Family of Socially Responsible Mutual Funds, the Calvert Foundation, and Spirit in Business, Inc.

We asked Terry to describe his vision of corporate transformation. "Currently, our multinational corporations give highest priority to the interests of a few—called the shareholders—at the expense of the many. That's an immoral contract with society. The moral imperative is to give priority to the good of all, and second priority to our own self-interest. Thus, we have a legal contract between corporations and governments that is fundamentally immoral. No matter how many restrictions we place on corporations, their priority is still the interest of a few at the expense of the many.

"The new corporation that's coming into existence is a corporation that will freely choose to give priority to the good of all of humanity. Once it figures out how to do this and do this well, such a corporation will have a tremendous ability to outperform all the other corporations because it'll be able to get tremendous customer loyalty. It will also demonstrate resilience during difficult times because everybody isn't just thinking about themselves, so people will tend to stick together. And it should, on every other basis, have the smarts to be able to outdo the other corporations.

Such is the brutalization of commercial ethics in this country that no one can feel anything more delicate than the velvet touch of a soft buck.

—Raymond Chandler

"I call this new form the *relationship corporation*. There's a board of trustees of only three or four people and they have only one job: to make sure the highest priority is the good of all. They delegate all of the responsibility for running the company under this principle to a board of directors— which is much like the current board of directors— responsible for setting policy and running the company. The board of trustees maintains the right to veto any decision made by the board of directors or management, and it has a representative sitting in at all meetings to see what's going on and to help them out. If there ever is a disagreement about what gives priority to the good of all, in terms of wages or product safety, or whatever, the board of trustees and the board of directors will meet to try to solve the problem.

"Further, the board of trustees commits itself to trying never to exercise the veto power. This will be something unique in our society: an eldering situation wherein the board of trustees reaches agreement with the directors to achieve the highest priority in all circumstances."

What will happen to profits in this new corporate paradigm? "The relationship corporation sets a ceiling on profits," says Terry. "Its highest priority is to end up with surplus profits that it doesn't have to pay to any investors. So it pays investors what it needs to pay them, whatever is necessary to raise capital or maintain capital. Same thing with bonds. It will only pay the interest rate it feels it needs to pay and it will redeem the bonds whenever it thinks it's best to redeem them. All the money in profits beyond that will be managed for the good of humanity in one or two ways: either by investing it in relationship investment banking firms, which will be about the business of buying more companies and converting them to be relationship corporations; or by donating it to charitable and education activities around the world."

Does Terry think that global evolution will encourage the positive transformation of corporations? "I think China will be the pivotal force. Americans tend to think the whole world is going to change to want to be like us, and so they think China is going to implode, as the Soviet Union did. But it's not going to happen. China is a very different kind of animal; it's very smart and has figured out a lot of things. A number of nations now realize that they have to get into competition with the multinationals because that's where the main game is being played. Norway, for instance, has taken action to end up with tremendous control over its private companies. And Russia is reorganizing to be like China. Hugo Chavez, the president of Venezuela, has figured out what's going on and he's starting to try to get South America to organize together and emulate China.

"Just think of the country as one corporation where all the people in the country work for the same company and they all happen to live on the campus of the company. In other words, a communist state is nothing but a Western corporation. But China has figured out that they should allow the creation of small enterprises because that encourages competition and a lot of good things flow from that. The smart companies that succeed and grow will only be able to sell to the government-owned multinationals. China, Inc. is going around the world and buying up natural resource companies. But unlike companies in the West, China will never be interested in selling these companies. Its interest is the long-term interest of its shareholders, that is, the Chinese people. If Western corporations are going to compete, they're going to have to establish the good of the people as their highest priority. So that's going to allow for the emergence of the relationship corporation. That's a flip that's going to happen rapidly."

TAKE THIS JOB AND LOVE IT

As you can see, big changes are afoot inside Corporate America. Positive changes. There are many companies who genuinely value their employees and their contributions. As the flip evolves, more and more corporate leaders and their businesses get on board to move away from the crumbling paradigm of the upside-down world.

Still, many people work in jobs they don't like because they feel trapped by circumstance. In fact, three-quarters of us are so unhappy, underpaid, or unappreciated that we are actively seeking employment elsewhere. Since a large part of our time is spent working, shouldn't we apply our skills to something we love, for a company we believe in?

Of course that's easier said than done. Granted, some of us do not have the skills, experience, or capabilities required to work our fantasy job, but we do have the ability to make the most of who we truly are. Ask yourself this: "What could I do to change my company for the better?" If you have a good list of ideas, take them to your supervisor. If you don't, envision a job you would love—and begin to take steps to find it. If you can't find it, create it.

Many of us are financially burdened by the material possessions we think we need to own. We've accumulated debt that we must repay and, even though we are working at a place we don't like, believe that we have no choice. But, as the chapter on flipping the mind revealed, there are many more choices than "either/or." Don't convince yourself that you must remain in a work situation that doesn't suit you. Work to change the environment, or move to a company that appreciates you and your talents.

Believe in yourself. If you aren't willing to stake your claim to an equitable wage for a good day's work, then who will? Many states, cities, and towns have implemented living wages higher than the minimum. Seek out those who will recognize and appreciate your gifts—whatever they may be. There are millions of entrepreneurial and socially responsible companies that would love to hire an honest, motivated person.

You have a right to work in the Right-Side Up world. Make the flip in your workplace. A more fulfilling life awaits!

FLIP TIPS

- Do not get your identity from your job.
- If you are unhappy at work, make the leap to a company you respect.
- Do your best work possible and leave the office each day with the knowledge that you made a contribution.
- Don't engage in gossip or the office rumor mill.
- Praise others when deserved.
- Make suggestions for improving processes and communication at your office.
- Unless absolutely critical, as in essential or emergency services, do not make yourself accessible by cell phone and pager after hours.
- Start a recycling program at your office.
- Find a local charity for your business to support.
- Encourage your firm to join the socially responsible business movement.
- Ride your bicycle or take public transit to work.
- Buy products from companies that share your values.
- Whenever possible, support local vendors.
- Invest in socially responsible funds (www.socialinvest.org).

TEN

FLIPPING THE TRIGGER

From Tribal Warfare to Global Tribe

Barry is confused. He is torn between what his fragmented mind fears and what his heart knows. His overstimulated senses are fed sound bite after sound bite in support of war, carefully designed to play on his insecurity. He finds himself harboring hostile thoughts toward people halfway around the globe whom he has never met. Even though he feels ill at ease about many aspects of the direction the United States is headed, he wanted to believe, perhaps needed to believe, that our leaders would get it right this time. The patriotic stirring lodged within him from years of reciting the Pledge of Allegiance in school and hearing the Star-Spangled Banner to commence every sporting event is powerful within Barry.

Our lives begin to end the day we become silent about things that matter.

—Martin Luther King

His life is in such shambles that Barry longs for something to believe in, to cheer on, to distract him from the mounting evidence that his life is spinning out of control. His frustration, resentment, and seething anger at his own circumstances are transferred to "evildoers" an upside-down world away. There is power in believing one lives in the greatest nation on Earth. Deep-seated masculine energy and pride well up into near defiant chest thumping at the thought of "bombing them back to the Stone Age."

It isn't hard to push his buttons. Barry's hostility is reinforced by angry rhetoric from politicians with hidden agendas, paid corporate shills acting as media analysts, and political flaks who callously believe the ends justify the means. He loves his country and is proud to be an American. In 2003, because of his insecurities about his job, his overextended finances, and his faltering relationships, Barry found himself secretly cheering for the impending war with Iraq. Like watching your favorite football team crush the competition, there is glory and pride, however hollow, in rooting your side on to victory. It is oddly empowering.

Barry bought into the political drumbeat and the media mantra, which went like this: The terrorists attacked us on September 11, 2001, so we attacked Afghanistan and then Iraq. But only a sliver of logic is needed to realize that fifteen of the nineteen terrorists on 9/11 were from Saudi Arabia and if any country had culpability it was the Saudis, not the Afghanis or Iraqis. Saddam Hussein, while evil and despicable by any standard, had nothing to do with attacking the United States. As the rationale for war changed from one excuse to another, those who believed the misinformation campaign feverishly backed the war. In the black-and-white thinking of the upside-down world, "you're either with us or against us."

For the majority of people around the world who knew the war was about oil and Middle East domination, fervor against war increased. The politicians and media ignored the pleas for peace. They casually dismissed the concerns of tens of millions of protestors worldwide as naïve and misinformed.

Truth be told, Barry didn't want to know the truth. He had bills to pay. There was trouble at work. In the upside-down world, fear-based minds rationalize and justify any action the government wants to take to keep us safe. It doesn't matter if it is fair or makes sense. Barry's willful sacrifice of his conscience is merely a natural extension of the commitments he broke to himself a long time ago, of the surrender of his potential, of the unrealized promise of his own life.

Barry doesn't have to fight the war. He can watch it on TV instead, away from the violence, the destruction, and the deaths of thousands of innocents. His bumper-sticker patriotism is slapped in red, white, and blue on the chrome of his SUV—United We Stand and Support Our Troops. On the eve of the second Gulf War, Barry made a batch of buttery popcorn, opened a beer, turned on CNN, and plopped down in his La-Z-Boy recliner for an evening of "shock and awe."

In Barry's world, the war has no consequence. Sure, he's paying more at the pump, more for his heating and electric, higher local and state taxes, and numerous social services have been cut, but that is the extent of Barry's sacrifice. The war had no real emotional consequence to Barry other than the inconvenience of higher bills and lower discretionary income.

Two years after the infamous stage-set "Mission Accomplished" claim by

George W. Bush on the aircraft carrier U.S.S. Lincoln, Barry has a nagging feeling that he was duped. He still doesn't want to believe it. The inner conflict is accosting him on all levels of his being. He can no longer ignore mountains of evidence.

Barry's naïveté dramatically changed one evening. Tom, his best friend, called choking back tears. Tom's brother had been killed in Mosul, Iraq, by a roadside bomb. For the first time in years, Barry cried. A flood of emotion washed over him as he could no longer reconcile his own self-denial. All the facts and all the lies lined up clearly for Barry, and his purposeful delusion was dispelled. The war in Iraq was a horrendous mistake.

FOOLED AGAIN

Millions of Americans have awakened to the deceptions of war as packaged by our leaders. Unfortunately, our most current war was sold to us in a fashion similar to all previous wars. Wrapped in the flag, amidst promises of democracy and freedom, we are manipulated into thinking that we are right, our cause is just. We are admonished that we must use our power to help the downtrodden in foreign lands, even if they don't want our help. We are browbeaten into believing that peace only comes through force and that, in the grand scheme of things, some people must be sacrificed for a greater good. But that argument doesn't justify the grieving of innocent civilians who have lost their children, partners, parents, and friends.

Anyone who has ever looked into the glazed eyes of a soldier dying on the battlefield will think hard before starting a war.
—Otto Von Bismarck

The war in Iraq is not an isolated incident, or a conflict that could not be avoided. We've been down this bombed-out road before. Let's take a quick peek at U.S. military interventions and covert actions since 1945. We aren't making any judgments whether these actions were justified or not, simply presenting a list:

China	1945–46, 1950–53
Philippines	1946–54
Korea	1950–53
Iran	1953
Guatemala	1954, 1960, 1967–69
Indonesia	1958

Cuba	1959–61
Peru	1965
Vietnam	1960–1975
Laos	1964–73
Cambodia	1969–75
Chile	1973
Grenada	1983–84
Libya	1986
Nicaragua	1981–90
Iran	1987–88 (U.S. intervenes, supports Iraq)
Panama	1989
Iraq	1990
Bosnia	1993
Haiti	1994
Sudan	1998
Yugoslavia	1999
Afghanistan	2001–
Philippines	2002
Iraq	2003–

"I believe in adequate defense at the coastline and nothing else. If a nation comes over here to fight, then we'll fight. The trouble with America is that when the dollar only earns 6 percent over here, then it gets restless and goes overseas to get 100 percent. Then the flag follows the dollar and the soldiers follow the flag. I wouldn't go to war again as I have done to protect some lousy investment of the bankers. There are two things we should fight for. One is the defense of our homes and the other is the Bill of Rights. War for any other reason is simply a racket."

So said Major General Smedley Bulter, USMC, the highest-ranking Marine of his day, in a speech in 1933. His book *War Is a Racket* (republished by Feral House, 2003) is a classic condemnation of war.

If it were true that we fight wars for benevolent means, why did we stand by and allow the recent genocide in Sudan; past genocides in East Timor, Cambodia, Rwanda, and Yugoslavia; or continually look the other way from various despots around the world who have brutalized their people?

IRRATIONAL DEFENSE

We would like to state unequivocally that we believe in a strong national defense to protect this great land. The military should be used to keep the citizens of the country safe and secure. However, waging war to serve capitalistic enterprises smacks of imperialism, regardless of how it is painted by our politicians. Our foreign policy is not as altruistic as our leaders want us to believe.

In 1795, James Madison said in *Political Observations,* "Of all the enemies of liberty, war is, perhaps, the most to be dreaded because it compromises and develops the germ of every other. War is the parent of armies; from these proceed debts and taxes . . . known instruments for bringing many under the domination of the few. No nation could preserve its freedom in the midst of continual warfare."

A common-sense look at the previous list of military interventions tells us that we have been in the midst of continual warfare since before World War II. It has become the American way of life. In fact, it is estimated that 7.5 million Americans (6 percent of the workforce) labor in support of the war economy, with another 7 million in retail and service sectors that indirectly depend on defense spending. That's approximately 12 percent of the workforce dependent on war for its livelihood.

So, how did we get here? The trail isn't hard to track; all we need to do is follow the money. As World War II was winding down and the lofty levels of defense spending with it, Charles E. Wilson, director of the War Production Board and, oh yeah, president of General Electric, proposed a permanent war economy as the answer to economic stability. So the thinking went that in order to have decent wages and a healthy economy, we have to kill people in other nations—on a regular basis.

How do we maintain our dominance in warfare and funding for the war economy? Your tax dollars and future debt funneled into the defense budget look like this:

Fiscal Year 2006	$441.6 billion
Fiscal Year 2005	$420.7 billion
Fiscal Year 2004	$399.1 billion
Fiscal Year 2003	$396.1 billion
Fiscal Year 2002	$343.2 billion
Fiscal Year 2001	$305 billion

Amazingly, in brazen sleight-of-hand, these numbers do not include money for wars in Afghanistan and Iraq or the budget for Homeland

Security. The next closest spender on defense is Russia at $65.2 billion, whom we outspent by six times. Then comes China at $56 billion and the United Kingdom at $49 billion. U.S. defense spending is thirty times larger than the combined spending of the seven "rogue" states of Cuba, Iran, Iraq, Libya, North Korea, Sudan, and Syria. This isn't a recent isolated development; we've outspent the rest of the world by vast amounts year after year.

So how much do we spend on, say, education or health care? Education, by comparison to defense spending, gets $60 billion of the U.S. budget, or approximately eight times less funding. Health care gets $51 billion. In the upside-down world we spend more to kill than we do to educate; we spend more to maim than we do to heal. So, what do you think our national priorities are—quality of life or quantity of death? These are your tax dollars being used to wage war. Again, a strong defense is good. But the evidence suggests that our leaders have taken this beyond reason.

Here's what President Dwight D. Eisenhower had to say on the matter in 1953: "Every gun that is made, every warship that is launched, every rocket fired, signifies, in the final sense, a theft from those who hunger and are not fed, those who are cold and are not clothed."

We used to wonder where war lived, what it was that made it so vile. And now we realize that we know where it lives, that it is inside ourselves.

—Albert Camus

But didn't the tragic events of 9/11 change everything? Actually not; what followed soon afterward was business as usual. Amidst the sorrow and the flag waving, massive amounts of war profiteering took place. Billions of dollars were diverted in the name of Homeland Security, but never made it to where it matters. Huge war budgets were approved with little oversight. Unparalleled corruption and cronyism, unmatched in modern times, smothered doing what was right and necessary. Tax cuts were given to the rich, and social programs for the less fortunate gutted. The politics of greed won again.

These are not just our conclusions. The General Accounting Office, the Inspector General, dozens of audits by watchdog groups, and countless media reports have documented gouging and profiteering at taxpayer expense and the expense of our collective health, safety, and security. No amount of blind loyalty and patriotism can hide the hideous truth. We've been sold out by our politicians and members of corporate America in the name of national security. It's upside-down and it's a disgrace.

Here's another reminder of U.S. intention from Major General Smedley

Butler, "I helped make Mexico, especially Tampico, safe for American oil interests in 1914. I helped make Haiti and Cuba a decent place for the National City Bank boys to collect revenues in. I helped in the raping of half a dozen Central American republics for the benefits of Wall Street. The record of racketeering is long. I helped purify Nicaragua for the international banking house of Brown Brothers in 1909–1912. I brought light to the Dominican Republic for American sugar interests in 1916. In China I helped to see to it that Standard Oil went its way unmolested."

> **Though force can protect in emergency, only justice, fairness, consideration, and cooperation can finally lead men to the dawn of eternal peace.**
>
> —Dwight D. Eisenhower

Still not convinced? Consider that U.S. armaments manufacturers are the world's largest exporter of weaponry with a 53 percent market share. This is accomplished through tax credits and outright grants to foreign countries. According to the Arms Trade Resource Center, the U.S. sold $177.5 billion in arms to foreign countries in the last decade. Twenty of the top twenty-five U.S. armaments clients in the developing world were either undemocratic regimes or ones with records of major human rights violations.

If we are a peace-loving nation, why are we exporting weapons to murderous regimes? Weapons create instability, insecurity, and conflict. Only the upside-down world holds the view that more violent means of destruction create peace. This is twisted logic at its worse.

THE UNDISPUTED HEAVYWEIGHT CHAMPION OF THE WORLD

We know you won't want to hear this; it's a bitter pill to swallow. Sadly, the number one aggressor on the world stage by far is the United States of America. Here's the evidence:

- The U.S. refuses to pay its dues to the United Nations.
- The U.S. is against the International Criminal Court.
- The U.S. has called the Geneva Convention, which protects the rights of prisoners, "quaint" and declared that we are not required to follow it.
- The U.S. refuses to sign the international treaty to ban land mines despite 177 other countries doing so.

- The U.S. refuses to sign an Internet "hate speech" ban.
- The U.S. refuses to sign the nuclear test ban treaty.
- The U.S. watered down a U.N. agreement against small arms trafficking.
- The U.S. refuses to ratify the nuclear reduction treaty with Russia.

The man who led the Allies to victory in Europe during World War II, President Dwight D. Eisenhower, said in 1961, "In the councils of government, we must guard against the acquisition of unwarranted influence, whether sought or unsought, by the military/industrial complex. The potential for the disastrous rise of misplaced power exists and will persist.

"We must never let the weight of this combination endanger our liberties or democratic processes. We should take nothing for granted. Only an alert and knowledgeable citizenry can compel the proper meshing of the huge industrial and military machinery of defense with our peaceful methods and goals, so that security and liberty may prosper together."

Eisenhower knew the dangers of unchecked authority. We are now living in the unfortunate reality of his prophetic warning.

ALL IS NOT LOST

> There never was a good war or a bad peace.
> —Benjamin Franklin

Mary knows in her heart that peace begins inside each individual. For years she viewed the politics of the nation with casual fascination but could not bring herself to vote for either Democrats or Republicans, as both seemed like different branches of the same political party: the Corporate Party. An astute student of history and human nature, Mary knows that both major parties rush to war on behalf of corporate interests. But she isn't radical; Mary doesn't feel like throwing bricks at city hall or trashing the leaders of this country.

She knows that the government is a reflection of the people. As above, so below. As below, so above. We are all a connected part of the whole. One. If our politics are corrupt, then it's because there is something in our leaders that is in ourselves as well. That is hard to admit. We have chosen ignorance over knowledge, silence over action. Mary also knows that most humans change for two reasons: for the promise of something better, or through the duress of crisis. It is a long, often painful process through which individual humans evolve to become wiser, better human beings.

In the run-up to the last war, Mary heard all the regurgitated sound bites at the office: "We can't afford to let the smoking gun become a mushroom cloud"; and "Saddam Hussein can launch a biological attack within forty-five minutes"; or "We have to fight the terrorists over there, so we don't face them over here."

She didn't buy any of it. She followed the logic and the money and dismissed the standard rhetoric packaged by the media. It's a simple formula: *The world has forty years of oil left at best. Iraq is sitting on top of the second largest supply on the planet. There is money to be made. Saddam is a villain so let's demonize him further and go take his oil—and control the Middle East at the same time.*

Mary did what she could to voice her opinion. She wrote letters to her elected representatives, attended rallies, and wrote letters to the editor. She used the Web to send information to as many people as possible. She meditated and prayed for peace. And even though our country went to war anyway and she feels saddened by the needless death and destruction, Mary takes solace in the fact that millions of people have had their consciousness awakened. Through crisis comes change.

> **We look forward to the time when the Power of Love will replace the Love of Power. Then will our world know the blessings of Peace.**
> —William E. Gladstone

For Mary, peace is a state of being. It starts with each individual and ripples out from there. If we, personally, are angry, violent, intolerant, racist, or insensitive, we abdicate our right to expect something better from others; and worse, we reinforce that this behavior is okay in others. It is akin to parents warning their teenager about the perils of smoking as they light up a cigarette. Humans of all ages in all nations see hypocrisy for what it is.

Mary sees great promise in the Web as the great equalizer for exposing lies and revealing truth. Those who seek to do bad deeds love to perform their malicious acts shadowed in secrecy. But the Web and the army of bloggers, interest groups, chat rooms, discussion threads, and websites shine light in dark corners and on deals made in smoke-filled rooms.

Mary realizes that while she is turned off by politics—and lacks respect for either party—she must get involved. She knows now that it makes a huge difference who is elected and governs our land. Her awareness has led her to become more actively involved in understanding the reasons for war— beyond the obvious greed of the last war—and she has vowed to become ardent in her desire to find peaceful solutions to conflicts in her life, and dedicated to becoming part of the solution in a Right-Side Up world.

DEEP ROOTS

Like Mary and millions of others, it is our belief that peace can be created by identifying and understanding the causes of war. By knowing what triggers this most violent of human behaviors, we can work to pull it out by its roots. The skeptics among us may scoff at the notion of peace on Earth, but we are hopeful. Later in this chapter, we will present successful illustrations that peace is not only preferable to violence and war, not only possible, but has already taken hold among many nations and many people.

Experts in the fields of nonviolent communication, social justice, conflict resolution, peace advocacy, and behavioral science have documented, in extensive fashion, the causes of war. It is clear that the reasons for war are complex and fluid:

- lust for power and material wealth
- economic disparity and inequality
- ideological differences based on intolerance of others' values or morals, and nationalism fueled by politicians and/or religious leaders
- conflicting religious beliefs
- ethnic and cultural differences based on long-running animosities and conflicts
- desire for natural, industrial, and technological resources

Some experts would likely define the above in much greater detail, but our task is to offer a broad view to show a better way—a flip. Those desiring a detailed examination can visit the Pugwash online website (www.pugwash.org). Check out their 50th Annual Conference for a paper on eliminating the causes of war.

A basic principle of life is polarity—the relationship of opposing energies or forces. It stands to reason that taking each cause of war in the above list and looking for its opposite may be a wise course. But human nature is not that simple. As we stated before, the reasons for war are complex and fluid. On the surface, it is logical to think that in order to stop war based on intolerance of ideological differences, we need to instill tolerance. Ah . . . easier said than done.

How is tolerance encouraged? We can suggest that showing that "we are all one" is a good start. Accentuating our similarities and finding common ground seems a good notion. Using methods of nonviolent communication, employing conflict resolution techniques, and educating children at an early age to be open and accepting of others also sounds reasonable. Exhibiting patience and understanding with people who may have rigid views and strong egos would be useful.

But to fully understand the origins of war, we turn to those who dedicate their lives to world peace. These are the heroes we should be celebrating. The Movement for the Abolition of War (MAW) website (www.abolishwar.org.uk) offers the following suggestions for creating a culture of peace:

- Educate for peace, human rights, and democracy.
- Counter the adverse effects of globalization.
- Advance the sustainable and equitable use of environmental resources.
- Eradicate colonialism and neo-colonialism.
- Eliminate racial, ethnic, religious, and gender intolerance.
- Promote gender justice.
- Protect and respect children and youth.
- Promote international democracy and just global governance.
- Proclaim active nonviolence.
- Eliminate communal violence at the local level.
- Enlist world religions in transforming the culture of violence into a culture of peace and justice.

The Movement for the Abolition of War takes it further and offers a plan for disarmament and human security. The idea is that we can be secure without the threat of annihilation. This makes great sense to us:

- Implement a global action plan to prevent war.
- Demilitarize the global economy by reducing military budgets and shifting resources toward human security programs.
- Negotiate and ratify an international treaty to eliminate nuclear weapons.
- Prevent proliferation and use of conventional weapons, including light weapons, small arms, and guns, and safeguard personal security.
- Ratify and implement the land-mine ban treaty.
- Prevent the development and use of new weapons and new military technologies, including a ban on depleted uranium and the deployment of weapons in space.
- Encourage universal adherence to and implementation of the biological weapons convention and the chemical weapons convention.

- Hold states and corporations accountable for the impact of military production, testing, and use on the environment and health.
- Build a civil society movement for the abolition of war.

Sound impossible? Read on as we show how people around the globe have found the courage to speak truth about power and change their societies' beliefs that violence is inevitable.

DON'T KNOW MUCH ABOUT HISTORY

Much has been written about humankind's unquenchable thirst for blood and destruction. In fact, there are those who espouse the belief that all life comprises stages of creation, maintenance, or destruction, so therefore our penchant for violence through war—the destruction part of the theory—is human nature and cannot be quelled. This is simply not true.

Consider the events of the Velvet Revolution, or as the Czechs prefer, the November Events of 1989, when massive demonstrations and work stoppages toppled the Communist regime of Gustav Husak. Without a shot being fired, the people of Czechoslovakia led by two groups, the Civic Forum and People Against Violence, overthrew their oppressors. Despite calls for retribution against the former Communist leaders, Vaclav Havel insisted that his newly elected government would not partake in the bloody repression that they had worked so hard to overcome.

> **True peace between nations will only happen when there is true peace within people's souls.**
> —Native American Proverb

After centuries of subjugation and decades of apartheid, the people of South Africa peacefully rejected the elected government and voted overwhelmingly to replace it with one that was more tolerant of all people. Nelson Mandela, previously imprisoned for life as a dissident, was elected president of South Africa. Rather than dwell on the inhumane slights done to him and his people as an excuse for retribution, President Mandela instead instituted the Truth and Reconciliation Commission (TRC). The Commission heard testimony from South African blacks, victims of violent acts, atrocities, and human rights abuses. The TRC provided an outlet for thousands of victims to be heard, and also allowed perpetrators to confess their crimes in exchange for immunity. This led to a time of great healing in South Africa and became the process through which democracy flourished.

If further evidence of a flip is needed, one only need look at Europe, which, after two devastating world wars that encompassed half a century, decided they had had enough bloodletting and needed to work toward common goals. Now, the European nations have formed the European Union, giving equal rights to all citizens of the member nations regardless of their country of origin.

Have you forgotten the great Soviet menace, which shadowed our lives and instilled fear in U.S. citizens for four decades? It was dismantled without violence by the visionary Mikhail Gorbachev, who saw that the constant competition of warmongering between the Soviet Union and the United States was an insane zero sum game which no one could win. President Gorbachev simply decided he wasn't going to play that game anymore—and he quit. End of the Soviet Union, end of the Cold War.

CONVERSATIONS ON THE BRIDGE

Let's hear what our experts on flipping the trigger have to say about bringing peace to a troubled world. In this section, Nobel Prize-winner Oscar Arias, formerly president of Costa Rica, describes how diplomacy can be used to broker peace. Marshall Rosenberg, a leader in the field of nonviolent communication, details the miraculous healing and bonding that can take place when people feel they are heard. And finally, Barbara Marx Hubbard speaks about the dividends paid by creating a cabinet-level position for the Department of Peace.

When you read about the dedicated work and open-minded views of these leaders, we are confident you will be as hopeful as we are.

A CONVERSATION ON THE BRIDGE WITH DR. OSCAR ARIAS

Oscar Arias (www.arias.or.cr) is the president of Costa Rica and a 1987 Nobel Peace Laureate. Dr. Arias holds international stature as a spokesperson for the developing world. Championing such issues as human development, democracy, and demilitarization, he has traveled the globe spreading a message of peace and applying the lessons garnered from the Central American Peace Process to topics of current global debate. The *New York Times* reported that Oscar Arias's "positions on Central American issues have become the standards by which many people in Congress and elsewhere have come to judge United States policy." In a similar way, he has come to take a leading position in international forums and discourse.

We asked him about his sources of inspiration: "I was inspired by the great peacemakers of history, such as Mahatma Gandhi and Martin Luther King, Jr., and began where they began—with a dream, a belief. This is what gave me the strength to confront the practical difficulties involved in the process of ending violence and turmoil in Central America. For as I learned from Gandhi and King, peace starts with conviction, ends with cynicism, and endures through sacrifice. If we do not first believe peace is possible, we will not be willing to do the hard work necessary to achieve it.

"Underlying the sheer moral necessity of bringing an end to the violence was my unwavering certainty that Central America could not develop economically if it was not at peace. It was in the best interests of the nations' leaders and their people to turn off the potholed road of autocracy and war onto the highway of democracy and development. It has been a rocky on-ramp, to say the least."

During the Arias administration of Costa Rica, the country maintained the healthiest economy and highest standard of living in the region. We wondered what Oscar's formula might be for raising the global standard of living. He answered, "This may seem obvious, but it is remarkable how closely tied prosperity is to peace.

> **One little person, giving all her time to peace, makes news. Many people, giving some of their time, can make history.**
>
> —Peace Pilgrim

Compare, for instance, the rates of economic growth in Central American nations during and after their armed conflicts of the 1980s and early '90s. From 1980–1990, the gross domestic product in El Salvador declined at an average annual rate of 0.2 percent. From 1990–2003, the rate of growth jumped to a positive 4.0 percent. In the 1980s, Guatemala's average annual growth rate was 0.8 percent, compared to 3.8 percent from 1990–2003. The greatest change came in Nicaragua, where GDP declined at an average rate of 1.9 percent between 1980 and 1990, but grew by 3.7 percent between 1990 and 2003.

"As mediocre as these economic recoveries have been, they are less heart-breaking than the total stagnation and deterioration experienced during the troubled times of armed conflict. It is a harsh but simple reality that if a country is at war, companies will be reluctant to invest there. Moreover, vast amounts of military spending could be better spent elsewhere. The world spends close to $1 trillion every year on weapons. And yet the United Nations Development Program (UNDP) estimates that it would only take $7 billion per year to provide 2.6 billion additional people with access to clean water, saving around four thousand lives per day. Debt forgiveness saves lives as well: according to another UNDP estimate, nineteen thousand children die every day in sub-Saharan Africa because governments must spend money on debt payment and servicing rather than on basic health care. Regions engaged in armed conflict need to go through the laborious processes of peace and demilitarization in order to raise the standards of living of their people."

Is there a way to demilitarize the entire planet? "Although a demilitarized planet seems painfully out of reach," Oscar comments, "I have always believed in setting big goals. Here is my vision: A hundred years from now, I would like my great-grandchildren to enjoy a world in which each government is democratically elected, is able to fulfill its people's basic needs, remains at peace with both its neighbors and its internal opposition, and uses the tools of economics and science to the benefit of all its people.

All the war propaganda, all the screaming and lies and hatred, comes invariably from people who are not fighting.

—George Orwell

"Although global arms expenditures continue to rise, there is a glimmer of hope that we may be moving in the right direction: International support for an Arms Trade Treaty (ATT) is growing. The ATT has its origins in the International Code of Conduct on Arms Transfers, signed by eight Nobel Peace Laureates in New York in 1997. Since then, a draft of a comprehensive, legally binding ATT has grown out of the principles set forth in the International Code of Conduct. The ATT, in summary, would prohibit the transfer of all arms that are likely to be used for violation of international law or human rights, or that significantly impair the goals of sustainable development. As of July 2005, over thirty governments have expressed their support for the ATT, including the United Kingdom, Costa Rica, Finland, Kenya, Spain, Colombia, Turkey, and Uganda. The sooner the treaty is implemented, the sooner lives will be saved. Will the planet ever be completely free of arms? Let's start with the ATT, and work from there."

A CONVERSATION ON THE BRIDGE WITH DR. MARSHALL ROSENBERG

Dr. Marshall B. Rosenberg is founder and director of educational services for the Center for Nonviolent Communication (www.cnvc.org), an international nonprofit organization. Nonviolent Communication training evolved from Dr. Rosenberg's quest to find a way to rapidly disseminate much-needed peacemaking skills. The Center for Nonviolent Communication emerged out of work he was doing with civil rights activists in the early 1960s. During this period, he provided mediation and communication skills training to communities working to peacefully desegregate schools and other public institutions.

Worldwide reactions to his work have been inspiring. Evaluations indicate that this training vastly strengthens the ability to connect compassionately with oneself and others, as well as to resolve differences peacefully. Reports also indicate that the benefit of the training not only is stable over time, but actually increases. We were curious to know how the early circumstances of Marshall's life placed him on the path to developing Nonviolent Communication. "As a child my family moved to Detroit just in time for the race riots of 1943. We lived in the inner city and for four days we couldn't go out of the house. We were locked in because there was violence going on in the streets; thirty people were killed in our neighborhood during that time.

"As a nine-year-old boy, locked in the house and being aware that I couldn't go out because of my skin color taught me that this is a world where some people can want to hurt you for no good reason. To accentuate this lesson, when I started school I found out my last name was a stimulus for hatred. When people heard my last name was 'Rosenberg' they were waiting for me after school and they treated me to some violence. As a child I kept wondering *why, why, why?* When it came time to decide what I wanted to do for a living, I chose to go to the university and study psychology. What I was looking for was just the answer to a couple of questions, the ones that I had ever since I was a child: *What makes some people compassionate no matter what their social conditions?* and *What turns other people to violence?*

"When I meet compassionate people in countries suffering horrible conditions, I'm always eager to ask them, 'What has helped you to stay compassionate in a world that contributes so much to violence?' The answer is that they didn't get disconnected. I think it's our nature to be compassionate. In exercises I've taught all over the world, I have asked people to think of something they did recently that enriched someone else's life. Then I ask them how they feel. And they feel wonderful. So, I'm convinced that is our nature; that we are created out of an energy which makes contributing to life our highest joy."

Marshall has found that this principle works even in war-torn countries where there is enormous strife and pain. "In places like Rwanda, Bosnia, Israel, and Palestine, we bring together people from both sides. In many situations, everyone participating has lost at least one member of their family. At the beginning, it seems impossible because both sides are in such pain. But once you can get each to see each other's humanity, it's amazing what you can do in a short time. For example, in Nigeria, I was working with chiefs from both sides of warring tribes—a Christian tribe and a Muslim tribe. My colleague told me as I walked in the door that it could be a little hot in there. He said, 'There's got to be at least three people in the room that know that somebody in the room killed a member of their family.'

> In order to rally people, governments need enemies. They want us to be afraid, to hate, so we will rally behind them.
>
> —Thich Nhat Hahn

And it was very, very tense at the beginning. I explained to them that our training is focused on human needs, and my job that day was to get everyone's needs on the table. I was confident that when we saw everybody's needs, we could find a way to peacefully resolve the conflict—which had to do in that case with how many places in the marketplace each tribe could display its wares.

"So I said, 'Let's start with telling what your needs are, whoever wants to start.' A chief from one of the tribes screamed across the table, 'You people are murderers!' And he was answered, 'You people have been trying to dominate us!' So, I asked for needs, and I listened to each side tell me what was wrong with the other. I wasn't surprised, because whether it's couples who are going through divorce or nations at war, people don't know how to connect with each other's humanity.

"Instead, they resort to diagnosing what's wrong with the other. So I have to loan them the skills. I loaned the skills to the chief who had screamed 'Murderer!' I helped him describe that as a need, which was pretty obvious. I said, 'Are you saying your need is for safety and you want to be sure that no matter what conflicts are there, that they be resolved somehow other than through violence?' And he said, 'That's exactly what I mean.' There was some more back-and-forth after that, but at one point one of the chiefs said to me, 'Marshall, if we know how to communicate this way, we don't have to kill each other.'"

A CONVERSATION ON THE BRIDGE WITH BARBARA MARX HUBBARD

Barbara Marx Hubbard (www.barbaramarxhubbard.com) has been a pioneer in positive options for the future of humanity for forty years. A public speaker, author, and social innovator, she is president and executive director of the Foundation for Conscious Evolution. She has been instrumental in the founding of many future-oriented organizations, including the World Future Society, New Dimensions Radio, Global Family, Women of Vision in Action, the Foundation for the Future, and the Association for Global New Thought.

Barbara was one of the original directors of the Center for Soviet American Dialogue and served as a citizen diplomat during the late 1980s. She has written many books, including *The Hunger of Eve, The Evolutionary Journey, The Revelation: Our Crisis Is a Birth, Conscious Evolution: Awakening the Power of Our Social Potential, Emergence: The Shift from Ego to Essence,* and *Ten Steps to the Universal Human.*

Barbara told us that her worldview began changing at an early age, when she witnessed a traumatic turning point in human history. "My flip was in 1945 when the U.S. dropped atomic bombs on Japan. I was fifteen and I suddenly saw that we were going to gain so much power that we could destroy our world. The question that came to me was: What is the meaning of our new power that's good? In my search to answer this, to make a very long story short, I began to see that the meaning of our power is the conscious evolution of our species on the one hand, or devolution and extinction on the other.

"When I say 'conscious evolution,' I mean evolving our own consciousness from passively receiving the way things are to actively guiding ourselves and our social evolution. I think this is the evolution from unconscious devolution to conscious choice. We're facing a mounting whole-system crisis because every single social system is breaking down. So there are individual flips, individual innovations, and individual breakthroughs in every system. You have to look at the crisis as evolutionary stress. And problems are evolutionary drivers. Nature forms whole systems in response to these crises, or the species goes extinct."

Barbara recently received an award for her work introducing a bill in Congress to create a Department of Peace. "The Department of Peace is the rallying point for a whole movement. What it's calling for is the voice of peace and nonviolence at the highest level of government. If it works, it would mean that the Secretary of Peace would be in on the meetings about violence and war, and that voice would be heard by whoever is the president of the United States.

"The State Department only follows the foreign policy of the administration. So the Department of Peace would have a special mandate to remind everyone in power of questions like, 'How could this problem be solved through nonviolence, through conflict resolution, through cooperation?'

> **If Tyranny and Oppression come to this land, it will be in the guise of fighting a foreign enemy.**
>
> —James Madison

That voice is not currently heard at the highest levels of government. But I see the possibility of even the military realizing it cannot produce security by force alone. That's clear in Iraq right now, where we have a very powerful military with no equal in the world bogged down by an insurgency. We have the ability to destroy any enemy, but we can't build peace. We can't build or rebuild a culture with our military. So I'm planning to meet with people in the military to see if there could be a sacred alliance between the peace movement and the new forces for security in the United States. The people in the military are so sophisticated, but they have to have a new strategy, a new purpose of providing security and peace."

It's a Matter of Culture

Believe it or not, there are peaceful societies to which we can look for inspiration. The Zuni tribe of the American Southwest, the Arapesh of New Guinea, the Semai of Malaysia, the Xingo of Brazil, the Kogi tribe of Peru, and the Buid of Mindoro—all are societies that accept the possibility of violence but stigmatize anger, violence, boasting, and arguing. They honor those who ascribe to generosity and gentleness. These are cultures that promote the importance of the individual to the greater good of all.

So, it can be done. It is a matter of culture. It is a matter of who and what we choose to be. It is matter of vision, of will, of heart.

If the United States turned its great power into a force for good, we would reap untold benefits. Our might could indeed stop all wars. We could support the United Nations in real peacekeeping efforts rather than token exercises with no impact. We could educate every child in our country, teaching them critical thinking and self-reliance, instilling confidence so that our leaders cannot mislead us into unnecessary conflicts. We could redirect a full 50 percent of the defense budget (and still outspend everyone else) toward the Apollo Alliance and create a strong, energy-efficient country that doesn't need foreign adventures to feed its energy addiction. We could eradicate poverty. We could focus our energies on cleaning up the environment. We could provide health care to every man, woman, and child in this great nation regardless of income. We could tend to the elderly and allow them grace and dignity in their twilight years. We could reduce violence in our own streets. We could put our attention on preventing drug addiction rather than incarcerating the addicts.

We can turn an upside-down world Right-Side Up in just a few short years. A dream, you say? A fool's errand? What is the upside-down alternative? More bloodshed? More dead innocents? More crying mothers and distraught fathers? More anger, rage, and retribution? More of the same is not an answer.

The flip is occurring. But this one, perhaps the most important of them all, requires you. It cannot happen without you. The world needs your commitment, your strength, your resolve, and your enduring love to make the flip toward worldwide peace. We all deserve a better world. Let's create it together.

FLIP TIPS

- Find peace within yourself.
- Reduce your exposure to violent TV shows and video games.
- Write or call your elected politicians on behalf of peaceful solutions.
- Learn nonviolent communication (www.cnvc.org).
- Question your elected officials.
- Realize that it is not unpatriotic to hold our leaders accountable.
- Support the brave men and women in the armed services.
- When you catch the media in a lie, call them on it.
- Don't purchase products from companies that promote aggression, such as defense contractors and their subsidiaries, oil companies, or companies that exploit indigenous populations.
- Join the online peace movement.
- If you are a person of faith, find out where your church stands on the issue of war.
- Support groups and causes that seek to eradicate poverty and educate people in developing countries.
- Travel abroad with an open mind.
- Sponsor a foreign exchange student—the exchange of cultures breaks down barriers and helps us all to see that we are One.

ELEVEN

FLIPPING THE LIGHT

From God-Fearing Believers
to Spiritual Human Beings

Barry was raised in a casual Christian environment. Churchgoing for the family was sporadic at best. His father didn't attend except for holidays, weddings, and the occasional funeral, but his mom found comfort in church. She appreciated the ceremony, the metaphor and symbolism, and the lessons of her faith. She loved the sense of belonging, of being part of something bigger than herself. As a kid, Barry used his dad's inconsistency about church as his excuse for not attending. In the tug of war between his mom's faith and his dad's ambivalence, Barry got a mild sprinkling of doctrine and dogma.

> **One often worships something as a substitute for understanding it.**
> —Raymond M. Smullyan

He didn't care for it. Without giving it a chance or even trying to understand the meaning and value of religion, Barry dismissed it. He decided the Bible was a fairy tale, a successfully marketed collection of fables written by men with an agenda. Barry didn't have to delve too far into the Bible to find the contradictions that would enable him to condemn it.

Lately, hearing the angry rhetoric of fundamentalist preachers and televangelists heaping blame on gays, feminists, and liberals for everything from hurricanes, floods, and tornadoes to the 9/11 terrorist attacks, Barry has lumped all people of faith into the same basket. He thinks anyone believing in God is foolish. His lack of belief is reinforced when he hears men of the cloth cozying up to politicians in order to make their moral authority law. Barry believes firmly in the separation of church and state as espoused in the Constitution, but he doesn't voice his opinion outside his living room or neighborhood bar. And even though the hypocrisy of politicized evangelists irks him, he will not get involved. He'll leave that fight to others.

Barry's life, stressed by work, bills, and a numbing daily pace, lacks meaning and purpose. He loves his family but feels emotionally distant. The inability to access and nurture his spirit leaves Barry hollow. He is lost, finding only fleeting comfort in physical activities—eating, watching TV, gorging on sports, sleep, work, and sex. Despite the great fortune of living in the richest nation on Earth, Barry is spiritually impoverished. He no longer knows what he believes, if anything.

MORE THAN 6.5 BILLION SERVED

By the time this book hits the market, there will be more than 6.5 billion people on the planet. And, we might add, there will be that many belief systems, all of them correct for the individual holding that belief at that place in time. Some believe in a wrathful god who will judge us and cast us into the sulfur-scented fires of hell. Others believe in a loving, all-knowing god who will lift us up to heaven upon our demise. Still others believe in neither heaven nor hell, but have strong faith in a Creator.

> I don't know what your destiny will be but one thing I know. The only ones among us who will be truly happy are those who have sought and found how to serve.
>
> —Albert Schweitzer

Those who have been exposed to a variety of belief systems and sects, such as Christianity, Judaism, Hinduism, Islam, Wicca, Paganism, Buddhism, and the Tao recognize a striking similarity in their primary messages. Not surprisingly, the original core spiritual essence of the world's major religions (now lost to many of them) is that God is inside each of us. This makes a lot of sense, for if God is the Creator, the origin of all life— and we come from God—wouldn't it be logical that He/She is inside each of us? How could we be separate from God as some suggest? Some of the human interpreters of this message, however, have taken that power from us by denying this truth.

Here's a little history. From a Christian standpoint, it all started back in 325 C.E., when Roman Emperor Constantine and a few Christians held a little soirée called the Council of Nicea. It was decided, amid mild protest, to change God from a loving, benevolent being to a wrathful, fear-based one. Welcome to the upside-down world.

Not content with simply putting people in a state of perpetual anxiety, the Council further decreed that God no longer resided on Earth in the hearts of humans and all living things; thus, they jettisoned him to the heavens. Goodbye pagan beliefs and our connection to Nature. Those clergy who didn't agree with the Council's pronouncements were executed. As one might imagine, the others fell into line rather quickly.

It also came to pass at the Council of Nicea, by a vote of 218 to two, that Jesus was elevated from man-prophet to Son of God. Within the year, Constantine ordered all works related to Jesus that differed from the newly established orthodoxy confiscated and destroyed. Constantine was no dummy; he knew that he could concentrate his power by sanctioning the Christian religion in his image. By 331 C.E., he commissioned a new and improved Bible. No version of the New Testament exists today that predates the fourth century. Therefore, the story of Jesus and his disciples as we know it was rewritten to accommodate the political ambitions of a Roman emperor.

We mention this theological history not because we seek to bash Christendom, but to show that our religious beliefs today have become corrupted from their original meaning. Similar distortions of the truth in other religions can be found as well, and are the subject of dozens of well-researched books. It doesn't matter which religion you choose—if Man is involved, the story has become falsified through a combination of innocent misinterpretations, intentional deceptions, lust for power, and numerous retranslations over the course of time.

Consider the example of the telephone game in which someone whispers a simple sentence into the ear of one person, who then passes it along to the next person, then the next. Everyone knows that the sentence comes out of the last person's mouth so jumbled and off-the-mark as to be laughable. How could we not expect that something as deeply profound and complex as the meaning of existence wouldn't be distorted after being translated from Hebrew to Greek to Latin to English over thousands of years?

As an example, the word "messiah" today does not mean what it did back in the time of Yahshua, a.k.a. Jesus Christ. According to the authors of Holy Blood, Holy Grail, the Hebrew term "messiah" applied to any anointed one. Thus, King David was a "messiah"—as were all the kings that followed. Before, during, and after the life of Yahshua, "messiah" was also the word for an expected deliverer or liberator. *Webster's Dictionary* still defines it as such.

The title of messiah was also conferred on the Roman-appointed high priest during the Roman occupation of Judea, and as such was a rather common term associated with a political office.

It was the Greeks who eventually brought Christianity to the fore as a religion, and gave Yahshua his surname. The Greek word for messiah is Christos, or anointed one. Yet the term Messiah in our twentieth-century language is a divine name associated directly with Jesus Christ. It is through the passage of time, shifting political motives, and translations of language over the course of sixteen hundred years that Messiah gained its divine connotation. You can see how one simple word, wrongly translated and applied, can have a tremendous impact upon belief. A long list of erroneous translations has turned the world upside-down for the major religions.

Now, we believe Jesus Christ existed. And Moses. And Buddha. And Muhammad. And Lao Tzu. And many other prophets, known and unknown. But while we believe that they were great prophets sent to Earth to fulfill purposeful missions, we also believe that they were people made into myths—their flaws glossed over so as to make their divinity appear unattainable by the average person. That way, your designated religious intermediary—priest, rabbi, guru, and the like—is in line to interpret the way to heaven for you.

MEMBERS ONLY, OTHERS NEED NOT APPLY

The more fundamentalist dwellers in the upside-down world insist upon strict interpretation of scripture and ancient texts of their respective religions. This separation-based thinking excludes those who will not follow their orthodoxy. Everything is black or white with no room for questioning the dogma. While we understand the appeal of this type of thinking for those with conservative values, it leaves the followers at the mercy of that specific religion's leaders.

My religion is kindness.

—The Dalai Lama

In the upside-down world, religion is used as a blunt instrument. We needn't recount the millions killed in the name of this god or that. There is a well-chronicled history of death and destruction over the last forty-five hundred years. But here are a few recent examples of separation-based rhetoric and the self-evident danger it poses. We chose fundamentalist Christian quotes, but we could just as easily have selected words from fundamentalist elements in other religions. These are exact quotes. We couldn't make this stuff up . . .

I want you to let a wave of hatred wash over you. Yes, hate is good . . . Our goal is a Christian nation, we have a Biblical duty. We are called by God, to conquer this country. We don't want equal time. We don't want pluralism.

—Randall Terry, Founder of Operation Rescue

The feminist agenda is not about equal rights for women. It is a socialist, anti-family political movement that encourages women to leave their husbands, kill their children, practice witchcraft, destroy capitalism and become lesbians.

—Pat Robertson

AIDS is not just God's punishment for homosexuals; it is God's punishment for the society that tolerates homosexuals.

—Jerry Falwell

Tolerance is the worst roar of all, including tolerance for homosexuals, feminists, and religions that don't follow Christ.

—Josh McDowell at a 1994 Youth for Christ rally

You say you're supposed to be nice to the Episcopalians and the Presbyterians and the Methodists and this, that, and the other thing. Nonsense. I don't have to be nice to the spirit of the Antichrist. I can love the people who hold false opinions but I don't have to be nice to them.

—Pat Robertson

I hope I live to see the day when, as in the early days of our country, we won't have any public schools. The churches will have taken them over again and Christians will be running them.

—Jerry Falwell

I really believe that the pagans, and the abortionists, and the feminists, and the gays and the lesbians who are actively trying to make that an alternative lifestyle, the ACLU, People for the American Way—all of them who have tried to secularize America—I point the finger in their face and say, "You helped this happen."

—Jerry Falwell, speaking on who's at fault
for the 9/11 terrorist attacks.

While it's true we don't have all the answers, we do know that any religion that espouses hatred or intolerance of others is not doing God's work. There are other forces at play here, but they are not spiritually based. This is unfortunate because many good people seek comfort in religion and deserve a faith that provides good counsel along life's journey. Instead, these upside-down leaders have hijacked belief to spread a message of fear.

24/7 ARMAGEDDON

In certain sects of fundamentalist Christianity, there are those who would wish us into Armageddon, a cataclysmic finale in which only the chosen survive. This doomsday scenario is at the heart of their faith, and only they have the answer.

Many are anticipating the end of the world. Tens of thousands are actually hoping for it, some are fervently praying for it. These apocalyptic upside-downers are banding together for the end of the world. They're building fall-out shelters, stockpiling C-rations, and studying survival manuals. They've even established survivalist communities on huge tracts of land. We have all seen the bumper stickers: IN CASE OF RAPTURE THIS CAR WILL BE UNATTENDED.

Their dark hope is that the Earth will be purged of the unholy, and only the "chosen" will be left to walk this great planet. Traffic will be lighter. The streets, even the highways, will be paved with gold. It'll be easier to find parking at the mall. There won't be any lines at the movie theater—and all movies will be G-rated. Gays and lesbians won't exist. Everyone will be alike; a world will be created in their own saccharine image. This apocalyptic scenario featuring punishment and reward is an excellent fear-based way of attracting followers.

This type of thinking—really a method of mind control—has been around for thousands of years. Ever since Man first learned to manipulate his fellow Man, the world has been coming to an end. A few people in every generation for the last several thousand years have perpetuated the scare that civilization was going to bite the big one if people didn't shape up, or at least cough up a few more bucks to appease the god of choice. Yet here we are.

The Goddess cultures that were wiped out from 3500 to 1000 B.C.E. faced their end of the world. The million or so Canaanites destroyed by the Tribes of Israel around 1650 B.C.E. experienced theirs. Countless societies and cultures have vanished from the land, yet the Earth continues to rotate on its axis. Let us not forget the untold creatures and species made extinct by Man *and* by Nature. The survivors of the bubonic plague, which destroyed one-third of European populations, certainly had their belief that things were pretty darn bad. The nine million Wiccans of the Middle Ages who were tortured and executed by the Catholic Church considered that time their Armageddon. The Native Americans of the 1800s who saw thirty million of their tribespeople die found their end of the world, as well. Those living through the horrors of the American Civil War undoubtedly felt that the end was near, as did people living in Europe during World Wars I and II. The twentieth-century victims of Spanish influenza, which killed an estimated twenty-five million people from 1918 to 1919, showed that the world situation was dire yet again. In our time, right now, let us not forget the thirty-five thousand children who die of starvation every day. Clearly, they are experiencing their own Armageddon, as are their relatives. Every generation has this. The world has its bitter, tragic moments—periods of time that decimate cultures and populations.

> I shall tell you a great secret, my friend. Do not wait for the last judgment. It takes place every day.
>
> —Albert Camus

The Earth will survive with or without humans, although most of us would prefer that humanity grow old gracefully with the Earth. With the flip from God-fearing believers to spiritual human beings, transcendence and ascension to a better world makes the future very bright indeed.

A SINGLE FAITH AND A WORLD OF POSSIBILITIES

Mary is a woman of authentic faith. She grew up in a household of spiritual seekers, one a Methodist, the other a wandering mind with a belief in "something." Her parents' open-natured searching encouraged Mary to cultivate a curiosity of her own. Over the course of her life, Mary's understanding of God has evolved. From her grateful childhood days of Sunday services in a moderate Christian church, Mary was well grounded in the principle of helping others. As her thoughts about the meaning of life developed through experiences with people of other faiths and people of no faith and exposure to religious books from many faiths, Mary's world expanded.

She studied philosophy and history, astronomy and astrology, and grew to understand that there are many ways to look at the world and the invisible realms beyond it. She has read the Bible many times. But she has also dipped her big toe in the reflective waters of the Koran, the Torah, the I Ching, Confucianism, Buddhism, Hinduism, and the Goddess cultures. She dove headlong into Akkadian, Sumerian, and Babylonian texts, such as the Epic of Gilgamesh—the story of the great flood written fourteen hundred years before the Bible. As a thinking woman Mary recognizes that many of the Judeo-Christian stories in the Old and New Testaments were borrowed from other cultures. Mary knows that while some stories of war and conquest are historical, most passages are meant as allegory. She has no illusions that the Bible was ever meant to be taken at its word, or never questioned.

Mary is a believer. She doesn't doubt the existence of higher powers or prescient beings, such as angels and guides operating in energetic realms that our five senses cannot perceive. Mary believes in spirit. She knows that spiritual essence pervades everything on the planet—from every person to a mighty mountain to the invisible world of neutrinos, the stuff of the universe.

Hope is a good breakfast, but it is a bad supper.
—Francis Bacon

Her belief in a Supreme Being does not conflict with her belief in evolution or the well-accepted science dating the universe at 13.7 billion years old. She is comfortable in a Right-Side Up world that values science and spiritual faith. Mary sees God as a benevolent power of love and creativity. And she accepts that others see God differently.

Mary lives her spirituality; she hears it in music, tastes it in pure water, breathes it in during a forest walk. She feels it in her laughter and her tears. To Mary there is an ever-present guide watching out for her, a benevolent presence helping her navigate the complexities of life on Earth.

Through meditation, yoga, and prayer Mary connects with her higher power and accesses a heightened state of awareness. To Mary this is a real daily communion, filling her heart and inspiring her actions. She believes it is a sacred blessing that all people can access if they so choose.

In this way, Mary's personal connection to the Creator makes Mary a cocreator in her life. She knows her thoughts are the primary source of her happiness or pain—and therefore is mindful of her choices. She is anchored by an unshakable faith and a belief in a world of possibilities.

Mary's open-ended faith, her desire to embrace life with a grounded spirituality, is common in many experiencing the flip today. In the Right-Side Up world, a misogynistic, vengeful god personified by a bearded white man sitting on a golden throne holds no province. Instead, a true spirituality has taken hold, a spirituality that is rooted within and radiates outward. Hundreds of millions of all faiths have returned to the belief that we are all one.

An article in the August 29, 2005, edition of *Newsweek* verifies the flip. The article states: "Americans are looking for personal, ecstatic experiences of God, and, according to our poll, they don't much care what the neighbors are doing." Done in conjunction with Beliefnet.com (www.beliefnet.com), the poll shows that eight in ten Americans believe that more than one faith can be a path to salvation. Further, 68 percent of evangelicals believe another faith can provide salvation. Seventy-nine percent of respondents considered themselves *spiritual* as opposed to *religious* (64 percent). This is a powerful shift, a flip to a healthier way of viewing the world.

People today are passionate about their pursuit of transcendent experiences to be in direct communion with God. The heightened interest in the mystical Kabala, the popularity of Zen and Taoist philosophies, and the open embracement of Nature-based faiths such as Wicca and Paganism all point to a positive flip taking place. The re-emergence of perhaps the world's oldest belief system, Hermeticism and its Emerald Tablet—which at one point rivaled Catholicism and Judaism before three hundred years of inquisitions and crusades forced it underground—is a warm and welcome sign. The truth ever flourishes.

Episcopalians are practicing Buddhist meditation. Catholics are studying the Vedas. Pagans are reading the Upanishads. Light workers are traveling the planet healing ailing areas ravaged by Man. People are taking spiritual vacations on cruise ships where workshops, seminars, and worship of many faiths are intermingled. Travel agencies specialize in trips to sacred sites and energy centers around the globe. Native American beliefs are proving to be in harmonious accord with Nature-based religions that are thousands of years old. People of all faiths have discovered that science and spirituality are intricately linked, with quantum mechanics actually reinforcing many of the basic tenets of Eastern and Native American beliefs.

Could it be that it is all connected? Again, when one strips away the man-made dogma and ritual, one finds that the core essences of all these religions are similar. We all come from the same stuff. We are one. The flip is on.

CONVERSATIONS ON THE BRIDGE

Now is an appropriate time to take a walk on the bridge and have a conversation with people of faith and insight. Through their lens we can see many ways of being in the world. Rabbi Zalman Schachter-Shalomi discusses how conscious faith can be used to heal and transform the planet. Native

American Elder Dhyani Ywahoo unveils the intimate and irrefutable connection between Nature, the Universe, and ourselves. Evolutionary biologist and futurist Elisabet Sahtouris explores the missing link between science and religion. Bishop Alden Hathaway gives an inspiring firsthand account of how faith in action, believing in God, can make a real difference in the lives of many. And finally, Her Holiness Sai Maa Lakshmi Devi illuminates and encourages us to remember the inherent divine love and divine light inside each of us.

A CONVERSATION ON THE BRIDGE WITH RABBI ZALMAN SCHACHTER-SHALOMI

Rabbi Schachter-Shalomi (www.rzlp.org) is the sage of a worldwide movement of Jewish renewal who encourages a meeting of his tradition with the psychological, ecological, and spiritual revolutions of our age. As the founder of the P'nai Or (Children of Light) religious fellowship and the rabbinic chair of ALEPH: Alliance for Jewish Renewal, Rabbi Schachter-Shalomi has inspired and guided a movement for an observant, deeply traditional Judaism that is at the same time gender-equal, environmentally aware (he coined the phrase "eco-kosher"), nonhierarchical, and grounded in renewed liturgy.

We asked the rabbi if he believes there is a spiritual flip underway. "When you go deep into meditation, you can arrive at the place where you can feel and hear the pain of the planet. The earth is sick and has emphysema as far as the atmosphere is concerned; blood poisoning as far as the water tables are concerned. So the issue is not so much transformation as healing. The first step is a change in our awareness, to realize that we are not at the center of everything, but rather, the planet is the center and we are like cells of that great organism.

"One thing any individual can do is to find time to be disconnected from the onslaught of the media. We are so constantly barraged by what the media are demanding and telling us that we never connect with our soul. That's why I'm so excited about our Shabbat. If you have a Shabbat where you don't turn on the TV and you don't make phone calls and you stay in a place where you can be in touch with your soul, that makes a great deal of difference. I feel it's not so much what you do in meditation as it is the fact that you're not faced with the barrage of the media. I don't think people can wake up as long as they're in the trance."

The rabbi believes that we can find the wisdom we need across the generations. "I think our mother, the Earth, is making us aware of the needs that she has and one of the needs that she has is for us to act on our wisdom. Elders are the wisdom keepers. Yet the wisdom of the past cannot handle the complexity of our life today. You take a look and see how kids take to computers, for instance, and it's really amazing. They can handle a lot more complexity than we can. And I think that's a wonderful thing. There is an arousing. There are children coming down to Earth; they speak of them as the Indigo Children. And that's just wonderful. There is a new spiritual sensibility emerging, but if you have ever seen a butterfly trying to get out of the chrysalis, it's an agony, a struggle. It's like a birth. And that's why in Judaism we speak of this as the birth pangs of the messiah. If you collaborate with it, it goes more smoothly."

A CONVERSATION ON THE BRIDGE WITH VENERABLE DHYANI YWAHOO

> There are only two ways to live your life: one is as if nothing's a miracle; the other is as if everything's a miracle.
>
> —Albert Einstein

Venerable Dhyani Ywahoo is the founder and spiritual director of Sunray (www.sunray.org), holder of the Ywahoo lineage, and Chief of the Green Mountain Ani Yunwiwa. Her training to carry the ancestral traditions began in early childhood, under the direction of her grandparents and elders. As holders of the sacred knowledge of their people, they passed to her the spiritual duty and blessing to carry the traditions on which the work and teachings of Sunray are based. The elders foresaw Ven. Dhyani's duty to be involved in the manifestation of world peace.

She recalled for us how her spiritual lineage shaped her life: "I am of the Ywahoo lineage. In the old time, there were people who were the priest craft of the Cherokee tradition, maintaining the temples and what we call the peace villages. Peace villages are modeled on the teachings of the Luminous One, or sometimes called the Pale One. He was born about twenty-eight hundred years ago in the Thunder Mountain of the Smokey Mountains, and was quite a remarkable person with a commitment to come whenever people needed him. He returned again in the 1500s, born among the Huron and known as the Peace Maker. You may know him through the stories of Hiawatha. Growing up, I had the direct awareness of the Luminous One as a flame within our consciousness. His reminders are that we are all relatives and that the ways in which we speak and act, how we interface not only with other people but also with other dimensions and other beings, is important.

"The Luminous One reminds us that we all have a spiritual responsibility to generate love, or as my grandmother said, we have a spiritual duty to be happy. Happiness was not considered your personal happiness, it was the harmony within the family clan and the nation, and harmony within our environment. As such, we've traditionally had a very strong belief in the power of mind to interface with the environment, and to bring forth a greater crop of abundance and also stabilization of the weather."

We asked Ven. Dhyani to elaborate on the connection between human consciousness and Nature. "It's very clear in the way we were taught that consciousness does have an impact on the environment. We were taught to gaze at the clouds and then to think of particular animal shapes, and the clouds would take on the shapes of the animals we thought of. So we had direct experience of the interrelationship of our mind and emotions with the environment.

Accept the things to which fate binds you and love the people with whom fate brings you together, but do so with all your heart.

—Marcus Aurelius

"In 1969, our elders decided to bring our teachings to the public because there had been many prophecies about these times and because people have forgotten what we call 'original instructions.' They have caused harm to themselves and the environment. In the Cherokee worldview, the environment and its health is an indication of our relationship and health with the seed of truth, the light that is in everyone. The environment responds to our emotions as our emotions respond to the environment.

"People have forgotten the connection of mind and matter. Our consciousness is definitely part of a dynamic dance with the elements which gives rise to the situations in what we call our world. The question is always asked, 'Who's dreaming us?' We call it a great mystery. Literally, it is a mystery because the moment you attempt to conceptualize or define it, you've stepped back from it."

We asked if the indigenous tradition perceives a battle between good and evil, or a struggle between ignorance and intelligence. "There certainly is a call to be awakened," says Ven. Dhyani. "There's a call to transformation. When we maintain the view of battling, then that perpetuates a dualistic view. We were encouraged as we grew up to recognize instead a dynamic dance of energy, and that what we contribute gives life to particular energy vortices. So untransformed anger and jealousy become the basis of an energy field that devours. In many teaching stories in Native American traditions, there are stories about the twins of positive and negative qualities who are part of this dynamic display.

"Without the attraction or repulsion of different charges, the four-dimensional world would not express itself as it does. So positive and negative energies create the dance. What has become distorted is the negative view of dominion over the elements, which are actually aspects of our own mind, which we are responsible to shape and guide in wholesome ways.

"So what's wholesome? It means recognizing a circle of relationship, that what we think or speak, what we do, always returns. Thus we are very clearly reminded of the importance of clarity in our speech and in our emotions. We don't run from the emotions of fear, anger, shame, blame but recognize them as energies which can ultimately reveal inherent luminosity."

How does Ven. Dhyani view the planetary flip taking place? "The shift is occurring as people awaken to an understanding of the mind as energy and energy potentials. They are also beginning to see that what is occurring on one side of the planet has an impact on the other side. And how we treat one another, and even how we view the world, are projections that can create negative, reactive states. For instance, the polluted water that flooded New Orleans after Hurricane Katrina is an example of the overflowing of unconscious ignorance. Holding back the river and thus depleting the deltas and further weakening the shoreline is another example of the ignorant expression of our relationship to water. This calls us to see very clearly that we cannot impose our priorities, that we must work with the elements.

"We can conceptualize a world of harmony and beauty. Visualize families, nations, the land in cooperative harmony and each one of us doing what needs doing. Conceptualize, visualize, energize, do what needs doing."

A CONVERSATION ON THE BRIDGE WITH DR. ELISABET SAHTOURIS

Elisabet Sahtouris, Ph.D. (www.sahtouris.com), is an American/Greek evolutionary biologist, futurist, and U.N. consultant on indigenous peoples. She is a popular lecturer, television and radio personality, author of *EarthDance, A Walk through Time: From Stardust to Us*, and coauthor with

Willis Harman of *Biology Revisioned*. Dr. Sahtouris has taught at the University of Massachusetts, M.I.T., and was a science writer for the *Nova/Horizon* TV series. Her vision is the sustainable health and well-being of humanity within the larger living systems of Earth and cosmos.

We asked Elisabet about how science has influenced our view of divine intelligence. "Western science is built on assumptions that we live in a non-living universe," she observes. "That's an unproven basic assumption, a mere belief. You assume that the universe is nonliving because you believe that to be the case. Only our culture thought up this concept of nonlife within which life has to emerge. There's logic behind the original choice to see Nature as nonliving mechanics because European men invented machinery and if the universe were nonliving and mechanical, then it would be easy for them to understand it. So they projected their machine-making creativity onto God Himself; they called God the 'grand engineer of the machinery of nature.' And then they said it was the other way around, of course, that men were created in God's image so that they too could create machinery.

"By contrast, in the Vedic view of things everything is consciousness. Within consciousness, ideas form and ideas become material realities in material worlds. They can do that; thoughts can condense into matter. The soul is our fundamental consciousness, but we also have bodies and there's no distinction between body and soul. Think of a piano keyboard: the low notes would be what we perceive as matter, and the high notes would be what we perceive as mind/spirit/consciousness. But the piano is one entity. You can't have low notes without high notes and still call it a piano, right? They're different keys on the same keyboard. To take it a little further, when you die you only play on the upper parts of the keyboard, so to speak. You leave behind the matter and it can be recycled into other things. Because it's all consciousness and it's all transformable."

Elisabet offers some interesting ideas on the recently controversial subject of evolution. "There is an arrow of evolution, I believe, toward complexity, and there's a cycle of evolution that begins with individuation. Whether it's a Big Bang giving life to lots of little dancing atoms or a world egg hatching into lots of creatures, classic creation stories are about individuation. In biological evolution, you find that young pioneer species are very grabby, taking all the resources and territory they can to establish themselves and knock out their competition. At some point in a long process, they learn that collaboration is more efficient than hostile competition. You don't find that insight in Darwinian theory. Darwin took his theory from Malthus, leading him to say everything in Nature is an endless struggle in scarcity. Even though Darwin himself observed a lot of cooperation, he didn't put that into his theory.

"We're at the stage that the ancient bacteria were after two billion years of hostilities, when they formed the nucleated cell as a cooperative that was thousands of times bigger than a single bacterium. It was so successful that we never had to reinvent or re-evolve another cell in two billion years. That happened at the midpoint in our past evolution. Now I think that globalization is exactly that same kind of process, where we find out that collaborating, even feeding your enemy, is more efficient, cheaper, and better for everybody than hostile competition. That is the real flip.

Unfortunately, in the creation versus evolution debate, we're seeing many scientists become as fundamentalist as the creationists—digging in their heels defensively rather than seeing that the scientific creation story, which is in two basic parts—physics and biology—is missing the second half in both cases. Physics says we live in a nonliving universe running down by entropy—which inspired people to think, 'No purpose, no meaning, and get what you can while you can because it's all going to pot.' And then there's biology, in which Darwin neglected to talk about cooperation in his theory."

Still, Elisabet has hope for the eventual spiritualization of science. "I think we will come to a modern version of Vedic science integrated with Western science that shows balanced physics and balanced biology and the sacredness of the whole. Because everything starts with consciousness, with awareness, with mind. That's what people have called 'God' throughout history. So, I believe that we will perceive all nature as sacred, alive, and participatory with ourselves as co-creators. Hopefully, we'll have a little more humility than to think we're superior to everything else that has evolved over billions of years longer than us, or our own billions of years of evolution."

> **In the Bible, the ones who were most certain about what they were doing were the ones who stoned the prophets.**
>
> —Bob Chell, University Lutheran Center

A CONVERSATION ON THE BRIDGE WITH BISHOP ALDEN HATHAWAY

Alden Hathaway, retired Bishop in the Episcopal Church of Pittsburgh, is the director of Solar Light for Churches of Africa (SLFCA; www.solarlight forafrica.org). He is a visionary who has worked tirelessly to put his faith into action for the betterment of others. Alongside Uganda's retired Bishop Masereka, now chairman of SLFCA, Bishop Hathaway has championed an ongoing effort to bring solar energy to orphanages, churches, and other facilities in Africa.

We asked Bishop Hathaway about the challenges of being in the ministry and being a social activist. "I've always believed in the fruit of good work. I believed in all of the great social issues that I was committed to in the sixties, and I still do. The only thing that I've changed my mind about is that we don't do this by our own will and intention or accomplish it on our own.

"We used to have a prayer when we were young radicals on the streets of Detroit and it went like this: 'Oh God, we pray that we are right for we are very determined.' But I realized that that wasn't it at all.

"As you open your heart more to the power and love of God, you're open to the things that God is doing and led into the care for the poor and care for people who are broken and torn by the world and also in the practical things, the opportunities that there are to really affect the things of God's love in the world."

We asked for an example of faith-inspired social action. "One great example is the solar project in Africa. I visited an orphanage that we had helped build there. As I stood admiring the building, it got later and later and the sun set and it got dark. Then I realized that this building had no electricity, no lights, and I could not imagine how in the world they could care for these children without any electricity.

"When I got home, I talked to my son who was an electrical engineer who understood solar technology. I said, 'Could we put some solar power into that little school? It's right on the equator.' And he said, 'Sure. Give me the dimensions of it.' He put together an array of equipment that would give light and power to that facility. And it was going to cost about eight thousand dollars. We raised that money through the church.

"As I traveled around, wherever I went, I told the story about the orphanage—and how you can use solar for anything and the wonderful thing about it is that it generates on site the amount of power needed. You don't need central generation and large transmission systems, so it's immediately applicable to people in remote areas.

"So far, we've installed about twenty-four hundred units in three different countries. Every summer we take a group of American young people over, and we train them alongside the African young people in terms of missionary service and practical application by way of solar light. This brings fundamental services like refrigeration or cell phones or televisions or computers, whatever. It really gives them a leg up.

"And this is an exciting thing for us, because solar power makes the difference. And the kids see this and they become advocates of it and a lot of them are patterning their careers to follow it up with one thing or another. In fact, we've got a couple of the young people who have finished their schooling and have come back to work for us now—both African and American."

Sounds like a great initiative to us; is it well supported? "I get frustrated in the United States because we haven't received the support we could use. But little by little people catch the vision. I speak about it all the time and I'm continually gratified by the way people are drawn into it, especially these young people. Institutions are hard to change, though, especially the aid industry—which is pretty well locked into bureaucracy and their way of doing things.

"We've tried to get our project picked up by one agency after another. I rather think it's God's will that we stay independent to keep this tension between the spiritual, the commercial, and the public. These three parties work well together in Africa. We don't understand it in America. We've got this tremendous separation between church and state. And I don't demean that. I'm all for religious freedom and the government not interfering in people's spiritual lives. But on the other hand, what we see in Africa is this wonderful cooperation in these three basic centers of human enterprise in life; the spiritual, the commercial, and the public or the governmental—working together to transform a society."

Know thyself.

—Socrates

Bishop Hathaway left us with these final words: "We are to bear witness to the whole of life. And all of it is transformed by spiritual vision. A vision of following Christ, who said, 'I am the light of the world,' and I believe He meant that literally.

"You don't go to Uganda or any place and see poor people and say, 'Oh yes, believe and have faith and things will get better,' when you've got the flashlight in your pocket and people are living in the darkness. They need for you to get that flashlight out and turn it on and share it with the people."

A CONVERSATION ON THE BRIDGE WITH HER HOLINESS SAI MAA LAKSHMI DEVI

Sai Maa Lakshmi Devi (www.humanityinunity.org) is a Divine Mother, spiritual teacher, and humanitarian. Honoring the many paths that connect us to God, Sai Maa teaches Oneness, Wholeness, Truth, and Love. Whatever our tradition, Sai Maa guides us to a deeper understanding and being of that which we choose. In addition to her spiritual teaching, Sai Maa is also a powerful advocate of interfaith understanding and cooperation. This is reflected in her collaborations and meetings with some of the world's foremost spiritual leaders from all religious traditions.

She shared with us some remarkable insights on the nature of form and consciousness: "As we take embodiment in physical form, our light, our consciousness, becomes denser. While becoming so dense, we forgot who we are. But before incarnation, what were we? We were light. We were beings of light. We were consciousness. You are the embodiment of God remembering. Do not limit the truth of who you are. See yourself as the sacred fire and know this is the truth. See yourself as the Christ Light, as the Light of Buddha, Moses, Mohammed, and all of the great ones. This is the truth. Own it.

"Move beyond the five senses. Through love, the self reveals itself. Only love will attract God. Instead of identifying with the physical body, identify with the eternal self, with the One who is breathing within. Say yes to the Light. Know that there is no separation between the you that is physical and the Light. It is your choice that creates separation.

This freedom from all attachment is the realization of God as Truth.
—Gandhi

"Humanity is yearning to be loved. You do not need anyone to love you. You are love at your essence. The reason people have a hard time experiencing love is that they are loving with attachment. We call it love, but it's not love. From attachment we create expectation, and from that comes disappointment, resentment, anger, and fear of loving. But divine love is your birthright, and you can reach this state; trust yourself. Be it."

How can the world progress beyond religious strife? "It is time for us to understand there is only one truth—the absolute, the God. There is only one, and the glory of God is within all religions. If you are a Catholic and you meet a Hindu and feel your religion is better, that is just your ego making comparisons. There is a lack of humility in all of us, even when it comes to religion. Some people claim to be spiritual, or to follow the teachings of a certain religion, but their actions speak differently. I think it is time we put spirituality into practice. By that, I mean love thy neighbor. How many neighbors can't stand their neighbors, or members of their own families? That is what we need to change. Human beings spend their time looking outwards. They forget the temple of God inside their heart."

How does Sai Maa view the global flip of consciousness that is now taking place? "Whatever is happening on the planet is our own creation that we have created for centuries. The Earth is cleansing herself. In cleansing herself she vomits, and whatever you hear is the cleansing. It is not negative. It's just all the terrible things that were put in her womb and are coming out now. People will eventually be so unsatisfied that they will have no other choice than turning to God, to truth. Everything will begin to fall apart. To achieve peace, we need love and forgiveness. But how many are ready to forgive?

"Move away from worshipping the material world and move toward finding Divinity within. Forgive others, forgive yourself. There is a great power when you forgive. The moment forgiveness happens, there is no guilt; there is no shame or discomfort.

"This is not the time to isolate yourself, but to open yourself and go beyond your fears. The human race is at a grand crossroads, stepping onto the great spiral path of enlightenment. This is a truly fabulous time to be on this planet. There is a golden opportunity to realize your fullness, your glorious potential to solve environmental, social, and medical issues. A collective willingness will allow the masses to move to a higher level of consciousness much faster than you would imagine—at the speed of love. Allow yourself to be transformed by love. Let the music of love melt your heart; let the abode of divinity fill your heart with love."

METAPHORS BE WITH YOU

Is it possible that the biblical Armageddon is a metaphor for the inner turmoil that occurs inside each person seeking to find his or her true spirit before the end of life's journey? We create our heaven and hell, our Age of Enlightenment or our personal Armageddon. All of us struggle with the balance between these two extremes—the yin and yang, the light and dark of the world. This is one of our grand lessons—to face life's challenges and discern which choice to make. Do you wish to live in a place of love and light, where the world holds out its arms and embraces you with friendships and treasured moments? Or do you wish to live in a place of fear, your own hell, filled with disappointment, suspicion, and self-doubt?

We abdicate our responsibility to ourselves, and others, if we rely on an outward being for our salvation. It has to come from inside us first. Find the god/goddess inside you. Become the potential that you are and then—if you find value in the ritual, dogma, and doctrine of religion—fine. Don't start by giving away your power, though, because you'll never find your bliss that way. Spirit is an individual province that no one else can define for you. Not your minister, your priest, your rabbi, your emum, your mullah—no one.

Bright spirits abound if we choose to see them. They teach our children. They serve our food. They work in shops, in offices, in hospitals, in homes. They can be found in literally every occupation, in every race, in both genders, in all religious beliefs, and in the nonbeliever.

Bright spirits share their wisdom and experiences in seemingly innocent actions: a smile, a hug, a short note, a gentle expression of gratitude. There is a light in their eyes, a sparkle. We've all met people who seem to shine no matter the circumstance. Some of us marvel at how they do it. Some of us may wish we could be more like these bright spirits who spread joy and kindness wherever they go.

Again, here is an obvious secret: we are *all* bright spirits. We can choose to look at life as filled with fantastic possibility, or as a constant struggle. We can see life as a wondrous adventure or merely a dull collection of days. It is up to us.

Each and every person can make a mindful choice as to which type of world they'd like to live in—one of love and light, or one of darkness and deceit. There are those who seek to manipulate the fears of others for personal power, financial gain, or to perpetuate their own fear. Please don't buy into the negativity. Martial law will not be declared, and Jesus isn't polishing his chariot of fire. These are dark fantasies. Don't give them power.

Now is the perfect time to shed ourselves of our collective fears. A time when millions of us stand up to the naysayers and doomsdayers and say, "No thanks, there is a better way." We can rise in unison and refuse to buy into the negative confusion that has overwhelmed our upside-down society for so long. We can sing our dreams in one voice to the Universe. We can offer our vision of a healthy Mother Earth, of harmony among all peoples, of peace and love, to the heavens in appreciation for this great gift of life. We can do this by living with integrity, honoring each other, revering our planet, and using her resources wisely.

People are essentially good. We want good things for each other and for the Earth. The flip is happening, a great awakening is in full blossom, and many are doing all they can to bring about enlightenment. What will you do as a participant? This is our age, our time. We stand at a vital threshold of humanity. What will we do with it? Will we cower in the darkness of our fears, hidden in the shadows of our doubts? Or will we step into the brightness of our individual potential, into the dawn of our destiny to live life with love and compassion?

If we are to transcend to an age of love, and away from our past of fear, we shall need to master intent. We have to employ mindful intent in all our decisions. Often, that which is supposed to give us comfort actually does the opposite. It causes us pain and discomfort. We are numb to the consequence, however, because we are told it is for our own good. Like an abusive husband who slowly degrades his wife until her self-esteem is so low she no longer believes in herself and is totally dependent upon him, so too can life grind one down if lived without mindful intent.

The most heinous and the most cruel crimes of which history has record have been committed under the cover of religion or equally noble motives.
—Gandhi

It is not a matter of tearing down the system, or trashing that which you wish to change. The challenge is to change ourselves individually and live in integrity, being a good person as best you can. This is far easier and more rewarding than one might think. It is far easier than struggling against the will of the Universe by repeating the same painful patterns we find ourselves trapped in. Eventually we get it.

Which do we want—Armageddon or Enlightenment?

It is our choice.

By choosing enlightenment, we become beings who make a difference. We can leave this world a brighter, better place than when we arrived. Isn't that a legacy upon which we can all agree?

FLIP TIPS

- Realize that you are an empowered, enlightened being capable of greatness.
- Learn to honor and accept the differences of others.
- Pray or meditate or both.
- Sing and dance with abandon—the gods love that kind of stuff.
- Smile earnestly at people you know and those you don't.
- Treat yourself and everyone else with respect.
- Practice nonjudgment.
- Never regret failure—celebrate the art of trying.
- Do the best you can—that is enough.
- Let your fears go—one at a time.
- Look for love—it's everywhere.
- Spend a day in silence.
- Attend religious services of a faith different from yours.
- Let your inner child come out to play—this life is far too short to be so serious.
- Give genuine thanks to everyone you encounter.
- Stare at your reflection in the mirror until you see your truth.
- Discover the metaphor of your life.
- Live with full abandon, without regret.

INDEX

Aburdene, Patricia, 174, 176–177
acceptance, self, 43
Acesulfame-K, 85
activism, 13
Adams, John Quincy, 149
"Advertising Ratios & Budgets" (Schonfeld & Associates), 63–64
Afghanistan, 137, 194
Africa, 226–227
AIDS, 53
Air America Radio Network, 70, 72–74
The Alchemist (movie), 68
ALEPH: Alliance for Jewish Renewal, 220
Alman, Brian, 43
American Academy of Child Adolescent Psychiatry, 63
American Health Association, 115
American Holistic Medical Association, 114
American Institute of Homeopathy, 103
American LIVES, Inc., 8
American Medical Association (AMA), 103, 104
Anderson, Ray, 174, 176, 177–180
Anderson, Sherry Ruth, 7
Apollo Alliance, 131–133
Arias, Oscar, 202–204
Armageddon, 216–217
Arms Trade Resource Center, 196
Arms Trade Treaty (ATT), 204
art, as inspiration, 11–13
Association for Global New Thought, 207
Australian National Government, 161
Aveda, 180
The Awakened Heart—Meditations on Finding Harmony in a Changing World (Robbins), 91
Awakened Media, 74, 75
awareness
  advanced, 29–30
  choiceless, 75
  conscious, 5, 8, 21, 33
  of emotional problems, 43
  of environmental issues, 29–30, 70, 71–72, 91
  of inner self, teaching, 166

media, exercise for, 61
  social, 152
ayurveda, 103, 112

Bain, Barnet, 69–71
Bangladesh, 155
bankruptcy, 106, 109, 150–151, 151, 156
Bankruptcy Abuse Prevention and Consumer Protection Act of 2005, 150–151
Baskin-Robbins, 91, 92
Batstone, David, 148
Begley, Ed, Jr., 134, 140–142
Beliefnet.com, 219
Beta Gamma Sigma, 73
Beyond Globalization (Henderson), 158
Bhopal disaster, 97
Bierce, Ambrose, 181
biodiversity movement, 91
Biology Revisioned (Sahtouris and Harman), 224
Biopiracy: The Plunder of Nature and Knowledge (Shiva), 97
brain. *See* mind
The Brain Book (Russell), 29
British Petroleum (BP), 72, 126, 130, 137
  Statistical Review of World Energy 2005, 128
Brookhaven National Laboratory, 83
Brower, Dave, 137, 141
Buddhist meditation, 219
Butler, Smedley, Major General, 193, 195–196
Bush, George W., 192
Bush administration (George W.), 64, 74, 94, 109, 126, 133
Buzzworm (magazine), 29

C. G. Jung Institute (Zurich, Switzerland), 115
California League of Conservation Voters, 140
Calvert Family of Socially Responsible Mutual Funds, 185
Calvert Foundation, 185
cancer, 85, 95–96, 114, 116, 117–118, 157
Cape Wind project, 139
capitalism, 176, 177
Carson, Rachel, 91

Casten, Liane, 62
Catholicism, 219
The Celestine Prophecy (movie), 68, 70
Center for Creative Parenting, 45
Center for Media Research, 63
Center for Nonviolent Communication, 205
Center for Responsive Politics, 150
Center for Soviet American Dialogue, 207
Centers for Disease Control and Prevention, 83, 86–87
Central American, 202–203
Central American Peace Process, 202
Chase Bank, 150
Chasse, Betsy, 66
Chavez, Cesar, 136
Chavez, Hugo, 187
Cheney, Dick, 128
Chevron, 126
Chez Panisse, 94
chi, 15, 103
Chicago Media Watch, 62
childbirth, 46–47
Children's Hospital Boston, 84
China, 137, 160, 187, 195
Chinese medicine, traditional (TCM), 103, 112, 118
Chittagong University, 155
choice, bridge of, 7
Chopra, Deepak, 112
Christianity. *See* religion
Cinemax, 63
Citibank, 150
Citizens for Clean Air, 159
Civic Forum, 201
Clean Water Act, 128
Cleveland Clinic, 116
Clinton administration (Bill), 177
clothes, organic, 153
CNN, 62
Coalition for Clean Air, 140
CO_2 emissions, 129, 130
Cold War, 202
Collins, Dianne, 25–27
Coming Apart (Kingma), 49
Community Supported Agriculture (CSA), 89–90
Conscious Evolution: Awakening the Power of Our Social Potential (Hubbard), 207
Conscious Healing (Selby), 28
consciousness
   and emotions, 54
   human, 29–30
   planetary, 32
Constantine, 212, 213
consumerism, 2, 8
Consumers Union, 151
Co-op America, 153–154

Corporate America
   corporations in, types of, 171
   environmental and social responsibilities, 177–182
   fraud and scandals in, 170
   fundamentalists in, 184
   gambling, legalized, 172–173
   growing, through people, 182–185
   as people, 170–171
   profit, hunger for, 172
   "relationship corporation," advent of, 185–187
   shopping with stewards exercise, 175
   spirituality in, megatrend towards, 176–177
   Triple Bottom Line, 174
Corporate Health Improvement Program (CHIP), 115
Costa Rica, 202, 203
Cousteau, Jacques-Yves, 138
Cousteau, Jan, 138–139
Cousteau, Philippe, 134, 138–140
Cousteau, Philippe, Jr., 138
Crawford, Lester M., 90
Creation, totality of, 23
Credit Union National Association, 154
Cultural Creatives, 8–9
Cultural Creatives: How 50 Million People Are Changing the World (Ray and Anderson), 7
Currency Network Office, 155
Current, 68
Czechoslovakia, 201

Daimler-Chrysler, 160
The Dancing Wu Li Masters: An Overview of the New Physics (Zukav), 30
Darwin, Charles, 224–225
De Angelis, Barbara, 7, 13–16
deBoer, Lee, 69
depression, 9–11
Devi, Sai Maa Lakshmi, 220, 227–229
Diesel, Rudolph, 135
Diet for a New America—How Your Food Choices Affect Your Health, Happiness, and the Future of Life on Earth (Robbins), 91
Douglas, Kirk, 66
Do You QuantumThink? (Collins), 25
Drobny, Sheldon, 70, 72–74
drug addiction and treatment, 53–55
duality, 4, 21, 22, 39
DVD clubs, 68

Earth Communications Office, 140
EarthDance (Sahtouris), 223
EarthEcho International, 138, 139
EarthSave International, 91
The Ecology of Commerce (Hawken), 178
education, spending, 195

Eisenhower, Dwight D., 195, 197
Embracing Your Power in Thirty Days (Y. King), 12
Emergence: The Shift from Ego to Essence (Hubbard), 207
Emotional Revolution, 56
emotions
   childhood imprints, 40
   consciousness of, 54
   dealing with, stages of, 43–44
   "emotional literacy," 55–56
   fear-based, 20
   freedom, 14–15
   healing, perceptive, 42
   influence of, in the womb, 45–47
   and male/female compatibility conflicts, 51–53
   physics of, understanding, 41
   professional help for, 38, 39
   repressing, and illness, 53–55
   resentment, 52
   resistance, 41
   resolution, of problems, 44
   and separation, 39–40
   traumas, 54
   see also feelings
energy
   Apollo Alliance, 131–133
   biodiesel, 134–136
   biomass, 131
   conservation, steps for, 143
   consumption, 124, 125–126, 127, 136–138
   divine, 15
   hybrid vehicles, 129, 153
   hydrogen, 131
   hydrogen, as energy carrier, 131
   legislation, 128
   living lightly on the Earth, 140–142
   9/11, affects on, 142
   renewable energy sources, 129–130, 138–140
   resources, and war, 5
   solar technology, 129–130, 226–227
   suppliers of, and profits, 126
   tidal power, 139
   universal interplay of, 22
   wind power, 130–131, 139
Energy Star appliances, 129
Environmental Media Association (EMA), 70, 71, 72, 140
Environmental Working Group, 86
Episcopal Church of Pittsburgh, 225
Episcopalians, 219
Erasmus, Udo, Foundation, 161
European Union (EU), 184–185, 202
The Evolutionary Journey (Hubbard), 207
Executive EQ: Emotional Intelligence in Business (Sawaf), 55
ExxonMobil, 124, 126

Fair Trade movement, 153
falling-apart process, 9
Fats That Heal, Fats That Kill (Erasmus), 95
FCC, 68
FDA, 85, 86, 87, 90, 102, 106, 107, 108
Federal Reserve, 149–150
feelings
   accepting, 41–42
   authentic, 52
   of connection, 42, 43
   control of, 47–48
   and emotional literacy, 55–56
   expressing, 37–39, 42, 44
   of separation, 42, 43
   and thoughts, differentiating, 47–49
   understanding, 45
   see also emotions
The Fifth Discipline: The Art and Practice of the Learning Organization (Senge), 182
"fight or flight" response, 22, 63
finances
   alternative currencies, 154
   bankruptcy, 106, 109, 150–151, 151, 156
   capital, spiritual, 161–162
   corporate responsibility movement, 158–161
   credit industry, 151
   debt, national, 149
   Fortune 500 companies, 161
   Gross National Product (GNP), 160
   Hierarchy of Need, 146, 147, 165
   interest rates, 145, 150, 151, 155–156, 186
   micro-credit concept, 155
   monetary system, global, 150, 156
   money, changing relationships with, 5
   poverty, 149
   retirement investing, 154
   scarcity to abundance, 153–156
   self-worth, universal ideas for instilling, 165–166
   service-devoted life, joy of, 162–164
   socially responsible investing (SRI), 154
   see also wealth
The Findhorn Foundation, 29
Finding True Love (Kingma), 49
Fitzgerald, Randall, 85
flipping your life, 2–6
flip tips
   for beginning your flip, 18
   for emotional flow, 58
   for energy consumption, 144
   for financial contentment, 167–168
   for food choices, 100
   for health care, 122
   for mindful media choices, 78
   for peace, finding, 210
   for spiritual enlightenment, 232

for whole thinking, 35
for workplace, fulfillment in, 189
The Florida Second District Court of Appeals, 62
The Food Revolution—How Your Diet Can Help Save Your Life and Our World (Robbins), 91
foods
    artificial sweeteners/preservatives in, 85–86
    biodiversity movement in, 97–98
    chemicals in, 84, 86
    cooking oils, dangers of, 95–97
    environmental connection, 91–93
    essential fatty acids (EFAs), 95
    food-borne diseases, 86–87
    "Frankenfoods," 87
    genetically modified organisms (GMOs), 87
    government intervention, and conflicts of interest, 87
    health care professionals, nutritional education of, 105
    junk-food addiction, 83–84
    labeling of, 90
    mercury in, 86, 108
    natural and organics, 89–90, 93–95
    processed, 5
    restaurant wars, 82–83
    in school cafeterias, 90
    two-dimensional view of, 81–82
fossil fuels, 124, 127, 130, 131, 135
Foundation for Conscious Evolution, 207
Foundation for Education in Emotional Literacy, 55
Foundation for the Future, 207
Fox News, 62
Francis, Linda, 31
"Frankenfoods," 87
Free Speech TV, 68
Friends of the Earth, 137, 140
Frist, Bill, 107
From Science to God (Russell), 29
Fuller, Buckminster, 21
The Future of Love: The Power of Soul in Intimate Relationships (Kingma), 49

gambling, legalized, 172–173
Gandhi, Mahatma, 203
    Seven Blunders of the World, 17
Garden State (movie), 68
gender roles, 51–53
General Electric, 194
Generation Environment, 72
genetically modified organisms (GMOs), 87
Getting Well Again (Simonton), 117
Global Family, 207
Global Green, 177
globalization, 180–181
global warming, 19, 29, 124–125, 159
    of the heart, 5

Good Morning America (TV news show), 135–136
Goorjian, Michael, 66
Gorbachev, Mikhail, 177, 202
Grameen Bank, 155
Gray, John, 45, 51–53
Green Money Journal, 154
Green Mountain Ani Yunwiwa, 221
Green Revolution, 97
Gross National Product (GNP), 160
Gulf War, 191

Hahnemann, Samuel Christian, 103
Hannah, Daryl, 134–136
happiness, responsibility for, 4
Harman, Willis, 224
Harvard Business Review (magazine), 159, 182
Harvard University, 161
Hathaway, Alan, Bishop, 220–225–227
Havel, Vaclav, 201
Hawken, Paul, 178
HBO, 63
The Healing Journey (Simonton), 117
health care
    homeopathy, 103
    naturopathy, 103
health care, in U.S.
    alternative medicine, 115–117
    chemistry, and better living, 106–108
    cost of, 104
    drug interactions, 108–109
    Eastern practices, 111
    guided imagery, 117–119
    holistic medicine, 103, 110–111
    insurance, 109–110
    "integrative medicine," 112
    medical bills, and bankruptcies, 106, 109, 151
    obesity, 84
    pharmaceutical industry's influence on, 105–108
    "principle of similars," 103
    professionals, education of, 105
    quality of, statistics, 103
    Three Horsemen of the Apothecary, 104–106
    touch therapy, 119–120
    women's health issues, treatment of, 113–115
Heal the Bay, 140
HealthSouth, 106
Healthtrac, Incorporated, 115
The Heart of the Soul: Emotional Awareness (Francis and Zukav), 31
Henderson, Hazel, 157, 158–161
Hierarchy of Need, 146, 147, 165
Higher Ground Productions, 7, 11
Hock, Dee, 183
Hollywood, 66, 68, 70–71

Homeland Security, 194–195
Hopi Indians, 27
How Did I Get Here? Finding Your Way to Renewed Hope and Happiness When Life and Love Take Unexpected Turns (De Angelis), 14
"how-to," 25
"how we got here," understanding, 14
Hubbard, Barbara Marx, 202, 207–208
The Hundred Year Lie (Fitzgerald), 85
The Hunger of Eve (Hubbard), 207
The Hunger Project, 162
hurricanes, 125, 223
Husak, Gustav, 201
Hussein, Saddam, 191, 198

IFTDO (International Federation of Training and Development Organizations), 161
Illusion (movie), 66
Immune System Activation (Selby), 28
Indian Ocean, tsunami in, 125
Indigo Children, 221
Industrial Revolution, 56
I Need Your Love—Is That True? (Katie), 10
Information Age, 56, 89
Inner Securities, Inc., 157
"Inside Wealth" (radio program), 157
Institute of Noetic Sciences, 29
Inter-Bank Research Organization, 155
Interface, Inc., 177
International Code of Conduct on Arms Transfers, 204
Internet, 69
Iraq, 192, 194
"it's-all-about-me" attitude, 22

Japan's Council for the Growth of Future Generations, 161
Jefferson, Thomas, 149
Johns Hopkins University School of Medicine, 53
Journal of the American Medical Association, 117
Judaism, 219, 221

Kabala, 219
Katie, Byron, 7, 9–11
Katrina, Hurricane, 125, 223
Kennedy, John F., 131
Kennedy, Robert F., Jr., 92
King, Coretta Scott, 11
King, Martin Luther, Jr., 7, 11–12, 91–92, 203
King, Yolanda, 7, 11–13
Kingma, Daphne Rose, 45, 49–51
Krieger, Dolores, 113, 119–120
Krishnamurti, 27
Kundalini Awakening in Everyday Life (Selby), 28
Kunz, Dora, 119

Lawrence Livermore National Laboratory, 127
Leach, Robin, 141
The Learning Channel, 68
Levin, Debbie, 70, 71–72
Lietaer, Bernard, 156
Lifestyles of the Rich and Famous (TV series), 141
LIME Media, 68, 69
Lindbergh, Charles, 150
Local Exchange Trading Systems (LETS), 154–155
love
    defined, 49–50
    fear, as opposite of, 22
    and intimacy, 56
    self, 15–16
Loving What Is: Four Questions That Can Change Your Life (Katie and Mitchell), 7, 10
Lovins, Amory, 137
Lovins, L. Hunter, 134, 136–138
Lovins on the Soft Path (movie), 136
Luminare-Rosen, Carista, 45–47
Luminous One (Pale One), 221–222

Madison, James, 194
Maine Medical Center, 113
Mandela, Nelson, 201
Mandell, Faye, 45
marriage tradition, 49–51
Masereka, Zabedee, 226
Maslow, Abraham, 146, 165
Massachusetts Institute of Technology (MIT), 161, 176, 182, 224
Mayo Clinic, 116
media
    advertising, 63–64
    authenticity in, 75–76
    cable/satellite programming, 61
    and children, affects on, 63
    conscious, 74–77
    diversified, 72–73
    entertainment, 61–62, 65–67
    environmental consciousness and, 70, 71–72
    in fast-food industry, 83
    film club movement, 68
    First Amendment, 62
    fulfilling experiences, desire for, 67–68
    guilty pleasures, 66–67
    honesty, in reporting, 73–74
    information, 62–63
    interactive exercise, 61
    Internet, 69
    limbic system controls, 63
    motion picture industry, 65–67
    movies, based on books, 68
    paranoia, media induced, 63
    radio, 64–65, 68–69, 73–74

as reflection of conscious, 69–71
  reform movement, 68–69
  television, 68
  "us *versus* them" mentality, 73
meditation, 27, 28, 111, 218, 219, 220
Meehan, Peter, 93
Megatrends 2000 (Aburdene), 176
Megatrends 2010 (Aburdene), 176
Megatrends for Women (Aburdene), 176
Men Are from Mars, Women Are from Venus
  (Gray), 51
The Men We Never Knew (Kingma), 49
mercury, 86, 108
mind
  calming techniques, 35
  flipping, 24–34
  limbic system controls, 63
  mastering, 27–28
  modes of, managing, 28
  stimulation of, 19–20
  study of, 21
The Mind of the Soul: Responsible Choice (Francis
  and Zukav), 31
Mitchell, Stephen, 10
modernism, 8–9
*Molecules of Emotion: The Science behind
  Mindbody Medicine* (Pert), 53
Mollner, Terry, 176, 185–187
Monsanto, 87, 92
Movement for the Abolition of War (MAW), 200
MSNBC, 62

National Academy of Sciences, 105
National Business Group on Health, 115
National Center for Complementary and
  Alternative Medicine, 116
National Geographic, 68
National Institute on Aging, 112
National Institute of Mental Health, 27, 53
National Institutes of Health, 53
Natural Capital Institute, 154
Natural Capitalism (Lovins), 136
Natural Capitalism, Inc., 136
Natural Resources Defense Council, 140
Navdanya, 97
neuroscience, 53
New Dimensions Radio, 207
New England Journal of Medicine (magazine), 109
Newman, Nell, 91, 93–95
Newman, Paul, 93
Newman's Own Organics: The Second
  Generation, 91, 93
Newsweek (magazine), 219
New York Times (newspaper), 7, 31, 176,
  202–203
New York University, 119

Nike, 180
Nobel Peace Laureates, 202, 204
Noggin (for children), 68
Northrup, Christiane, 113–115
Norton, Edward, 72
Nova/Horizon (TV series), 224
nutrition. *See* foods

Ocean Thermal Energy Conversion (OTEC), 139
Ohio State University, 112
Organic Consumers Association, 90
Oxford Centre for Environment, Ethics, and
  Society, 155
Oxygen (cable station), 68
oxytocin, 52
ozone depletion, 141

Paganism, 219
Paradigm Group II, 72–73
Paradigms in Progress (Henderson), 160
parenting, 45–47
*Parenting Begins Before Conception: A Guide to
  Preparing Body, Mind, and Spirit—For You
  and Your Future Child* (Luminare-Rosen),
  45–46
The Passion of the Christ (movie), 70, 71
peace villages, 221
Pelletier, Kenneth R., 115–117
People Against Violence, 201
peptides, 53–54
"perception is reality," 24
personal growth, 8
Pert, Candace, 45, 53–55
Pew Research Center for the People & the Press,
  62, 134
pharmaceutical companies, 106–108
Pharmaceutical Research and Manufacturers of
  America, 107
Picard, John, 178
P'nai Or (Children of Light), 220
Political Observations (Madison), 194
pollution, 5, 93, 124, 135, 141, 159, 160
poverty, 149
President's Council on Sustainable Development,
  177
"principle of similars," 103
"profit over people" priority, 5
Project Censored (perennial news book), 62–63
Prometheus Radio Project, 69
psychiatry, 55
psychoanalysis, 54
Pugwash online website, 199

quantum leap concept, 25–26
quantum mechanics, 25, 219
The Quantum Self (Zohar), 161

The Quantum Society (Zohar), 161
QuantumThink, 25

Raatz, John, 70, 74–77
Ray, Paul, 7–9
reality, 24–27, 30–34
    new, 30–32
*Reclaiming Our Health—Exploding the Medical
    Myth and Embracing the Source of True
    Healing* (Robbins), 91
Reebok Apparel and Retail Group, 180, 181, 182
Re-inventing the Corporation (Aburdene), 176
religion
    Armageddon, 216–217
    belief systems, 5–6, 212
    creation v. evolution debate, 225
    "messiah," defined, 213–214
    Native American beliefs, 219, 223
    Nature-based faiths, 219
    prophets, 214
    science and, missing link between, 225–227
    separation-based rhetoric, 214–215
    spiritual v. religious, 219
    theological history of Christendom, 212–213
    see also spiritual enlightenment
Research Foundation for Science, Technology,
    and Natural Resource Policy, 97
The Revelation: Our Crisis Is a Birth (Hubbard), 207
Robbins, John, 91–93
Robertson, James, 155–156
Rocky Mountain Institute (RMI), 136, 137
Rocky Mountain Media Watch, 63
Rosenberg, Marshall, 202, 205–207
Rothschild, Mayer, 150
Royal Dutch Shell, 126, 130
Russell, Peter, 24, 29–30

Safe Drinking Water Act, 128
Sahtouris, Elisabet, 220, 223–225
Santa Cruz Predatory Bird Research Group, 93
Santa Monica Baykeeper, 140
Santa Monica Mountains Conservancy, 140
Saudi Arabia, 191
Sawaf, Ayman, 45, 55–56
Schachter-Shalomi, Zalman, 219, 220–221
Schonfeld & Associates, 63
The Seat of the Soul (Zukav), 30–31
Second Bank of the United States, 149
Selby, John, 24, 27–28
Self-Powerment: Towards a New Way of Living
    (Mandell), 47
Self-Powerment Model, 47
Senge, Peter, 176, 182–185
separation, 39–40
September 11, 2001, terrorist attacks, 142, 191,
    195, 211

Seven Blunders of the World (Gandhi), 17
Seven Masters, One Path (Selby), 28
Shell Hydrogen, 137
Shiva, Vandana, 91, 97–98
Showtime, 63
Sideways (movie), 68
Silent Spring (Carson), 91
Silverstone, Alicia, 71
Simonton, Carl, 113, 117–119
Social Funds, 154
Social Investment Forum, 154
socially responsible investing (SRI), 154
Society for Organizational Learning (SoL), 182,
    183
Solar Light for Churches of Africa (SLFCA), 225,
    226
*The Soul of Money: Transforming Your Relationship
    with Money and Life* (Twist), 163
Soul Stories (Zukav), 31
South Africa, 201–202
Soviet Union, 187, 202
Spirit in Business, Inc., 185
Spiritual Cinema Circle, 68
spiritual enlightenment
    connection between Nature, Universe and our-
        selves, 221–223
    conscious faith, and planet transformation,
        220–221
    faith in action, believing in God, 225–227
    flip tips for, 232
    inner love and light, 227–229
    open-ended faith, 217–218
    see also religion
SQ: Spiritual Intelligence, the Ultimate Intelligence
    (Zohar), 161
Star Group, 25
Statistical Review of World Energy 2005, 128
*Stolen Harvest: The Hijacking of the Global Food
    Supply* (Shiva), 97
Sunray, 221
Surgeon General's Office, 117
Swedish National Parliament, 161

Tam, Marilyn, 176, 180–182
Taoist philosophies, 219
Tauzin, Billy, 107
Ten Steps to the Universal Human (Hubbard), 207
*Therapeutic Touch: How to Use Your Hands to Help
    and to Heal* (Krieger), 119
Thimerosal, 107
thinking, whole
    authentic power, 31–32
    awakening, 27
    balance, finding, 22–23
    cognitive, 28
    either/or, 26

environmental issues, 29–30
exercise for, 33
"observer effect," 26
opposites, play of, 22
self-centeredness, 30
separation-based, 26
stimulation, brain, 19–20
Thoreau Institute, 140
Thunder Mountain of the Smokey Mountains, 221
TIME magazine, 136
The TM Technique (Russell), 29
Toyota Prius, 129
traditional Chinese medicine (TCM), 103, 112, 118
transformation, personal, 13–14
Travis Air Force Base, 117, 118
Tree People, 136–137, 140
True Love (Kingma), 49
Trusteeship Institute, Inc., 185
Truth and Reconciliation Commission (TRC), 201
tsunami, in Indian Ocean, 125
Twist, Lynne, 157, 162–164

U.S. Census Bureau Survey of Health Care and Social
Assistance (2003), 102
U.S. Congress
bankruptcy laws, 109
Department of Peace, 208
medical industry lobbyists, 107
Office of Technology, 159
U.S. Department of Health and Human Services, 115
U.S. Environmental Protection Agency (EPA), 86, 87
Uganda, 204, 226, 227
UNESCO, 161
Union Carbide, 97
Union of Concerned Scientists (UCS), 125
United Nations Development Program (UNDP), 204
University of Arizona School of Medicine, 115–116
University of California School of Medicine (USCF), 115
University of Massachusetts, 224
University of Michigan, 112
University of Oregon Medical School, 117
Upanishads, 219
The Upanishads (Russell), 29
USA Today poll, 56
USDA, 80, 87
USW Incorporated, 169

Vedantam, Shankar, 108
Vedas, 219
Velvet Revolution (November Events of 1989), 201
Ventana Wilderness Sanctuary, 93
The Violence of the Green Revolution (Shiva), 97
Vioxx, 105–106
The Visioneering Group, 74
vulnerability, 56

WAG, 148
A Walk through Time: From Stardust to Us (Sahtouris), 223
warfare
arms expenditures, 196, 204
causes of, 199, 200
defense spending, 194–196, 203–204
demilitarization, 204
Department of Peace, cabinet-level position, 207–208
disarmament and human security, plan for, 200–201
economy and, 194
energy resources and, 5
gouging and profiteering, at taxpayer expense, 195–196
nonviolent communication, 205–207
peace, through diplomacy, 202–205
tolerance, encouraging, 199–200
U.S. aggression in, 192–193, 196–197
War Is a Racket (Butler), 193
War Production Board, 194
Washington Post (newspaper), 108
Waters, Alice, 94
The Way of the Peaceful Warrior (movie), 68
wealth
class separation, 148–149
imbalance of, 158
inner, cultivating, 157–158
pursuit of, 147
values, skewed, 147
worry, and net worth, 148
worth, defining, 148
What Dreams May Come (movie), 70
What the Bleep Do We Know? (movie), 66, 68
Wicca, 219
Wilson, Charles E., 194
Wisdom Media Group, 70
WISDOM WorldView Award, 70
Wolfowitz, Paul, 98
women
health of, 113–115
issues of, 8
Women of Vision in Action, 207
Women's Entertainment, 68
Women to Women, 114

Woodrow Wilson Fellow, 115
Woodward, Joanne, 93
The Work, 11
World Bank, 98
The World Business Academy, 29, 161
The World Economic Forum, 161
World Future Society, 207
World Heath Organization (WHO), 80, 103,
    115, 116
World Meteorological Organization, 125
World War II, 9, 194, 197

YPO, 161
Yunus, Muhammad, 155
Ywahoo, Dhyani, 220, 221–223

Zen, 219
Zimco Advisors, 157
Zimmerman, Stu, 157–158
Zohar, Danah, 157, 161–162
Zukav, Gary, 24, 30–32

ABOUT THE AUTHORS

JARED ROSEN is an author, artist, and thought leader. He is the coauthor of *Inner Security and Infinite Wealth*, the cofounder of Inner Securities Inc., and the developer of Whole Self Management. In addition, he is the founder of Dreamsculpt, a consulting group focused on catalyzing authentic and soulful expression in the entertainment and media industry.

Jared has dedicated his life to building a world where love is recognized as the highest standard. He lives in Sonoma County, California, with his family.

DAVID RIPPE is founder and president of Celestia International, a strategic marketing communication and creative services firm. He is the author of *The Journals* trilogy under the pseudonym, R. T. Stone.

David enjoys a peaceful lifestyle centered on family, meditation, activism, music, reading, and travel. He strives to embrace the energetic flow of all things. "We each walk our own path, find our own light. Hopefully, we can laugh at ourselves on our journey of discovery."

MORE WAYS TO FLIP!

To read the in-depth conversations with our Flipsters, and additional interviews with Flipsters whose wisdom we couldn't fit into this book, please visit our website at www.theflip.net. You won't be disappointed.

Here you will also find additional resources, exercises, Flip Tips, and groups to aid you on your journey to the Right-Side Up world. We'll see you there!

Flipping Your Life
Dr. Paul Ray—www.culturalcreatives.org
Byron Katie—www.thework.com
Yolanda King—www.yolanda-king.com
Dr. Barbara De Angelis—www.barbarade angelis.com

Flipping the Mind
Dr. Dianne Collins—quantumthink.net
John Selby—www.johnselby.com
Dr. Peter Russell—www.peterrussell.com
Gary Zukav—www.zukav.com

Flipping the Emotions
Dr. Carista Luminare-Rosen: www.creative-parenting.com
Dr. Faye Mandell—namastepublishing.com/mandell.asp
Daphne Rose Kingma—www.daphnekingma.com
Dr. John Gray—www.marsvenus.com
Dr. Candace Pert—www.candacepert.com
Ayman Sawaf—www.aymansawaf.com

Flipping the Channels
Barnet Bain—www.the celestineprophecy movie.com
Debbie Levin—www.ema-online.org

Sheldon Drobney—www.airamericaradio.com
John Raatz—www.thevisioneeringgroup.com

Flipping Burgers
John Robbins—www.foodrevolution.org
Nell Newman—www.newmansownorganic.com
Udo Erasmus—www.udoearasmus.com
Dr. Vandana Shiva—www.vshiva.net

Flipping Pills
Dr. Christiane Northrup—www.drnorthrup.com
Dr. Kenneth R. Pelletier—www.drpelletier.com
Dr. O. Carl Simonton—www.simonton center.com
Dr. Dolores Krieger—www.therapeutic touch.org

Flipping the Switch
Daryl Hannah—www.grassolean.com
L. Hunter Lovins—www.hunterlovins.com
Philippe Cousteau—www.earthecho.net
Ed Begley, Jr.—www.edbegley.com

Flipping the Coin

Stu Zimmerman—www.insidewealth.net

Dr. Hazel Henderson—
www.hazelhenderson.com

Dr. Danah Zohar—www.dzohar.com

Lynne Twist—www.soulofmoney.com

Flipping the Corporation

Patricia Aburdene—
www.patriciaaburdene.com

Ray Anderson—
www.interfaceinc.com

Marilyn Tam—
www.howtousewhatyouvegot.com

Dr. Peter Senge—www.solonline.org

Terry Mollner—www.calvertfoundation. org

Flipping the Trigger

Dr. Oscar Arias—www.arias.or.cr

Dr. Marshall Rosenberg—www.nnvc.org

Barbara Marx Hubbard—
www.barbaramarxhubbard.com

Flipping the Light

Rabbi Zalman Schachter-Shalomi—
www.rlzp.org

Venerable Dhyani Ywahoo—
www.sunray.org

Dr. Elisabet Sahtouris—www.sahtouris.com

Bishop Alden Hathaway—
www.solarlightforafrica.org

Her Holiness Sai Maa Lakshmi Devi—
www.humanityinunity.org

Hampton Roads Publishing Company

. . . for the evolving human spirit

HAMPTON ROADS PUBLISHING COMPANY publishes books on a variety of subjects, including metaphysics, spirituality, health, visionary fiction, and other related topics.

For a copy of our latest trade catalog, call toll-free, 800-766-8009, or send your name and address to:

HAMPTON ROADS PUBLISHING COMPANY, INC.
1125 STONEY RIDGE ROAD • CHARLOTTESVILLE, VA 22902
e-mail: hrpc@hrpub.com • www.hrpub.com